D0907396

Fabric of an Exhibition:
An Interdisciplinary Approach

Preprints of a Conference
Textile Symposium 97 – Fabric of an Exhibition:
An Interdisciplinary Approach
Ottawa, Canada
September 22 to 25, 1997

Organized by the Canadian Conservation
Institute and the North American Textile
Conservation Conference

Canadian Conservation Institute
Ottawa, Canada
1997

L'étoffe d'une exposition :
une approche pluridisciplinaire

Les prétirages de la conférence
Symposium 97 – L'étoffe d'une exposition :
une approche pluridisciplinaire
Ottawa, Canada
du 22 au 25 septembre 1997

Organisé par l'Institut canadien
de conservation et la North American
Textile Conservation Conference

Institut canadien de conservation
Ottawa, Canada
1997

© Government of Canada, 1997

All rights reserved. No part of this publication may be reproduced or transmitted in any form or by any means, electronic or mechanical, including photocopying, recording, entering in an information storage and retrieval system, or otherwise, without prior written permission of the publisher.

PRINTED IN CANADA

Available from:
Extension Services
Canadian Conservation Institute
1030 Innes Road
Ottawa, Ontario
K1A 0M5

Canadian Cataloguing in Publication Data

Main entry under title :

Fabric of an exhibition : an interdisciplinary approach = L'étoffe d'une exposition : une approche pluridisciplinaire

Articles in English with abstracts in French and English
"Textile Symposium 97, Ottawa, Canada, September 22 to 25, 1997"
ISBN 0-660-60261-X
Cat. no. NM95-59/6-1997

1. Museum techniques — Congresses.
2. Textile fabrics — Conservation and restoration — Congresses.
3. Costume — Conservation and restoration — Congresses.
I. Canadian Conservation Institute.
II. Title: L'étoffe d'une exposition, une approche pluridisciplinaire.

AM151.T47 1997   677.0075   C97-980236-9E

© Gouvernement du Canada, 1997

Tous droits réservés. La reproduction d'un extrait quelconque de ce livre, par quelque procédé que ce soit, tant électronique que mécanique, ou par photocopie, microfilm, bande magnétique, disque ou autre, sans l'autorisation écrite de l'éditeur est interdite.

IMPRIMÉ AU CANADA

Vendu par :
Services de diffusion externe
Institut canadien de conservation
1030, chemin Innes
Ottawa (Ontario)
K1A 0M5

Données de catalogage avant publication (Canada)

Vedette principale au titre :

Fabric of an exhibition : an interdisciplinary approach = L'étoffe d'une exposition : une approche pluridisciplinaire

Articles en anglais et résumés en français et en anglais.
"Symposium 97, Ottawa, Canada, du 22 au 25 septembre 1997.
ISBN 0-660-60261-X
N° de cat. NM95-59/6-1997

1. Muséologie — Congrès.
2. Textiles et tissus — Conservation et restauration — Congrès.
3. Costume — Conservation et restauration — Congrès.
I. Institut canadien de conservation.
II. Titre: L'étoffe d'une exposition, une approche pluridisciplinaire.

AM151.T47 1997   677.0075   C97-980236-9F

Cover illustrations and session dividers taken from:

Stockham, Peter ed. *Old-Time Crafts and Trades*. Dover Publications, Inc. New York: 1992.

Stockham, Peter ed. *Early Nineteenth-Century Crafts and Trades*. Dover Publications, Inc. New York: 1992.

Illustrations en couverture et divisions entre les séances tirées de :

Stockham, Peter ed. *Old-Time Crafts and Trades*. Dover Publications, Inc. New York: 1992.

Stockham, Peter ed. *Early Nineteenth-Century Crafts and Trades*. Dover Publications, Inc. New York: 1992.

This publication is printed on Mohawk Satin which conforms to the specifications set out in ANSI Z39,48-1992, "American National Standard for Permanence of Paper for Publications and Documents in Libraries and Archives".

La présente publication est imprimée sur du papier «Mohawk Satin» conformément aux spécifications de la norme ANSI Z39,48-1992 qui porte sur la permanence du papier utilisé pour les publications et les documents de bibliothèques et d'archives.

Table of Contents/Table des matières

1. Exhibition Perspectives
Perspectives en matière d'exposition

2. Exhibiting the Historic House
La maison historique en exposition

3. Considerations for the Long-term
Considérations à long terme

4. The Exhibition Environment
Les facteurs ambiants d'une exposition

5. Travelling a Collection
Le déplacement d'une collection

6. Support and Presentation
Support et présentation

7. Expanding Roles
Rôles en expansion

8. Demonstrations
Démonstrations

9. Posters
Affiches

Foreword

The first biennial North American Textile Conservation Conference — Symposium 97 — is the result of an unprecedented effort by textile conservators in the United States and Canada working together to develop a conference on the important topic of exhibiting textiles. Conferences organized by this group are intended to take the broadest possible approach to a topic in order to include the participation of curators, scientists, museum designers, art historians and other professionals. Symposium 97 succeeds in this by bringing together specialists from around the world to share their experiences on exhibiting textiles.

The goals of the North American Textile Conservation Conference are to organize meetings that explore issues relating to textile preservation. Supported by a different host institution each time, future meetings will also change locations within North America. Published conference papers will accompany each meeting. While these goals are ambitious, this first conference demonstrates that through the hard work, assistance and cooperation of many, we can share our experiences and advance the field of textile conservation. As well, the preprints will make this information accessible to an even wider audience.

The founding of this group was rooted in the desire to improve communication among textile conservators. The number of North American conferences that deal exclusively with themes related to textile preservation had declined, and the time seemed appropriate to develop a new organization to sponsor such meetings.

Throughout the planning and development of Symposium 97, Steering Committee members received generous support from their institutions. A special acknowledgment must be given to the Canadian Conservation Institute for its support, and to other members of the local organizing committee. They have generously and enthusiastically given their time and resources to making this event successful.

The Steering Committee is pleased to announce that the next North American Textile Conservation Conference, Symposium 2000, will be hosted by the Biltmore House textile conservation staff in Asheville, North Carolina. Biltmore House is the stately home of George Washington Vanderbilt, grandson of Commodore Cornelius Vanderbilt. Constructed in 1895, the house is nestled in the scenic Blue Ridge Mountains. The meeting will take place amidst the lovely floral display of the mountain springtime. We hope you will plan to attend.

Jane Merritt for the Steering Committee

Avant-propos

La première conférence biennale nord-américaine sur la conservation des textiles — Symposium 97 — est le fruit des efforts sans précédent de restaurateurs de textiles des États-Unis et du Canada, qui ont travaillé ensemble pour élaborer une conférence sur cet important sujet qu'est la mise en exposition des textiles. Les conférences organisées par ce groupe sont conçues pour traiter un sujet de la manière la plus vaste possible, afin que des conservateurs, des scientifiques, des concepteurs, des historiens de l'art et d'autres professionnels y participent. Symposium 97 y parvient en réunissant des spécialistes des quatre coins du monde pour qu'ils se communiquent ce que l'expérience leur a appris dans le domaine de la mise en exposition des textiles.

L'objectif de la Conférence nord-américaine sur la conservation des textiles consiste à organiser des rencontres portant sur des questions liées à la préservation des textiles. Les futures rencontres, dont chacune sera parrainée par un établissement hôte différent, se tiendront à divers endroits en Amérique du Nord. Les communications faites à chaque rencontre seront publiées. Bien que cet objectif soit ambitieux, cette première conférence montre que, grâce aux efforts, à l'aide et à la collaboration de beaucoup de gens, nous pouvons mettre en commun le fruit de notre expérience et faire des progrès en conservation des textiles. Les prétirages des communications rendront cette information accessible à un auditoire encore plus vaste.

Le désir d'améliorer la communication parmi les restaurateurs de textiles est à l'origine de la création de ce groupe. Le nombre de conférences nord-américaines portant exclusivement sur des thèmes liés à la préservation des textiles ayant diminué, le moment semblait bien choisi pour créer une nouvelle organisation qui parrainerait de telles rencontres.

Pendant toute la période de planification et d'élaboration de Symposium 97, les membres du Comité de direction ont été fortement soutenus par leurs établissements. Il faut remercier tout particulièrement l'Institut canadien de conservation de son appui, ainsi que les autres membres du comité organisateur local. Ils ont donné avec générosité et enthousiasme du temps et des ressources pour faire de cet événement une réussite.

Le Comité de direction a le plaisir d'annoncer que la prochaine conférence nord-américaine sur la conservation des textiles, Symposium 2000, sera organisée par le personnel en conservation des textiles de Biltmore House située à Asheville en Caroline du Nord. Biltmore House est la résidence de George Washington Vanderbilt, petit-fils du Commodore Cornelius Vanderbilt. Construite en 1895, la résidence est nichée dans les pittoresques montagnes Blue Ridge. La conférence aura lieu parmi le paysage florissant du printemps en montagne. Nous espérons que vous vous joindrez à nous.

Jane Merritt pour le Comité de direction

Acknowledgments

Steering Committee, North American Textile Conservation Conference
Deborah Bede, Minnesota Historical Society
Julia Burke, National Gallery of Art, Washington
Linda Eaton, Winterthur Museum
Patricia Ewer, Biltmore House
Michaela Keyserlingk, Canadian Conservation Institute (CCI)
Catherine C. McLean, Los Angeles County Museum of Art
Jane Merritt, US Department of the Interior, National Park Service
Chris Paulocik, The Costume Institute, Metropolitan Museum of Art
Sara Reiter, Philadelphia Museum of Art
Suzannne Thomassen-Krauss, National Museum of American History, Smithsonian Institution
Deborah Trupin, New York State Bureau of Historic Sites
Cara Varnell, Los Angeles County Museum of Art

Local Organizing Committee for Symposium 97
Renée Dancause, CCI
Jane Down, CCI
Tara Grant, CCI
Sherry Guild, CCI
Helen Holt, Canadian War Museum
Julie Hughes, Canadian Museum of Civilization
Michaela Keyserlingk, CCI
Lucie Thivierge, Parks Canada
Season Tse, CCI
Jan Vuori, CCI
Janet Wagner, CCI

Special thanks to CCI management and staff who have given their generous assistance.

Authors
The organizing committee thanks the authors for their manuscripts and cooperation. Additional thanks are given to session chairs, and poster and demonstration presenters.

Editorial Team
Edwinna von Baeyer, CCI
Linda Leclerc, CCI
Sophie Georgiev, Design and Layout, CCI

Program Assistance
Christine Bradley, CCI
Denise Levesque, CCI

National Gallery of Canada
courtesy of Dr. Shirley Thompson

Bursary and Financial Assistance
Institute of Textile Science
Dupont Canada Inc.
Lincoln Fabrics Limited
Dominion Industrial Fabrics Company
Textile Conservation Newsletter

Remerciements

Comité de direction, Conférence nord-américaine sur la conservation des textiles
Deborah Bede, Minnesota Historical Society
Julia Burke, National Gallery of Art, Washington
Linda Eaton, Winterthur Museum
Patricia Ewer, Biltmore House
Michaela Keyserlingk, Institut canadien de conservation (ICC)
Catherine C. McLean, Los Angeles County Museum of Art
Jane Merritt, US Department of the Interior, National Park Service
Chris Paulocik, The Costume Institute, Metropolitan Museum of Art
Sara Reiter, Philadelphia Museum of Art
Suzannne Thomassen-Krauss, National Museum of American History, Smithsonian Institution
Deborah Trupin, New York State Bureau of Historic Sites
Cara Varnell, Los Angeles County Museum of Art

Comité organisateur local pour Symposium 97
Renée Dancause, ICC
Jane Down, ICC
Tara Grant, ICC
Sherry Guild, ICC
Helen Holt, Musée canadien de la guerre
Julie Hughes, Musée canadien des civilisations
Michaela Keyserlingk, ICC
Lucie Thivierge, Parcs Canada
Season Tse, ICC
Jan Vuori, ICC
Janet Wagner, ICC

Remerciements particuliers aux gestionnaires et aux employés de l'ICC pour leur aide généreuse.

Auteurs
Le comité organisateur remercie les auteurs pour leurs manuscrits et leur collaboration. Merci également aux présidentes de séances, aux présentateurs d'affiches et de démonstrations.

Équipe de production
Edwinna von Baeyer, ICC
Linda Leclerc, ICC
Sophie Georgiev, conception graphique et mise en page, ICC

Aides à l'organisation
Christine Bradley, ICC
Denise Levesque, ICC

Musée des beaux-arts du Canada
grâce à la permission de Mme Shirley Thompson, Ph.D.

Bourses et aide financière
Institut des sciences textiles
Dupont Canada Inc.
Lincoln Fabrics Limited
Dominion Industrial Fabrics Company
Textile Conservation Newsletter

Introduction

Textile Symposium 97 - Fabric of an Exhibition: An Interdisciplinary Approach takes place from September 22 to 25, 1997 in Ottawa, Canada. It is the first biennial North American Textile Conservation Conference sponsored by textile conservators in Canada and the United States. Symposium 97 is organized locally by the Canadian Conservation Institute (CCI) and the federal Department of Canadian Heritage with generous input from the Steering Committee. Presentation of symposium papers and posters takes place at the National Gallery of Canada. Demonstrations of professional techniques are offered at the Canadian Conservation Institute, and tours of CCI, Laurier House and the Canadian Museum of Civilization are given.

In many ways, textiles represent the most personal record of human material history. As a result, textiles on display provide an attractive and imaginative human experience. But the conflict between access and preservation remains an ongoing concern. Textile artifacts on exhibition are very vulnerable. As well, museums are undergoing rapid changes as they try to cope with permanent exhibitions and increased demands for temporary and travelling exhibits. New attitudes towards exhibitions challenge curators, designers and conservators to question long-held professional assumptions.

The theme for Symposium 97 was chosen in recognition of the fact that exhibiting textiles demands close cooperation between conservators, designers, and curators as well as scientists. In arranging the program, the steering committee sought papers from a diverse group of professionals representing this broad spectrum of interests and activities. The sessions were planned to provide conference participants with the opportunity to exchange information and to benefit from each other's knowledge and experience.

The program covers new and innovative approaches and solutions to problems faced daily by conservators, designers and curators. Symposium presentations deal with a wide range of topics from contemporary exhibits to long-term displays, exhibition environments, historic houses, travelling exhibits, support and presentation, and expanding professional roles.

These preprints for *Textile Symposium 97 - Fabric of An Exhibition: An Interdisciplinary Approach* should contribute to finding solutions for the problems encountered when exhibiting textiles. Organizers of this symposium hope that it will deepen mutual understanding and cooperation among professionals responsible for exhibits of historic textiles.

Michaela Keyserlingk, *Chair, Symposium 97*

Introduction

Le *Symposium 97 sur les textiles - L'étoffe d'une exposition : une approche pluridisciplinaire* se tient du 22 au 25 septembre 1997, à Ottawa, Canada. C'est la première conférence biennale nord-américaine sur la conservation des textiles parrainée par des restaurateurs de textiles du Canada et des États-Unis. Symposium 97 est organisé dans la région par l'Institut canadien de conservation (ICC) et le ministère du Patrimoine canadien avec l'aide généreuse du Comité de direction. Les communications et les affiches préparées pour le symposium sont présentées au Musée des beaux-arts du Canada. Il y aura aussi des démonstrations de techniques professionnelles à l'Institut canadien de conservation, ainsi que des visites guidées de l'ICC, de la Maison Laurier et du Musée canadien des civilisations.

De bien des façons, les textiles sont les témoins les plus intimes de l'histoire des produits de l'activité humaine. Une exposition de textiles est donc une activité intéressante et qui frappe l'imagination. Cependant, le conflit entre l'accès et la préservation demeure une préoccupation constante. Les textiles en exposition sont très vulnérables. De plus, les musées, qui tentent de s'occuper d'expositions permanentes tout en répondant à une demande accrue d'expositions temporaires et itinérantes, sont en train d'évoluer rapidement. Les nouvelles attitudes à l'égard des expositions forcent les conservateurs, les concepteurs et les restaurateurs à mettre en question des principes de conservation établis depuis longtemps.

Le thème de Symposium 97 a été choisi parce qu'exposer des textiles nécessite une étroite collaboration entre les restaurateurs, les concepteurs et les conservateurs ainsi que les scientifiques. Pour organiser le programme de la conférence, le Comité de direction a demandé des communications à un groupe diversifié de professionnels représentant cette gamme étendue d'intérêts et d'activités. Les séances ont été planifiées de manière à permettre aux participants à la conférence d'échanger des renseignements et de profiter des connaissances et de l'expérience de chacun.

Le programme englobe des approches et des solutions nouvelles et novatrices en réponse à des problèmes rencontrés tous les jours par les restaurateurs, les conservateurs et les concepteurs. Les exposés portent sur des sujets très divers tels que les expositions contemporaines, les expositions de longue durée, les facteurs ambiants des expositions, les maisons historiques, les expositions itinérantes, les supports et la présentation, ainsi que les rôles professionnels en expansion.

Les prétirages rédigés pour *Symposium 97 sur les textiles - L'étoffe d'une exposition : une approche pluridisciplinaire* devraient aider à trouver des solutions aux problèmes posés par la mise en exposition des textiles. Les organisateurs de ce symposium espèrent qu'il favorisera la compréhension mutuelle et la collaboration entre les professionnels chargés des expositions de textiles historiques.

Michaela Keyserlingk, *Présidente, Symposium 97*

1

Exhibition Perspectives
Perspectives en matière d'exposition

Can High Productivity be Productive?

Jonathan Ashley-Smith

Victoria and Albert Museum
Cromwell Road
London SW7 2RL United Kingdom
Tel.: 0171-938-8568
E-mail: jonathan@vam.ac.uk

Lynda Hillyer

Victoria and Albert Museum
Cromwell Road
London SW7 2RL United Kingdom
Tel.: 0171-938-8591
E-mail: lyndah@vam.ac.uk

Abstract

Accessibility is the essential element which promotes the understanding and enjoyment of a museum's collections. For the general public, this access is achieved through permanent gallery displays and temporary exhibitions. Increasing demand for temporary exhibitions, which will travel to a number of venues and the need to keep changing the "permanent" displays, have presented new challenges to the Textiles Conservation Section at the Victoria and Albert Museum. This paper examines the experience gained during three major projects carried out over the past six years. There have been changes in attitude and responsibility, as well as the development of new skills and techniques. These changes are discussed in the context of the V&A's mission and attitudes to productivity, preservation and access.

Productivity?

The title of this paper is intended to indicate that the Textile Section of the Conservation Department at the Victoria and Albert Museum (V&A) is highly productive, that is, the textile conservators undertake a satisfyingly large number of tasks in a year. Meeting deadlines for a large number of loans, exhibitions and gallery openings satisfies the organisers of these events and so automatically pleases the head of the Conservation Department. It may not necessarily satisfy the conservators who interpret it as undesirable pressure.

High productivity measured by performance indicators such as 'quantity of objects treated' is likely to appeal to the civil servants who regulate the flow of public money. It is easy to measure like the indicator 'number of museum visitors through the doors'. This is widely acknowledged as lacking any qualitative dimension, pays no regard to academic progress, and totally ignores long-term outcomes. However, because the information is reasonably easy to gather, it becomes the dominant indicator. In time, museum directors adopt policies that satisfy that criterion in order to maintain income from government. Eventually such behaviour becomes so commonplace that it is difficult to remember why the indicator was thought so inadequate.

A performance indicator should be chosen to measure the success of a policy, but now the policy has been designed to meet the performance indicator. An inappropriate measure turns out to be ideal. The senior managers of a conservation department might easily fall into the same trap, believing that high productivity was an admirable goal in its own right.

So the title of this paper asks "Can successfully meeting the criteria of an inadequate performance indicator actually result in long-term benefit to the collections, to the conservators and to the profession"?

Context

The Victoria and Albert Museum has 145 years experience of displaying textiles. Since the Museum was founded in 1852, the collections of textile-related material have grown at an average rate of 800 objects a year, leading to a diverse assortment of around 120,000 objects. Visitor surveys have consistently shown that the most popular attraction is the display of historic dress. Temporary exhibitions relating to current or recent fashion in dress are always well attended.

At the V&A there is one major curatorial department specialising in the collection and interpretation of textiles and dress. However there are five other departments in the Museum with substantial textile holdings relating to furniture, theatre, childhood, India and the Far East. The Textile Section of the Conservation Department has to respond to the needs of these separate collections.

Each curatorial department is responsible for the organisation of storage for its collections and for the regulation of access. Each has its own proposed programme of loans and changing displays. From time to time one curatorial department may be the centre of a major gallery refurbishment or a major temporary exhibition. From time to time curatorial departments contribute to centrally organised travelling exhibitions or temporary displays containing objects from a number of different collections. Many of these projects are concurrent and may have deadlines that are close in time.

The Conservation Department is a conduit through which all these projects, real or proposed, must pass. The main thing that restricts the flow is the size of the conduit. To a limited extent the flow can be controlled by imposing or relaxing standards and by regulating the degree of job satisfaction. Different objects require varying degrees of conservation treatment, some lasting a few hours, some lasting months or even years (Table 1). It is inevitable that the Textile Conservation Section is always working on a large number of simultaneous projects at different stages of completion. It is common for a conservator to be working on several objects concurrently.

Table 1

Distribution of treatment times for textile conservation from a sample of 1690 samples

% of Treatments	Time Taken (hrs) per Treatment
57	5
29	15
11	60
2.8	500
0.2	1600

Preservation and Access

The Conservation Department is an integral part of the Museum. The work of any part of an organisation must assist rather than resist the aims of that organisation. If preservation and access are seen as separate activities within a museum, it will appear that they are in conflict. However it is possible to arrive at a state of mind where the two processes are integrated harmoniously. In her 'systems view', Suzanne Keene[1] arrives at a definition of a museum that begins to do this: "A system to permanently maintain an irreplaceable and meaningful physical resource and to use it to transmit ideas and concepts to the public". This suggests a role for a conservation department as maintaining a non-renewable resource which is destined for use.

The mission of the V&A is to "increase the enjoyment and understanding of art, craft and design through its collections". The underlying assumption is that there will always be collections to act as the medium for communicating understanding and enjoyment. The message of the mission statement is that the Museum sees its major purpose in the relationship between the objects and the audience, not in the objects by themselves. Preservation of the artefacts is not a sufficient reason for the existence of the Museum.

If a museum were a static and isolated collection of objects in varying states of decay, it would be relatively easy to sort out the conservation priorities. A general condition audit could be followed by more detailed surveys of groups of artefacts at risk. Once everything had been done to

optimise conditions of storage and display, practical intervention could begin with the least stable objects and continue until every object was stable and in optimum visual condition, beautifully displayed or safely stored. This is the simplistic scenario that has led government auditors to berate national museums about conservation backlogs.[2]

Taking the V&A as an example, there are nine full-time conservators in the Textile Section. With our present understanding of the state of the collection, and our more accurate knowledge of the distribution of past treatment times, it can be predicted that the nine conservators working full-time would complete all the necessary treatments in about 40 years. This is the definition of a 'backlog'; the time it would take to deal with all outstanding work if you ignored all other calls on your time. This is a finite period and it is imaginable that, if only there were more conservators, the whole sorry mess could be cleared up in a few years. This illusion is born out of a desire for tangible personal achievement, a desire to see completion rather than contentment at being a temporary part of a continuous process.

The reality is different from the illusion for a number of reasons:

- The staff resource cannot be devoted exclusively to practical intervention. Senior staff spend time planning, supervising and training. Junior staff spend time being appraised and being trained.
- The collection is not static. In achievable display and storage conditions there is still deterioration; conservation materials and treatments have limited lifetimes.
- The museum is not static. New objects are acquired. To avoid excessive exposure, objects are rotated between storage and display. To reach new and greater audiences, and to tell new stories, there are temporary exhibitions, renewed displays and loans out.

It is possible to build a simple computer model that calculates the effect of various factors on the 'backlog' and progresses this through time. In the real dynamic system in which objects decay, treatments do not last forever and the museum continuously interacts with its audience, the calculation of the apparent backlog for textiles objects at the V&A increases from 40 to about 150 years. At the end of 40 years, even though some 40,000 treatments have taken place, the 'backlog' remains at about 150 years. If it is true that conservation treatments only last for a limited period of time, say a few decades, then it is obvious that the work can never be completed. All the objects that are treated eventually revert to the category of objects awaiting treatment.

The dynamic model indicates that eliminating backlog is not a meaningful major aim unless museums radically alter their mission. Objects pass through the Conservation Department, not so we can tick another object off our list, but as part of their continuous maintenance, allowing them to be used and re-used as resources for emotional and educational experiences.

In a dynamic system, we cannot deal with problems in the logical order proposed for the static illusion. The criteria for prioritising treatment are not solely object condition, but also the date the piece is needed for exhibition. Condition audit and detailed survey must be carried out as a continuous interactive process in parallel with preventive programmes and interventive treatments. The management problem is not about doing things in the logical order but about achieving a balance between a number of concurrent continuing activities.

Changing displays, loans and exhibitions do not interfere with the work of the Department, they are an essential part of the work.

Constant Change in Permanent Displays

As recently as ten years ago it was assumed that the lifetime of a gallery design was at least 25 years and that the same objects would remain on display until finances allowed a re-think, a fresh design and a total refurbishment. The Nehru Gallery of Indian Art, which opened at the V&A in 1990, broke with this traditional view. The design accommodated the plan that parts of the display would change at regular intervals to protect light-sensitive material from over-exposure and to allow more of the Museum's large Indian collections to be made accessible to the public.[3] Other galleries in the Museum, such as the Dress Collection, have areas for small changing displays, but these are distinct from the main thematic exhibition. The aim with the new gallery was to allow parts of the various display sequences to be changed while ensuring that the condensed story of Indian art retained its coherence.

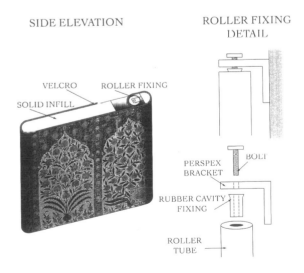

Figure 1. Roller and Perspex bracket system used for patkas (sashes) incorporated into a former to display a qanat (continuous tent hangings).

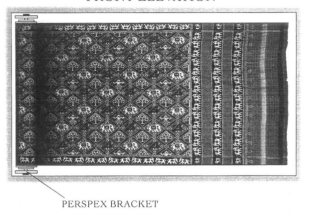

Figure 2. Roller and Perspex bracket system used on a board to display a patola (double ikat sari length).

The first display in the newly refurbished gallery involved 85 textiles and took three years to prepare. During this period, conservators worked closely with the designer and with the technical workshops to develop a range of mounting systems. A roller system used for items such as patkas (sashes) was incorporated into formers and boards so that very much larger textiles could be successfully displayed within limited space. The simplicity of the system eased handling during changes of display and in many cases the rollers could be used for storage (see Figures 1, 2).

The first re-display was originally planned to take place after one year but, because of pressure on the curatorial and conservation sections, a period of two years between rotations was thought to be more manageable. The first rotation required the treatment of 20 major textiles. Because of the length of time needed, work had already started on some items for the second cycle. The intricate early 19th century paijama and gown referred to as the costume of the Queen of Oudh (Figures 3, 4) required 2000 hours of work over a period of four years.[4]

Most textile objects cannot be displayed forever without obvious changes in colour and dangerous weakening of the fibres. Even at low levels of illumination with no ultraviolet content, some form of rotation policy becomes necessary for all textiles. The factors that dictate how frequent that rotation can be are: the ease with which an object can be removed without destroying the didactic or visual coherence of the display, the time to safely store the displaced object, the availability of a suitable replacement and the time necessary to research and prepare the replacement. Curators and conservators may decide to choose material that will not need much treatment which can be more easily fitted

Figure 3. The Queen of Oudh's costume on display in the Nehru Gallery of Indian Art.

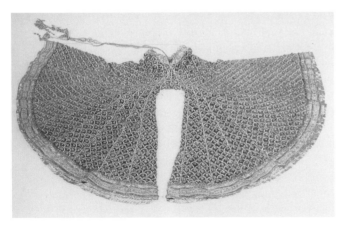

Figure 4. The elaborate paijama from the Queen of Oudh's costume before conservation.

into a crowded programme. However this would mean that certain difficult objects will never be displayed no matter how interesting they may be. It also means that senior conservators are never challenged and junior conservators never learn to rise to a challenge. The curators of the Indian and South East Asian Collection have a wish list of objects that

are possible candidates for the rotation programme which also provide challenging conservation projects.

For conservation reasons, there should be more frequently changing displays, yet the policy adds a permanent addition to the flow of proposals to the Conservation Department; a call for higher productivity. Even so, the programme to date has produced lasting benefits. The development of systematised mounting methods has saved time in the preparation of a number of exhibitions, gallery schemes and loans since then. The Nehru project was among the first where there was a permanent conservation representative on the project team. This makes the conservator more aware of the problems that other members of the team have to face. Working closely with the designer helped develop a lasting relationship that has saved time and arguments in later exhibitions. Working more closely with the curators made conservators more aware of collections management problems and allowed conservation input into storage methods in the reserve collection. Despite pressure of time the programme stimulated research into problems such as the removal of rust stains from iron mordanted chintzes and provoked a review of the use of adhesive treatments in the section.[5,6]

Travelling Exhibitions

Between 1992 and 1995, the V&A organised five major exhibitions, each containing several hundred objects, which travelled to a number of venues in Japan. The planning for the repetition of packing, unpacking, mounting and dismantling involved careful consideration of the choice of objects, the accurate assessment of current condition and of future risks. Before the objects travelled, all the venues were checked to see whether they could maintain the environmental parameters specified in the loan agreement and to assess the difficulties of delivery and installation. During the exhibitions and while the objects were in transit, the conditions in the galleries, display cases, packing cases, and vans were recorded. Vibration measurements showed that there were only slight shocks and that these occurred mostly during the mechanical handling of the packing cases, less so while the cases were man-handled, and not at all during transit in the air-ride vehicles.[7]

There was a long lead-in to the project, which allowed plenty of time to select appropriate objects. Selection, of course, implies inspecting a large number of objects, only a few of which will be deemed suitable. This time-consuming selection process must take place at an early stage and cannot be postponed until other work is out of the way. At first the choices were quite conservative for textiles, costume and very large objects were rejected. The borrowing organisation used the same handlers throughout and had hired a resident conservator to help with condition-checking. As confidence grew in the integrity of this team, more adventurous choices were made for later exhibitions. With hindsight, some choices were too adventurous - objects with metal threads or sequins which were susceptible to damage by vibration or abrasion by even the most gentle of packing materials.

In addition to inspection and practical intervention the conservators had further duties. Couriers, who would be different at every transfer, were given training in handling techniques, and in understanding the potential for damage and its early recognition. The Japanese conservator, who would be present at every stage, was shown the methods of packing and mounting of complex exhibits. V&A conservators acted as couriers for some changes of venue.

A number of lasting benefits arose from this experience. Perhaps the most valuable was a clearer understanding of the risks of travel. The large number of objects and the repetition of transfers meant that a swift standard method of condition-checking was needed, this can now be used for other loans. A great deal of effort went into devising standardised methods of mounting that allowed handling by non-specialist staff. The experience of designing Perspex mounts and working with Ethafoam bodies has been useful for later displays. It has been possible to incorporate some of the mounted and framed objects prepared for loan in a newly refurbished textile study room.

Borrowing Material for Exhibition

In 1996, the Museum organised a major temporary exhibition about the life and work of William Morris. There was a long planning lead time. For the final 18 months, a member of the Conservation Department worked with the exhibition curator, the exhibitions officer and the designer to ensure the flow of information between the exhibition team and the specialist conservators and conservation scientists.

As a responsible borrower, the Museum had to assess the risks of receiving objects from sources that had no immediate access to conservation expertise. Past experience had taught that objects from historic houses and churches are most susceptible to environmental damage, moving from generally cold and damp surroundings to a warm and comparatively dry museum. The people responsible for the contents of such institutions may be willing to lend without having the skills to assess whether the objects are stable enough to travel or strong enough to be displayed effectively.

The costs of V&A staff assessing the condition of objects before they travelled to the Museum had to be weighed against the time that might be spent hurriedly making the object fit for exhibition once it had arrived. Nearly all the textiles to be borrowed for the William Morris show were viewed *in situ* by a V&A conservator. Where treatment was needed, specifications were agreed to and work carried out by colleagues in the private sector.

A conservator advising an exhibition designer has to have the safety of the object in mind and seek to avoid unnecessary intervention before and after the exhibition. The display method must fully support the object. A textile which is mounted on a board will not be subject to potentially damaging stresses but its essential qualities of drape and fluidity are lost. For this exhibition, in a section evoking the environment of a workshop, some textiles were simply laid in cases. In other sections, a deliberate attempt was made to demonstrate the natural form of the textile by mounting on specially shaped formers (see Figures 5, 6).

Textile conservators are very worried about open display. The showcase or glazed frame is a proven protection against dirt and pollution. The presence of dirt amongst the textile fibres may possibly be damaging, and it is certain that the attempts to remove any soiling are risky if not destructive. In this instance, a positive decision was made to show a proportion of the textiles in the open with only

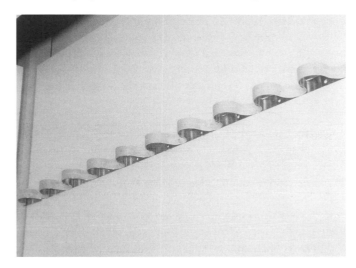

Figure 5. Wiggly former constructed of aluminum and faced with Velcro.

Figure 6. William Morris velvet curtain supported on a wiggly former.

the protection of the air-conditioning. In this way, it was possible to give some impression of the cohesion and variety of Morris designs which would only be apparent when seen in room settings. Moreover, some carpets were displayed with furniture placed on them, something that would disturb a conservator with the sole interest of preventing any long-term damage.

For conservators to cooperate in displaying textiles in ways that would traditionally be thought of as unsafe needs a flexible way of thinking that involves a barely conscious analysis of costs and benefits. For a brief period, a textile in sound condition and displayed unsupported will not be damaged; a textile unprotected in an open exhibition space will not become detectably dirty. The risks, the costs of damage and future treatment are small. There are immense potential benefits. A great many visitors will see textiles in context, textiles that act like textiles. The Morris exhibition was a huge success attracting 216,159 visitors in four months.

The success of the Conservation Department's contribution to this exhibition was the result of accumulated experience from other exhibitions and displays. It stemmed from early involvement in planning and the development of good working relationships with exhibition staff and designers over a period of years.

Conclusion

Each of the three projects discussed contributed to, and benefited from, a continuous process of learning by experiment and experience. They proved the value of developing long-term relationships built on trust of other people's professionalism. They were not always welcomed as additional demands for higher productivity, but were productive of new attitudes, new ideas and opportunities for staff development. Whether this was despite the pressure or because of it is difficult to judge.

The system is dynamic not just because there is a constant flow, the nature of the flow changes year by year. It is easy to feel that the pressure has increased to a point where necessary tasks are being left undone and unnecessary risks are being taken. However there is no one point in the past to use as a benchmark, the notions of necessity and of risk are changing too.

Endnotes

[1] Keene, Suzanne. *Managing Conservation in Museums.* Oxford: Butterworth-Heinemann in association with the Science Museum, 1996, pp. 76-94.

[2] National Audit Office. *Management of the Collections of the English National Museums and Galleries. Report by the Comptroller and Auditor General.* London: Her Majesty's Stationery Office, March 1988.

[3] Swallow, Deborah. "Conservation and Rotating Displays in the Nehru Gallery of Indian Art," *V&A Conservation Journal*, vol. 5 (1992), pp. 8-9.

[4] Hillyer, Lynda. "The Queen of Oudh, Conservation and Research," *Costume in Context*, Postprints of the UKIC Textile Group Meeting, March 1996.

[5] Potter, Jenny. *A New Method of Removing Rust Stains from Indian Chintz.* Research Project (unpublished). RCA/V&A M.A. Conservation Course (Textiles), March 1994.

[6] Hillyer, Lynda, and Boris Pretzel. "Research in Progress. A Re-evalution of Adhesives - work in progress at the V&A," *Newsletter of the Working Group of Textiles. ICOM Committee for Conservation*, Number 2 (1993).

[7] Discussion of the environmental risks involved in these exhibitions can be found in: Ashley-Smith, Jonathan, D. Ford, and N. Umney. *Let's be Honest: Realistic Environmental Parameters for Loaned Objects.* Preventive Conservation: Practice, Theory and Research. Preprints to the Ottawa Congress, 12-16 September 1994, pp. 28-31, and also Ashley-Smith, Jonathan. *Let's be Honest.* Accessible in the Ethics section of Conservation On Line on the World Wide Web at http://www.palimpsest.stanford.edu And also, Ashley-Smith, Jonathan. *Consider the Benefits, Calculate the Risks.* 1995. Accessible in the Ethics section of Conservation On Line on the World Wide Web at http://www.palimpsest.stanford.edu

Résumé

Les niveaux de productivité élevés peuvent-ils être productifs?

L'accessibilité est un élément crucial qui favorise la compréhension et l'agrément des collections de musée. Dans le cas du grand public, l'accès doit être assuré grâce à des expositions permanentes et temporaires. La demande croissante en expositions temporaires, qui se déplacent d'un endroit à l'autre, et la nécessité de modifier régulièrement les expositions «permanentes» présentent des défis nouveaux pour la section de conservation des textiles du musée Victoria & Albert. Dans l'article, on examine l'expérience acquise au cours de trois grands projets menés ces six dernières années. La démarche et les responsabilités ont changé, des compétences et des techniques nouvelles ont vu le jour. Ces changements sont traités dans le contexte de la mission du musée Victoria & Albert et des attitudes face à la productivité, la préservation et l'accès.

Textile Conservation, Exhibit and Storage Design for the Commonwealth's Flag Reinstallation Project

Betsy Gould

Boston Art Conservation
9 Station Street
Brookline, MA 02146 USA
Tel.: (617) 738-1126
Fax: (617) 734-5490
E-mail: bgould@ bosartconserv.com

Abstract

The purpose of this project is to provide a practical balance between exhibition requirements and stable long-term preservation for the flag collection of the Commonwealth of Massachusetts. The project incorporates seven phases:

1. research and assessment of the display cases to provide proper exhibition conditions,
2. display case modification design,
3. mock-up of design,
4. modification construction,
5. survey to assign conservation and curatorial priorities,
6. storage improvement, and
7. conservation treatment of an initial 48 of the collection's 300+ flags.

Introduction

The Commonwealth of Massachusetts holds a collection of 300 military flags, which were on exhibit at the State House in Boston from 1865 to 1987. In 1900, the Hall of Flags was built as a memorial in which to hang the Civil War flags. The hall is a large circular space of sienna marble in which there is a stained glass dome, murals depicting civil war scenes, and eight semicircular niches into which all 300 flags were divided. They have been displayed there vertically on their poles until 1987. Since the 1980s, conservation planning and treatment has been ongoing. In 1987, the mural paintings were treated, the stained glass dome is now scheduled to be treated by October 1997, and furthermore, the architectural finishes are currently being analyzed for future treatment. In 1984, the flags were initially examined, condition reports written, and they were returned to their niches. In 1987, the flags were removed from display and placed in temporary storage until proper exhibition conditions could be executed, conservation treatment performed, and stable long-term storage provided.

Boston Art Conservation was contracted for the Commonwealth's flag reinstallation project. The contract is for 18 months which began June 1, 1996 and runs through November 1997. At the time of this writing (January 1997), my partner, Paul Messier, and I, are eight months into the work. The purpose of the project is to provide a practical balance between exhibition requirements and stable long-term preservation of the collection. The project is multifaceted and incorporates the following phases which make up our plan: (1) research and assessment of the eight semicircular display case niches in order to provide proper exhibition conditions, (2) display case modification design, (3) in-situ mock-up of the display case modification design, (4) display case modification construction, (5) a survey of the flags to assign conservation and curatorial priorities, (6) the improvement of the current storage facility to create proper conditions for long-term storage and preservation, (7) conservation treatment and mounting of an initial 48 of the Civil War flags.

Phase 1: Research and Assessment

When the flags were placed in storage in 1987, the glass fronts were painted black, and hung with a transparency of a flag. To access the display case niches, we needed to remove the glass plate panels, because the only entrance was through a small rear door. While removing the glass fronts, it became apparent that all eight niches were not identical. The four inside niches were one-quarter the size of the outside niches, and finished with marble facing, while the larger outside niches were painted plaster walls. After researching the history of the Hall of Flags, it became evident that the smaller niches had been designed for the placement of sculpture, which related to the flags' history, and it was the larger ones which were intended for the flags' display. Over the years, as the number of flags increased from the original Civil War flags, all eight niches were used to accommodate the growing collection.

Environment

Before we could proceed with the display case and storage modification plans, our initial concern was to study and evaluate the environment. There have been precedents of high temperature and humidity in the niches and in storage. There was a water leak in a niche, which unfortunately went unnoticed for an unknown period of time, causing extreme mold growth and the need for an environmental specialist to be called in to exchange and filter the air from the case. There have also been instances of theft, and vandalism of a display glass. These are concerns of all public institutions with collections to protect. But in a public building having open access such as the State House, without a security staff specifically appropriated to the collection, or a permanent ongoing staff who can be responsible for the daily monitoring and maintenance of the collection, we thought it imperative to have a system installed that is able to provide the highest level of monitoring.

Temperature, relative humidity, visible and ultraviolet light along with issues of security, assuring a quick response to disaster situations (i.e., flood), and threats of theft or vandalism were issues we wanted addressed. The only on-site equipment available were two hygrothermographs. With nine sites to monitor, the eight niches and storage, equipment needed to be purchased. After researching the options of hygrothermographs, remote data loggers, and the Hanwell wireless system, we choose to recommend that the State purchase the Hanwell system. For both the immediate environmental concerns with regard to our display case modification recommendations, and long-term monitoring, it was the most efficient system. From a single location using a personal computer, it has the ability to monitor all cases with easily maintainable remote wireless sensors. It is an active rather than passive system, as it has the capacity to record, analyze, and interpret the information immediately, and can be programmed with alarms for situations needing immediate attention. We have scheduled its installation for early March. The specific requirements for temperature, humidity, pollutant filtering, light and ventilation will be recommended after the monitoring system has been installed, data collected and analyzed.

Phase 2: Display Case Modification Design

Our initial proposal consisted of two display options using all eight niches. In our revised plan we eliminated the small niches for flag display. This had historical intent and conservation considerations. The plan met preservation parameters, and it was in keeping with the architectural aesthetics of the Hall of Flags. Aside from historical considerations, the small niches presented severe display difficulties. They allowed only vertical pressure mounts which would require double glazing, one for the external glass, one for the pressure mount. Also, a third of the flags, the largest ones, could not be displayed because 12.5 cm (5 in.) of the flag would be obscured on either side of the case opening. If the small niches were to be used, the flags displayed in the large niches would also have to be vertically mounted. The necessary exception being that the largest flags would always have to be displayed in the large niche, singularly at an angle, thus simultaneously creating two display techniques, losing display consistency.

Decreasing the Niche Size
When assessing the four large niches, one of our initial concerns was the large quantity of air volume. The 388.2 m^3 (1,254 ft.^{3}) made it difficult to create

a manageable microenvironment. Because of this, we decided it was necessary to modify the niche to less than one half its size by creating a case within a case, with an air volume of 187.2 m^3 (624 ft.^{3}).

The decreased niche size would ease the management of its environment and allow the implementation of a passive rather than an active air handling system using silica gel. The gel will first be conditioned to the required relative humidity or a little higher to allow for air exchange. The effectiveness of this as a way of controlling case humidity depends to a large extent on the airtightness of the case; if the leakage rate is too high, then the silica gel will be unable to compensate. The gel maintains the humidity level for a variable period of time, depending on both the leakage rate and the external conditions. The cases will be sealed to prevent as little air exchange as possible. About 42 pounds of silica gel per modified sealed case will be needed. It will be divided into four tubes spaced throughout the case. Part of every batch will be conditioned every display rotation, or three times a years. Like the monitoring system, a system needing as little daily monitoring and maintenance as possible is required.

Light
The light levels were a concern, because after the treatment of the stained glass dome, the natural light levels emitted within the hall will become considerably higher. We plan to maintain levels in the cases no higher than five to 10 footcandles (50 to 100 lux), and have an ultraviolet filter incorporated into the display glass, but if the levels are extremely high we may have to take further measures. We plan to have a flexible lighting system, which is directional and features variable intensities housed externally from the sealed case, hidden in the false ceiling of the new smaller case to lessen any radiant heat.

Support Mounts
It is a parameter that after conservation treatment the flags be handled as infrequently as possible, because of their fragile condition, and the fact that the personnel responsible for handling them may not be trained in handling extremely fragile textiles. Our solution is to have rigid support mounts, which we have designed to serve both display, transport, and storage. This system of a single, permanent mount for each flag insures that they will be handled as little as possible. For ease and consistency, we divided the flags into thirds according to size, thus creating three standard mount sizes. The mounts are a dimensionally stable board made with a poplar frame, 1.25 cm (1/2 in.) honeycomb core with a 0.4 mm (.016 in.) aluminum skin on both sides. A padding, which is laid on the face of the board, is cut out in the center based on the individual dimensions of each flag, creating a well. The display fabric is stretched over the face of the board, and the flag is placed in the well, so it does not protrude from the surface of the mount. While the flag mounts are in transit from

storage to the display site an acrylic cover will be screwed into the mount to protect the flags and allow them to be carried vertically. Once they are installed in the display case the protective cover will be removed.

Mount Display

The display unit will consist of a metal armature which is secured to the niche wall. Attached to vertical members will be horizontal brackets. These brackets will be able to be moved up and down or adjusted to a desired display angle. The mount boards are secured to the metal brackets, and will allow the mount to appear to "float" in the display case. The angle of the board, and the nap of the chosen display fabric will hold the flags in place.

Display Rotation

When this project is completed, 48 of the collection's 300+ flags will have been treated. We had to take into consideration that this may be the only number of flags available for rotation for an unknown period of time, until more flags are able to be treated. Considering this, we have scheduled a four-year rotation per flag: 1 flag displayed per large niche = 4 flags per rotation x 3 rotations yearly = 12 flags per year x 4 years = 48 flags. Display time any more frequently than every four years is risking too much exposure to light, handling, and change of environment, all of which accelerates degradation to the already fragile textiles, even in optimum display environments.

Phases 3 and 4: In-situ Mock-up of Case Modification Design and Case Modification Construction

In one niche, using foam core, wood strapping, and paint, we built an in-situ mock-up of our modification plan. Following the architectural lines of the hall we created a false ceiling and floor, and following the curve of the semicircular niche, decreased the walls by about 30 cm (1 ft.). We built the display armature of the wood, and made foam core mounts in the three standard mount sizes. We are now engaged in interviewing architects to work with us in drawing up our plans for construction, and to assist us with the lighting specifications. Construction of the niche modification is scheduled to begin in July.

Mount Transport

One of the logistical problems we face with the mounted flags is the transport of the largest mount from the storage area to display in the Hall of Flags. The storage vault is several stories below ground, and not equipped with a freight elevator. The only access is two three-story cinderblock and cement stairwells, one of which is too small, even for restructuring. The second one can be modified by cutting a notch in the cement floor, and installing a hydraulic pulley system to transport the mounts with as little vibration as possible. Other modifications, including an elevator built into the storage vault are being explored,

but budget restraints are constricting. The option of rolling the large flags for transport is not an option we are willing to explore because of their fragility, and again we must consider the fact that the staff responsible for the display rotation may not be conservators or trained personnel. Therefore, permanent mounts which serve display, transport, and storage are a preservation necessity.

Phase 5: Conservation and Curatorial Priority

The 48 Civil War flags for this project will be chosen from the collection after a survey and examination of the flags is performed for both conservation and curatorial priorities. The examination is scheduled for April. At that time, an on-site conservation facility will be established.

Phase 6: Storage Improvement

The storage vault itself will need improvement, and the environment is of great concern. The vault is near an area which has been known to flood periodically, and the temperature remains low and the relative humidity high. In 1989 a new HVAC system was installed in the State House, but it does not function adequately enough for the storage vault. Further analysis and our specific recommendations for improving the environment will be done in the spring after the new monitoring system has been installed and data collected.

In 1987, when the flags were taken out of their niches, open temporary storage shelving units were created of baked-enamel finish steel angle iron, which was cut into various needed lengths. The shelving material or "pallets" were a double-walled, acid-free cardboard. In 1989, because of the construction of the HVAC system, the flags were rolled, and again placed into another temporary storage situation. This time, into boxes constructed of wood, double-walled, acid-free cardboard and lined with Mylar. The collection is now still stored in these boxes, two or three rolled flags per box.

It is projected that after the environmental recommendations have been implemented, the new storage units will be installed. We are now studying various systems, but the option of choice will probably be for baked enamel finish cases, but for more permanent storage, ones that are fully enclosed, sealed, and with sliding drawers which will accommodate the flags on their permanent mounts.

Phase 7: Conservation Treatment

Once the niche construction is under way, the storage system designed, chosen and implemented, conservation treatment will begin. This is scheduled for summer 1997. The collection is generally in fair to poor condition. Considerable damage and fading has been done, caused from years of being exhibited in conditions of exposure to uncontrolled light and heat. Damage was also caused by the flags hanging unsupported on their poles. There are diagonal folds and creases caused by this hanging position, which are virtually permanent. The interior of some of the flags is stretched, that fullness is also permanent and must be considered when mounting and storing.

Many of the flags have been previously treated in the 1920s by Mrs. Ritchie and her daughter who specialized in the "interlock stitch." This technique was done on flags both in poor and good condition, flags of either silk, wool, or cotton, painted or unpainted. It stabilized at the time many fragments in poor condition, but has created problems in others. The flags were attached by this stitch to a backing, and the needleholes have caused splitting to develop along the lines of the stitch, especially in the silk, and painted silk flags. It is not my intent to remove these stitches, as the potential damage would de-stabilize the flags even further. Other than this, my plans for specific treatment will depend on the individual condition of each of the chosen flags.

Conclusion

In September, at the time of the Symposium, the multifaceted aspects of this project will be coming together, and they will secure as a whole the long-term preservation of the Commonwealth's flag collection. At that time, I will discuss the updates and progress we have made with this project over the course of the next eight months.

Résumé

Conservation, exposition et mise en réserve des textiles dans le projet de réinstallation des drapeaux du Commonwealth

L'objectif du projet est de fournir un compromis pratique entre les exigences en matière d'exposition et celles de la préservation à long terme de la collection de drapeaux du Commonwealth du Massachusetts. Le projet se répartit en sept étapes :

1. *recherche et évaluation des vitrines d'exposition en vue d'assurer des conditions adéquates de présentation;*
2. *étude de la modification des vitrines d'exposition;*
3. *fabrication d'un modèle modifié;*
4. *fabrication des vitrines modifiées;*
5. *étude visant à établir la liste des priorités de préservation et de conservation;*
6. *amélioration de la mise en réserve;*
7. *traitement de restauration d'un premier groupe de 48 drapeaux de la collection de plus de 300 pièces.*

Textile Exhibition Practices in the Philippines

Evelyn T. Elveña

Chemistry and Conservation Laboratory
National Museum of the Philippines
P. Burgos Street
P. O. Box 2659
Manila, Philippines
Tel.: 527-12-33
Fax: 527-03-06

Abstract

The National Museum of the Philippines is mandated by the government to protect and preserve the rich cultural heritage of the country. One of its objectives is to preserve national treasures whether they are movable or immovable objects, and includes textiles. The Chemistry and Conservation Laboratory undertakes research and preservation of all types of objects. Since its establishment, the laboratory has analyzed and conserved hundreds of textile specimens. The staff also assists in setting up textiles for exhibits in private or government museums. Most museums in the Philippines collect, preserve, and exhibit textile objects and artifacts using textiles. Collections are varied and include ecclesiastical cloth, archaeological and ethnological textiles, and even contemporary textiles. This paper discusses the different techniques used for properly exhibiting, lighting and mounting textiles at the National Museum and at the San Agustin Church Museum. Recommendations for upgrading display methods are also included.

National Museum Exhibition Techniques

The items displayed at the National Museum range from costumes, blouses, skirts, malongs, blankets, trousers, belts, headgears, to bags. Their fibers are made up mostly of cotton, piña, ramie, linen and abaca. Decorations on these textiles include shells, metals, sequins, beads, buttons, and tassels.

a) For costumes

Costumes are displayed on mannequins and hangers padded with pre-washed white cotton cloth. They are enclosed in a glass case which serves as protection against dust, dirt and handling.

b) For small, flat textiles

Small, flat textiles are mounted on plywood that has been sprayed with varnish in order to seal off the acid gases emitted by wood, thereby protecting the object from harmful chemicals. A plastic cover is used to protect the object from dust and dirt. This method prolongs the life of the object considerably.

c) For long, flat textiles

An alternative way of exhibiting long, flat textiles is to hang the object from a rod: one end of the textile is rolled and sewn, while the other end extends to the floor of the showcase, or the textile hangs freely.

d) For archaeological textiles

Upon retrieval from an archaeological site, the textile is given conservation treatment. It is wrapped in acid-free paper. Very fragile fragments are placed between sheets of glass. Upon arrival at the Chemistry and Conservation Laboratory, the textile is given immediate treatment. It is cleaned and its fibers are aligned. For the final treatment,

Figure 1. Textiles on padded hangers.

Figure 2. Textiles on mannequins.

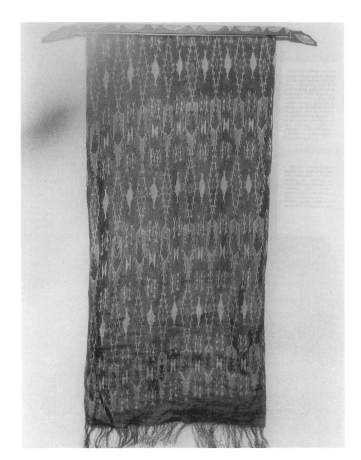

Figure 4. Rod used to hold the textiles.

Figure 3. View of a showcase for the textile exhibit.

it is sewn on to a pre-washed cotton support, then mounted on a wooden stretcher and covered with Mylar plastic for exhibit. The cover must not touch the object in order to prevent static electricity.

San Agustin Museum Textile Exhibit

The San Agustin Museum is one of the oldest churches in the Philippines and is now included on the World Heritage List. It is situated in Intramuros, Manila, which is a pre-Spanish restricted area.

The textile collection ranges from ecclesiastical vestments and church furnishings. Vestments include capes, chasubles, dalmatics, albs, stoles, collars, belts. Other objects include altar cloth, humeral veil, chalice veil and burse. In 1994, the conservators of the National Museum undertook the setting up of the exhibit of the San Agustin Church Museum in time for the Papal visit of Pope John Paul II.

The majority of the textiles are either embroidered or intricately decorated with silver and gold threads. Prevalent colors are green, orange, violet, blue, beige, yellow, black, red orange and peach. Raw materials used for weaving are cotton, abaca, silk, and pineapple fibers. Accessories include beads, sequins, tassels, cords and metallic threads.

Most of these museum objects are in stable condition. Others have heavily deteriorated and need minor and major restoration.

a) Flat objects

The technique used in exhibiting flat objects is the Velcro system. It is a two-part fastening system consisting of hook and loop tapes which when pressed together, will interlock forming a strong bond. The Velcro tape is cut to a desired length, then a sleeve made of muslin cloth is prepared and folded. The looped Velcro is machine-stitched onto the sleeve along the selvage and across the two ends. Using a running or herringbone stitch, the looped Velcro with muslin sleeve is attached to the reverse side of the object. Because of the multi-layers, the stitches penetrate both lining and textile to prevent sagging. Stitching is executed with care so that it will not be obtrusive. The hooked Velcro is just stapled onto the panel boards since it is considered to be safe enough because it will not be in direct contact with the object. Mounting is done starting from the center working out towards the ends. The Velcro tape is sewn by machine onto a larger tape, which can be sewn by hand on the piece to be mounted.

The pile (soft) Velcro strip should be attached to the tapestry and the hook strip nailed or stapled onto a wooden batten cut to the size desired and then sanded.

b) Heavy and huge textiles

Textiles with metallic thread and heavy adornment are exhibited in horizontal cases angled at 30 degrees. This technique considerably eliminates the stress on the fabric. The principle of rest is a very effective way of protecting large pieces and heavy textiles for exhibit.

c) Long, light objects

Some light objects are displayed on a rod and freely hang. In the case of long textiles, the end portion is made to rest on the floor. This minimizes stress upon the object. A rod is threaded through a casing on the back of the object. A casing strip is machine-stitched to a length of carpet stripping the full width of the top edge of the textile. The casing should allow the rod to be inserted easily, and should allow enough material so that it does not lie flat against the carpet stripping. The stripping along the

Figure 5. Velcro system for displaying textiles.

Figure 6. Horizontal display technique.

upper edge of the textile is carefully hand-stitched. If the object is already backed, this stripping is stitched to the upper edge of the backing. The non-rusting rod is drawn through the casing.

d) Vestments

These textiles which are multi-layered and have heavy metallic embroidery should be mounted properly. They can be displayed on mannequins padded with pre-washed, white cotton cloth. Others may be hung using polyester-padded hangers. Polyester padding is used because of its long-term stability. Pads soften and distribute the weight of the object while hanging on display, and therefore minimize stress to a certain extent. Glass cases are fabricated to protect against dust and handling.

Mounting Techniques

Stretcher Frame For Weak Textiles:

1. A stretcher made of wood is prepared. The size will depend on the dimension of the object to be mounted.

2. A pre-washed cotton cloth is tacked into the four sides of the stretcher.

3. Damaged areas are secured to its backing fabric by a series of conservation stitches. Sewing is carried out on a flat surface and stitches should be relaxed so that no tension is created on the fabric, which can break old fibers.

4. After carefully stitching the object onto the cloth, the supported material is removed from being tacked in the stretcher. Then it is placed in a wooden frame. It is covered with plastic which serves as protection against dust and dirt in such a way that it will not touch the object.

Figure 7. Rod for display purposes.

The procedure is as follows:

4.1 Lay the finished object on a clean, flat surface.

4.2 Put the 2.5 cm (1 in.) thick wooden frame (treated with insecticide and varnished) over the supported object.

4.3 Tack the four sides of the support cloth to the frame loosely so as not to produce strain on the object.

4.4 Put acid-free paper at the back of the framed object, attach the labels and cover with plastic.

4.5 Store in a clean, well-ventilated room.

Factors to be Considered for Display

Time - The length of time greatly affects the physical and chemical properties of the item on display. Longer exposure to the internal stresses, the environment, pests and man increase the chances of textile damage. Therefore, some action must be taken in order to avoid fading of colors and weakening of textile fibers and other photo-chemical degradation.

Lighting - The National Museum and the San Agustin Church Museum usually use fluorescent lamps with ultraviolet (UV) filters in order to eliminate UV rays. Blinds are placed on windows to protect the exhibited textiles from direct sunlight. More often than not, lights are left on only when there are visitors viewing the exhibits. This practice minimizes the duration of light exposure and heat — thus, the probability of deterioration is lessened, and the life of the textiles as well as the dyes present are prolonged. The effect of continuous exposure to light is detected when the unexposed part of the object is compared with the exposed portion. Light levels must be maintained at 50 lux.

Observations

1. Museums apply different techniques in exhibiting textiles. Any display design is acceptable as long as it is applicable to the textiles and within international conservation standards. The display of textiles must be presented in an artistic manner and must always consider the safety of the textiles.

2. At present, only the textile exhibits of the San Agustin Church Museum apply the Velcro system and the horizontal showcases for display.

3. The correct way of displaying is very important for better viewing of the textiles. Objects must be presented in an artistic way while at the same time considering their safety. The types, dimensions, and the weight of the textile determine the exhibition techniques to be adopted.

Recommendations:

1) Information on the different techniques of displaying museum textiles should be widely disseminated.

2) The conservator and exhibition officer should consult each other regarding the planning of an of exhibition.

3) The exhibition officer must gain some knowledge on conservation/preservation requirements of textiles.

4) The conservators should be trained in the exhibition of textiles and other artifacts utilizing textiles.

Action Taken

1. A Training Course on the Conservation of Museum Textiles was held from November 12-29, 1996. This was sponsored by the National Commission for Culture and the Arts (NCCA) and the National Museum of the Philippines, implemented by the Philippine Association for Scientific Conservation of Cultural Property, Inc. (PASCON), a society of practicing conservators.

References

Ballard, Mary. "Restoration and Preservation of Textiles: Rotating Display," *Art and Antiques*, pp. 42-43.

Canadian Conservation Institute. "Stitches Used In Textile Conservation," *CCI Notes 13/10*, Ottawa: Canadian Conservation Institute, April 1986.

Canadian Conservation Institute. "Hanging Storage for Costumes," *CCI Notes 13/5*, Ottawa: Canadian Conservation Institute, September 1983.

Canadian Conservation Institute. "Velcro Support System for Textiles," *CCI Notes 3/4*, Ottawa: Canadian Conservation Institute, September 1983.

Elveña, Evelyn and Jesusa Avenido. "Report of the Textile Conservation of Ecclesiastical Vestments of the San Agustin Museum," unpublished, 1996, pp. 10-14.

Elveña, Evelyn. "The Conservation of a Bilaan Belt," *National Museum Papers*, vol. 5, no. 1 (1995), pp. 50-53.

Merrimack Textile Valley Museum. "Museum Display of Textiles," *Textile Conservation Notes*, no. 13, pp. 1-7.

Résumé

Pratiques d'exposition des textiles aux Philippines

Le Musée national des Philippines a reçu du gouvernement le mandat de protéger et de conserver le riche patrimoine culturel du pays. À ce titre, l'un de ses objectifs est de préserver les trésors nationaux, qu'il s'agisse de biens culturels meubles ou immeubles, y compris les textiles. Le laboratoire de chimie et de conservation entreprend des recherches et des travaux de préservation sur des objets de tous genres. Depuis sa fondation, le laboratoire a analysé et conservé des centaines de textiles. Le personnel contribue aussi à la préparation des textiles en vue de l'exposition dans des musées privés ou publics. La plupart des musées des Philippines recueillent, préservent et exposent des textiles et des objets comprenant des éléments textiles. Il existe plusieurs genres de collections, notamment des étoffes ecclésiastiques, des textiles d'intérêt archéologique et ethnologique et même des textiles contemporains. Dans l'article, on traite des diverses techniques employées pour exposer, éclairer et monter convenablement les textiles au Musée national et au Musée de l'Église San Agustin. On formule aussi certaines recommandations pour moderniser les méthodes d'exposition.

A Once-in-a-lifetime Opportunity: Planning and Building New Permanent Exhibitions at the Armémuseum, Stockholm

Annika Castwall af Trolle, Lena Engquist Sandstedt and Anna Zillén

Armémuseum
Box 14095
104 41 Stockholm, Sweden
Tel.: 08-788 95 60 kansli

Abstract

This paper will describe the transformation of the Armémuseum into a new museum. It recounts the history of the Armémuseum and the trophy collection, which was moved to the Armémuseum in 1960. The collection has been documented from the 17th century. During this time, the attitude regarding what to display, how and why has changed. We will also describe the pedagogical intentions of the new museum and how we are going to realise them. What a challenge!

The Armémuseum is situated in central Stockholm by "Artillerigården" (the Artillery Yard) established in the 1640s as the main depot for the field artillery of the realm. After a century the original, wooden houses were replaced by masonry buildings, still standing. From the end of the 18th century, the establishment was used by an artillery regiment, which moved out in 1879. Then it was decided to turn part of the main building into a museum - Artillerimuseum. In 1932 the museum was closed for rebuilding and the name was changed to the present one, which was more adequate. Over the centuries, trophy cannon, armouries from the Royal Castle, collections of models and other military objects had been gathered at the yard, and the museum had in reality been a museum for the whole army. The museum was reopened in 1943.

The first embryo of the Trophy Collection can be discerned as early as 1611, when some Danish colours were displayed in the Cathedral of Stockholm for propaganda purposes. They were quietly removed the next year, probably to be recycled as Swedish colours. The trophy colours, standards and guidons were stored in the Royal Castle during most of the 17th century. Different alternatives of storage and exhibitions were discussed but came to nothing. Sweden's many wars continuously increased the number of trophies. Their existence was rather obscure, however, and the fact that they were depicted as early as the 1680s indicates that they were decaying. In connection with this documentation, the collection was moved to a private palace in Stockholm (serving as Royal Palace while building a replacement for the old palace that was destroyed by fire in 1697). There they remained for the greater part of the 18th century. For a short period, they had been stored in Fredrikshov, another royal residence.

At the beginning of the 19th century they were moved to an orangery in the royal garden, where the sunlight flowed in through large windows. The awakening of national romanticism meant a renewed interest in the trophies. In 1817 they were - ceremoniously and with military honours - transferred to the church where most Swedish kings are buried. Quite a number were exhibited in trophy arrangements. The church was ravaged by fire in 1835, but most of the trophies were saved. About a century later, in 1906, the major part was moved again, this time to the Royal Armoury in the Royal Castle. In 1960, the Trophy Collection was moved to the Armémuseum. The year after, it was put on show for the first time in its new surroundings. It took the form of a temporary exhibition: "The Figurative Language of Colours." Part of the exhibition was permanently mounted in the Trophy Room, which was inaugurated in 1964. The Trophy Collection today contains nearly 4,000 items: mostly colours, standards and guidons, but also other kinds of trophies: drums, kettledrums and keys to fortresses and towns.

When the exhibition opened for the first time, in 1879, the museum saw as its goal to exhibit the objects "whereby the public and especially the inquisitive officers are given an opportunity to gain knowledge of these monuments from our ancestors' struggles and labours in the service of the fatherland." The result was a massive agglomeration of military objects with the sole purpose of reminding us of a glorious past. It was an international phenomenon, most national military museums, founded in the 19th century represent a romanticized picture of their own armed forces.

The museum reopened in 1943 under its new name, Armémuseum. That there was a war going on can be deduced from the museum's instruction: "The different trophies remind us of victories, essential for our nation and its independence, won by the officers' diligence and the men's courage and endurance... We shall not, however, let these glorious memories merely beguile us into a hollow conceit regarding our ancestors' feats but rather by them draw strength, should destiny befall Sweden once more, that we will be able to sacrifice everything in order to pass our country as free and independent to our descendants as we once inherited it from our ancestors." Once again the triumphs and victories of the Swedish army were enhanced, but nothing was said about the living conditions of the humble men in the rank-and-file.

The Armémuseum's present instruction says that the museum shall: "endeavour to spread information about the defence in older times and the defence's significance for the evolution of society."

Over the last couple of decades, a new generation of historians has taken an interest in war, regarding it as part of a larger context. This so-called "War and Society" school defines war and military activity as an integrated part of society at large.

A government report on the activity of the Swedish museum, run by the state, made in 1994, maintains that "the museums ought to make use of their possibilities to tie phenomena from different areas together and create an understanding of connections and totalities."

The new exhibitions in the Armémuseum will be created in accordance with the report's spirit. The authentic objects will be displayed as they are, without additions or completions. The original objects, tangible links to our ancestors, will speak for themselves. Their appearance when they were actually used, how, in what circumstances, and for what purpose will be shown by replicas and reconstructions in more or less elaborated scenes. The exhibitions are meant to address all senses, not only the eye. Every reconstruction will be preceded by extensive research and because the museum is a military one, we have access to voluminous archives dating from the 1670s onwards.

The new trophy exhibition will be created in accordance with the general guidelines for the museum. When first exhibited, they were symbols for martial success. Then, after a period of oblivion, they were revived in order to stir up sentiments of romantic nationalism by reminding the nation of its heroic past. When the chauvinistic feelings faded away, interest was focused on the historic, textile and artistic values of the colours. The exhibition will occupy three rooms. One room (the biggest) contains a permanent display of colours, standards and guidons taken in the 30-Years War and the Great Nordic War. The exhibition illustrates how size, technique, material and iconographic message varies with time and place. Another room will be reserved for temporary exhibitions, for instance "How to Preserve a Colour" or displays of seldom-seen objects like lock covers and drum covers. In between those two rooms there will be a hall where the function and importance of the colours will be explained. The trophy rooms will be entered through the appropriate part of the museum, the one that deals with the 30-Years War.

Textiles, such as colours, are rather fragile things and decay quickly if not taken care of. They have not been handled with care except during the last century. As symbols of the enemy's defeat, they were dragged in the dirt. Then they were simply rolled up and stored. Displayed in the church, they hung completely unsupported. Natural decay and their own weight caused them to slowly fall apart. Wire nets underneath caught most of the rags but fragments fell to the floor. Some of them happened to be swept up and stuffed into kettle-drums, there to be retrieved 150 years later. Conservation started at the end of the 19th century. Crepeline was introduced as a fabric for conservation in the mid-1920s. Crepeline-supported colours were allowed to hang vertically, but this resulted in grave degradations after only a couple of decades. The changing exhibiting technique caused them to be replaced in the 1980s by copies carried out in Scannachrome.

In the exhibitions to be, not one colour will be exhibited vertically. They will all lie on sloping supports of some kind. The material has, at present, not been decided upon. Different solutions have been discussed: either that the colour rests on a supporting board covered with cloth of neutral hue, resting on Perspex, making the colour seem suspended in the air, or laid out on a rest covered with black textile in order to have the colour "stand out." The glass in the showcases will be Optic White except at the entrance, where anti-reflex glass will be used.

The Trophy Collection workrooms are located in a recently renovated building with super-modern air conditioning ... that never worked properly. That experience and the fact that the exhibition building is a more than 200-year-old structure of extreme sturdiness and bulk with great capacity to level out occasional changes in humidity and temperature brought up the question of what kind of installation for climatic control to choose. In cooperation with Jan G. Holmberg (Comnord Sweden AB), expert on climate control from the Conservation Institute of National Antiquities, the Armémuseum has put together the temperature and humidity measurements that have been recorded continuously in the building since 1973. The analysis of this data should form a foundation upon which a sensible decision can be made.

The measurements show that the air temperature varied from 17° to 23°C and that the RH readings fluctuated between 30% and 60%, the curves changing very slowly. The results support our opinion that ventilation with filtered air should be utilized instead of a big climate control installation. The exhibition rooms, the auditorium and the restaurant will have their own separate ventilation systems adapted to the lighting in order to evacuate the heat from the lamps.

The showcases will be slightly pressurized and permit easy access. Some 70% of the glass will be anti-reflex. The light will not exceed 50 lux in showcases holding sensitive objects. Fibre-glass optics have been contemplated because it does not emit UV or heat radiation.

The museum was closed in 1993, every single object was computer coded and put in evacuation storage. The new museum is planned to reopen in late 1999. Planning and building completely novel exhibitions in a renovated building equipped with the latest system for controlling electronic functions, such as light and sound, is an equally exciting and frightening task. A totally new museum! What a challenge!

Acknowledgements

We would like to thank our colleagues at Armémuseum, Leif Nilsson, Leif Pettersson, Svante Folin, Erik Wahlberg and especially Lke Blix.

References

Blix, Lke, Svante Folin and Leif Nilsson. "The brochure and synopsis of the new exhibitions of Armémuseum."

Holmberg, Jan G. "Klimatmätningar vid Armémuseum, Stockholm," 1995.

Jacobsson, Thorsten. "Frln artilleri - till Armémuseum, Armémusei meddelande 1938."

Pira, Folke. "Statens Trofésamling, Armémusei meddelande 1938."

Seitz, Heribert. "Statens Trofésamling, Armemusei meddelande 1960."

Spak, F.A. "Artillerimuseum Koncept - Handlingar 1877-90."

Résumé

Une occasion unique : planification et construction de nouvelles expositions permanentes à l'Armémuseum de Stockholm

Dans cet article, on décrit la transformation de l'Armémuseum en un nouveau musée. On y expose l'histoire de l'Armémuseum ainsi que de la collection de trophées qu'il a acquise en 1960. La collection est documentée depuis le XVIIe siècle. L'attitude face à la sélection des pièces et à la méthode d'exposition a évolué au fil de l'histoire du musée. On explique aussi les objectifs pédagogiques du nouveau musée et les moyens qui seront déployés pour les réaliser. Il s'agira sans aucun doute d'un défi de taille.

Behind the Seams of an Exhibition

Christine Paulocik

The Costume Institute
The Metropolitan Museum of Art
1000 Fifth Avenue
New York, NY 10028-0198 USA
Tel.: (212) 570-3908
Fax: (212) 570-3970

Abstract

The conservation laboratory at the Costume Institute of the Metropolitan Museum of Art, New York, primarily focuses on exhibitions. The range of this work includes: Institute shows; out-going loans for other museums; participation in shows for other departments of the museum either as artifact rotation or an out-going loan for a traveling exhibition where costume is an integral part of a bigger show. In order to accomplish this ambitious program, we have learned to prioritize tasks and streamline the installation process. This paper focuses on my experiences with Institute shows that are usually conceived to examine various elements in the history of costume using the artifacts from its outstanding collections. I realized that in the eight years since I came to New York, I have completed over 20 Institute exhibitions ranging from the blockbusters like "The Age of Napoleon," and "Théâtre de la Mode," to simpler retrospectives like "Madame Grès," and "Bloom."

The Institution-Exhibit Personnel

The Metropolitan Museum of Art is a large institution with an established framework of personnel to carry out their numerous shows. For each exhibition, a designer, assigned to the department, works with the curator to determine the overall look of the installation and coordinates the different steps in the process.

A lighting designer works with a team of lampers to set up illumination in the galleries. Riggers are required to move large items such as columns. The Registrars department coordinates in-coming and out-going loans, and accommodates couriers. The Editorial department works with the curators on the publication or video accompanying the show. Public relations deals with advertising and press previews. Installers, who are a part of Objects Conservation, build special mounts.

There are many separate components of a show, but all are co-dependent upon the others. One is dealing with a staff that is both union and professional. Union members have clearly defined job descriptions and schedules that must be accommodated. This is the group of people set up to help your department put on an exhibition.

Figure 1. Two gowns exhibited in the show, "Fashion and Dialogue." A satin Dior dress from 1954 at the left. The evening cape at right by Charles Frederick Worth, late 19th century.

Exhibition Issues

A conservator is faced with many issues when dealing with an exhibition: time, money, manpower, treatments, mannequins, and materials. First of all, everyone wants the exhibition to look good. Can you improve the appearance of the garment with a treatment? Will the curator be satisfied with diminished stains rather than eradicated ones? Costumes can be among the most difficult types of artifacts to display well. The three-dimensional structure requires interior support to define the shape and function of a garment, but mechanical stresses occur each time mannequins are dressed and undressed or mounted. Can the piece withstand the handling? Will this garment fit on a mannequin? Can we afford a suitable mannequin that we may only use for this show and never again? Do we have the time to custom-make an Ethafoam support?

Sometimes a costume lacks components that are necessary to complete the story. When is it appropriate to fabricate a substitute for these components? Since costumes are susceptible to environmental deterioration and light degradation over time, rotation is necessary. How long should the show be up, and will the public ever stop complaining that the galleries are too dimly lit for proper viewing?

Funding and budgets are issues. What should be included? Can we afford new mannequins? Do we have any money to do wigs? Time is another factor to consider and often a source of frustration. Do we have the time to conserve all of these pieces before the show opens? If not, which ones should get top priority? Lead time is essential, otherwise limitations are already imposed on the overall level and extent of the artifact treatment. If curators choose the pieces only a few weeks before the show, it is very difficult to accommodate all their requests on such short notice. Exhibitions place rigorous demands on staff time.

For the purposes of this paper, I will describe pieces that are pre-1950 as "historic." Generally, the historic pieces are the garments that require more involved treatments. Unfortunately, these are also the artifacts that the dressers usually want to start with first since they are often the most complicated to build bodies for. Good communication and negotiating skills are a must. Accommodating reasonable, or special requests requires tact and flexibility.

It is also important that the conservator be involved in meetings with the Design department when ideas and materials are chosen for the show. The conservator can assist in determining suitability, but the priorities that are a concern to the conservator may not necessarily be those of the curator, designer or installer. The conservator's recommendations are often overruled. Therefore, the ability to negotiate, compromise and cooperate are key elements to maintain successful work relationships.

Conservation is a multi-faceted, service-oriented discipline. When should a conservator merely recommend or absolutely insist on standards? There may be ethical considerations the conservator must address when recommendations are not followed. We face many conflicting issues of care and handling versus safety and preservation of the artifacts. With differing philosophies regarding mounting and design, frustration is inevitable. When is it time to compromise? If you give an inch will they take a mile? Should a conservator be a member of the "Conservation Police" or just a sniper for flagrant misdemeanors? Should conservators be willing to trade and compromise or should they demand only absolutes? When pushing too hard for strict conservation controls, the conservator may be forced out of the loop altogether. Reality may triumph over theory due to

practical limitations. These are all questions I have asked myself a hundred times. The sobering truth has been, although you have none of the authority you have all of the responsibility. A departing conservator from the Met left me with some valuable words of wisdom, "Choose your battles, you can't fight them all."

Mandate

The mandate expressed by our Director, Philippe de Montebello, was to have a state-of-the-art suite of galleries at the Costume Institute that would be open all year with no down time. The curator has chosen to install three shows a year with accompanying publication. Each show includes the treatment of hundreds of artifacts a year. With limited turnaround time in the galleries between exhibitions, we have streamlined procedures for installation and de-installation in order to accomplish our ambitious program.

The Exhibition

Now that I have highlighted some of the issues facing exhibit conservators, I will discuss the specifics of an exhibition. Although every show has its own variables, the process is consistent. Solutions have evolved as a response to problems and are then incorporated in the next exhibition. In the following portion of the paper, I will explain the inner workings of an exhibition, who does what, when and how, beginning with artifact selection and concluding with the final placement of the wigs and accessories.

Once the curator determines the theme of the show and artifact selection begins, it is imperative that the conservation staff be involved in the early stages of the exhibit planning. One major issue of contention often is the artifact list for the exhibition. This list allows the conservator to have an idea of the workload ahead in order to determine schedules. An artifact list is critical, but rarely in my experience available until the show is up.

It is essential that the curator communicate with the conservators. A common situation that must be accommodated is the consideration of loan artifacts. The curator barters the conservator's time to obtain an object from a lending institution. Therefore, a requirement of the loan is that the object be conserved by the staff in the lab.

Treatment

The racks of costumes start arriving in the lab, and garments are triaged according to condition, assessing treatment options and determining those that require remedial, intermediate or full treatments. After discussions with the curator, the pieces are prioritized and work schedules established. Sometimes a piece is rejected because there just will not be the time to complete the treatment. At this point, it is important to have the dressers review the chosen artifacts. They will assess whether the garments will fit on the available mannequin. Believe me, many artifacts we had toiled over under demanding time constraints only brought frustration when they would not fit on any mannequin and could not be used.

Treatments can range from the what we call the "Volkswagen," or remedial, to the "Cadillac," or deluxe. Each show presents its own range of conservation problems to consider and solve. With "Infra-Apparel," we were dealing with sheer lingeries where every stitch appeared like a Frankenstein scar on the surface of the garment. What do you do with acres and acres of organza, pleated and draped in lavish confections that has yellowed and become crispy with age?

Other shows like "Orientalism" made us pause and contemplate our treatment options. In this case, we were dealing with 18th-century painted silk garments. In fact, our research provoked so many questions that it resulted in the Costume Institute hosting a Symposium and a subsequent publication, "The Conservation of 18th-Century Painted Silk Dress."

"Bloom" forced us to explore the problems of some contemporary garments constructed of inherently unstable materials such as unvulcanized latex rubber or plastic. With the current trend towards the use of these products in high fashion, we are seeing these problems more and more often. The deterioration of the Koji Tatsuno latex rubber dresses embedded with real leaves and flowers prompted a week-long consultation with Scott Williams of the Canadian Conservation Institute. Scott worked with us to evaluate the potential problems with our 20th-century collection. The brainstorming session identified our problems, established simple methods of plastic identification, outlined guidelines for their treatment and storage, and made us reassess our collection policy regarding certain materials.

Mannequins

A major factor for consideration with a costume exhibition is the choice of suitable mannequins that properly support the garments and achieve the period silhouette. Not only are mannequins expensive, as much as $1,500 each, but there is not just one perfect model available that satisfies all the necessary requirements. We are very fortunate that the Costume Institute has built its mannequin collection from our exhibition program through the years, resulting in a large pool to fall back on with a wide range of periods, sizes and shapes. The down side to this wonderful resource is that we now have a storage problem for the hundreds of figures.

Approaches to mannequins are varied, but we generally work with abstract faces and minimal detailing, which focuses the attention on the costume rather than on the mannequin.

Figure 2. The Costume Institute has built up a large resource of mannequins through the years.

There is a wide range of commercially available mannequins reflecting different historic periods and shapes. We deal with many different companies such as Pucci, Goldsmiths, or Wacoal. We often use the Wacoal mannequins from Kyoto for historic pieces, Schlappi mannequins from Pucci for more contemporary pieces, or dressmaker forms from

Figure 3. We sometimes use dressmaker's forms to exhibit costume. On the right side, a French gown ca. 1770s and on the left, a chevron-patterned dyed pony-skin coat from 1960s by Frank Stella and Jacques Kaplan.

Bernstein. For the exhibition "Fashion and Dialogue," supermodel Christy Turlington donated her time to become the new face of the Museum's mannequins. Most recently for our "Christian Dior" show Associate Curator, Harold Koda worked directly with the Pucci company to come up with a suitable figure custom-designed with narrow hips and wide shoulders. As you can imagine, this all comes with a high price tag.

Sometimes it is necessary for us to refurbish old mannequins. For about $200 you can have them stripped and repainted. Mannequins are modified by decapitation, limb removal, breast reduction or stomach surgery. These radical amputations are often necessary in order for a garment to fit properly and achieve the correct silhouette.

Mounts

We use many different types of support systems for the display of costume and accessories. In addition to mannequins, we also use a wide range of different support systems. For the "Mme Grès" show, we built invisible mounts based on figures developed at the Fashion Institute of Technology by conservator Shirley Eng for the Charles James dresses in their collection. They are constructed out of layers of wet buckram applied over a plastic covered dressmaker's dummy. After removal from the dummy, the buckram shape is still slightly damp and modifications can be made by cutting and reshaping sections of the bust or waist. Once the buckram is completely dried, it can be covered with batting and a final layer of fabric. The Madame Grès costumes appeared almost to be floating on these mounts.

Sometimes we have to resort to carving Ethafoam to get a correct body form. We have used all kinds of techniques of construction like the disk type or the intersecting silhouette mannequins by Denis Larouche. We like this type of mount because of the versatility of the technique with applications for torsos to be used with sweaters, corsets, bodices, or additions for carving limbs or supports for hats.

Dressing

The volume of shows and outgoing loans that we deal with every year has necessitated a separate area within the department that deals with dressing. Although in instances where the piece is fragile or problematic, the artifact is dressed by conservation.

Ideally the mounting of the costume should be a collaborative effort between the curator, dresser and conservator. Mannequin selection is determined at the beginning of the exhibit planning stage. The time involved in dressing a mannequin can be considerable, and one must remember that the ideal is to provide interior support and shaping, but at the same time minimize the handling and mechanical damage to the piece. Solid underpinnings result in less

Figure 4. Corset forms of carved Ethafoam.

Figure 5. Dressers preparing mannequins for an exhibition.

damage and a more accurate final appearance. The installers begin dressing at least a month in advance in order to complete the work in time.

The dressing process always begins in the same way with the garment protected from the mannequin with a pair of pantyhose cut at the crotch and pulled over the head. Twill tapes are stitched to the waistband and tied under the crotch. Other twill tapes are basted at the neckline so that the stocking can be cut without it running. Each leg portion of the pantyhose is used to cover an arm. The pantyhose becomes an outer layer of skin that is padded inside with layers of polyester Fiberfill to add shaping to the garment.

Through the years, we have built up a resource of reproduction semi-boned corsets based on ones in the collection. Muslin hip pads of different sizes and shapes add dimension to 18th-century gowns. The dressers use corsets, bras, petticoats, crinolines and panniers, modern and reproduction to achieve the correct silhouette.

Figure 6. Reproduction undergarments like these panniers are based on pieces from the collection and used in costume preparation.

These underpinnings are placed over the pantyhose and used as a foundation for the period shape. Buckram or layers of tulle are used to build volume under the skirts. Ribbon wire can be stitched to the edges of either material in order to achieve further shaping.

Once the mannequins have been dressed, the completed figures are transported to the storeroom and placed in the aisles where a protective layer of paper has been laid down on the floor. The mannequins are then covered with Tyvek or acid-free paper until the galleries are finished and they can be placed.

De-installation

We must, of course, remove the current show before we install the new exhibition. The mandate expressed by the director is to have a suite of costume galleries always open to the public. This has resulted in a very limited turnaround time between exhibitions, which can be as short as a week. With these time restrictions, we have evolved a synchronized method to remove the shows often in as little as four hours. The process is very efficient with each staff member assigned a specific job.

Our shows have ranged from 75 to over 235 mannequins fully dressed and accessorized. Dressing sheets were developed to attempt to track the artifacts used on each figure. Each sheet contains pertinent information: artifact description, accession number, loan pieces, installation pieces, areas of weakness on the artifact, use of dressing techniques and materials. The dressing sheet is a useful tool for identification purposes and dressing information. When the conservators go to undress the artifact, they are alerted to areas of potential weakness.

On the final day of the show, rolling racks, carts, carrying boards, hangers are all assembled and when the last visitor exits, the process of de-installation begins. Dressing sheets are matched to the artifacts and hung around the neck of each mannequin. Loan pieces are clearly identified with a large red sticker affixed to the dressing sheet. Loan pieces without couriers are undressed by the conservators working in teams of two with the curatorial staff. Costumes that are Costume Institute artifacts are undressed by another team working with the collections manager. Each group works with a selection of costume racks and Metro carts that, once filled, are removed to our classroom. Other carts are identified and set aside for accessioned accessories or installation pieces. Mannequins that are going to be used in the next show are clearly marked and remain with their underpinnings intact.

Once the figure is undressed, a team follows which strips all the remaining underpinnings, including the corsets, crinolines, petticoats or panniers. Tables are set aside for each type of material and grouped according to classification. Tulle and batting is removed and placed in bags to be reused for other shows. Wigs are removed and grouped according to period. Mannequins are assembled according to type as are hands, arms, legs and heads. Protective stockings with batting in the toes are placed on the feet of the mannequin to prevent damage to the toes. As a final protective measure, large plastic bags are used to cover the rest of the mannequin before their removal to mannequin storage.

Installation

Now that the show has been de-installed, we begin the preparation of the galleries for the next exhibition. Initial phases of installation include construction of decks, plastering, painting, silk-screening, installation of photos, or murals. Ideally, all these segments of the process should be completed before the artifacts can be brought out into the galleries.

Storyboards are a big help when planning and installing a show. They are used as a reference by the people involved with the show. The artifacts for the show are photographed. Each gallery is designated with a large cork board upon which the photos are pinned and organized. The curator can move the pieces around in order to develop story lines or determine placements. In this way, the technician knows by viewing the boards which mannequin goes where in the exhibition. The dressed figures can be very heavy and unwieldy and are moved only as absolutely necessary to reduce the potential for mechanical damage.

Team work is essential and a great technician is a bonus. The decks in the galleries are papered to prevent scuffing the freshly painted surfaces. Each mannequin is transported by two people. The storyboards indicate where they should be placed in the gallery. After final adjustments with the curator, the mannequins are secured by being spiked into the platforms. This heavy, awkward job involves at least three people. The group of spikers are followed by another team which removes the protective paper from the decks.

Finishing Touches — Wigs, Accessories
Once the figures are completely secured, the final process of additions to compliment the overall look of the costume commences. It can be difficult to get 100 mannequins to appear related to each other. Through the years, we have attempted many techniques like painting all the mannequins the same color, or obscuring their faces with knots of colored pantyhose. Often we use the abstract approach to hair in order to provide the correct period look to the costume.

Every type of material has been used including metallic fabric, ribbons, tulle, leaves, net, papier-mâché, or paper rope. Originally, the wig material was applied directly to the head of the mannequin using double-sided tape. Since we always had trouble removing the adhesive residue from the mannequin head, we came up with another technique. Once the proper mannequin has been chosen, buckram skull caps are made to fit that head shape. These can be mass produced and later trimmed down. Using the skullcap as a base, the wig material is applied to the buckram using an archival grade hot glue from University Products.

Figure 7. Wigs are made using a buckram skullcap with rope paper applied for hair.

With the wigs in place, the curator selects accessories that compliment and give the costume the correct period look. These must be supported and attached carefully. Fans, purses, jewelry etc. can be lifted quite easily and pose a security issue unless protective showcases are used. Through the years, the installation department has built up a resource stock of shoes, gloves, lace, feathers, and stockings that are not artifacts but rather installation pieces. It would be unusual for a collection to possess suitable shoes for every period and size necessary. The accessioned shoes often do not fit the mannequin feet properly and a tremendous amount of mechanical damage can occur to these delicate artifacts. Over time, a range of shoes has been purchased in various, colors, sizes and shapes that could be used to compliment the costumes. They are stored in clear plastic shoe boxes according to date and color for ease of retrieval.

Sometimes, to complete the look of the garment, we need to produce a facsimile component or use an installation piece. The piece is based on period research and a curatorial decision. For example a collar might be constructed using installation materials. The non-accessioned pieces are labeled and identified on dressing sheets that accompany the costume.

We also display accessories as separate decorative objects utilizing our vitrines in the theme of the show. In past shows we have highlighted corsets, hoops, crinolines, hats, shoes, handbags, fans, or gloves. It is usually necessary to provide an interior support that can range from a carved Ethafoam mount to a Plexiglas fan support.

At this point in the exhibition, everything has been placed and final adjustments are made. Labels are matched to each artifact and placed in the appropriate vitrine. The lighting designer and his crew of lampers work systematically through each gallery adjusting and refining the placement of lights. Platforms are vacuumed, showcases cleaned and everything is ready when the press come trooping down the grand staircase to view the exhibition.

Showcases

When I first arrived at the Costume Institute, the mannequins were exhibited on raised platforms and protected from the public with sensors and security guards. Weekly maintenance of the platforms and garments was necessary due to dust accumulation. In 1992, the Costume Institute was re-configured into new exhibition galleries which occupied less than half of the old space. At the same time a new heating, ventilating and air-conditioning system was installed. Five major display areas and four supplementary vitrines were built and enclosed with special glass walls, in order to protect the artifacts.

The platforms in each gallery were adjustable and therefore one could see four or five mannequins at different levels at one time. The difference has been remarkable, since we installed floor to ceiling glass showcases. Their use in combination with the new HVAC system has drastically reduced our problems with dust and dirt. Even during the "Christian Dior" show when our security guards were counting 1,000 people per hour did we see any negligible amounts of dust on the platforms.

Conclusion

Any exhibition from conception to execution involves a large group of people with conflicting priorities. Each group must work in conjunction with one another, and although their duties intersect, their priorities may not necessarily be the same. I hope that I have succeeded in conveying the complexity of an exhibition. I cannot stress enough the necessity of teamwork and flexibility on the part of those involved with the show. I have been very fortunate for the past eight years to work closely with Rita Kauneckas and Debbie Juchem.

Bibliography

Larouche, Denis. "Intersecting Silhouette Mannequins," *Textile Conservation Newsletter*, Spring Supplement 1995.

Palmer, Alexandra. "Mannequins for the Royal Ontario Museum Costume Gallery," *Textile Conservation Newsletter*, Supplementary to the TCN, Spring 1988.

Paulocik, Christine and Sean Flaherty. *The Conservation of 18th-Century Painted Silk Dress*. Vol. 1, The Costume Institute, The Metropolitan Museum of Art and the Graduate Program in Costume Studies, New York University, 1995.

Suppliers

Mannequins
Bernstein Display
24-60 47th Street,
Astoria, N.Y. 11103 USA
Phone: (718) 545-7311

Wacoal Corp.
29 Kisshoin Nakajima-Cho,
Minami-Ku,
Kyoto, Japan

Goldsmith
10-09 43 Street
Long Island City, N.Y. 11101 USA
Phone: (718) 937-8476
Fax: (718) 937-4525

Pucci International
44 West 18th Street
New York, N.Y. 10011 USA
Phone: (212) 645-2020

Coroplast
Archivart
7 Caesar Place
Moonachie, N.J. 07074 USA
Phone: (201) 804-8986

Insect Pins
Ward's
5100 W. Henrietta Road
P. O. Box 92912
Rochester, N.Y. 14692-9012 USA
Phone: (716) 328-7830

Ethafoam
George H. Swatek, Inc.
1095 Edgewater Avenue
P. O. Box 356
Ridgefield, N.J. 07657-0356 USA
Phone: (201) 941-2400

Quilt Batting
Leiderman & Co., Inc.
1001 Newark Avenue
Elizabeth, N.J. 07208 USA
Phone: (908) 820-9700

Buckram
Eagle Buckram Inc.
951 West 2nd Street
Hazelton, Pa., 18201 USA
Phone: (717) 455-0911

Résumé

Sous les coutures d'une exposition

*Le laboratoire de conservation de l'institut des costumes
(Costume Institute) du Metropolitan Museum of Art, à
New York, se concentre avant tout sur les expositions. La
gamme de ses travaux va des expositions de l'Institut aux
prêts à d'autres musées, en passant par la participation à
des expositions d'autres départements du musée, soit par la
rotation des objets, soit par les prêts à l'extérieur pour les
besoins d'expositions itinérantes comprenant des costumes.
Afin de réaliser ce programme ambitieux, nous avons
appris à classer nos tâches par ordre de priorité et à
rationaliser le processus d'installation.*

*Dans l'article, je traite de mes expériences personnelles
des expositions généralement conçues afin d'examiner les
divers éléments de l'histoire des costumes à l'aide d'objets
des collections remarquables de l'Institut. Je suis arrivée
à New York il y a huit ans et, depuis, j'ai mis la main à
plus de 20 expositions de l'Institut, allant des expositions
d'envergures comme «The Age of Napoleon» et «Théâtre
de la Mode», à des rétrospectives plus modestes comme
«Madame Grès» et «Bloom».*

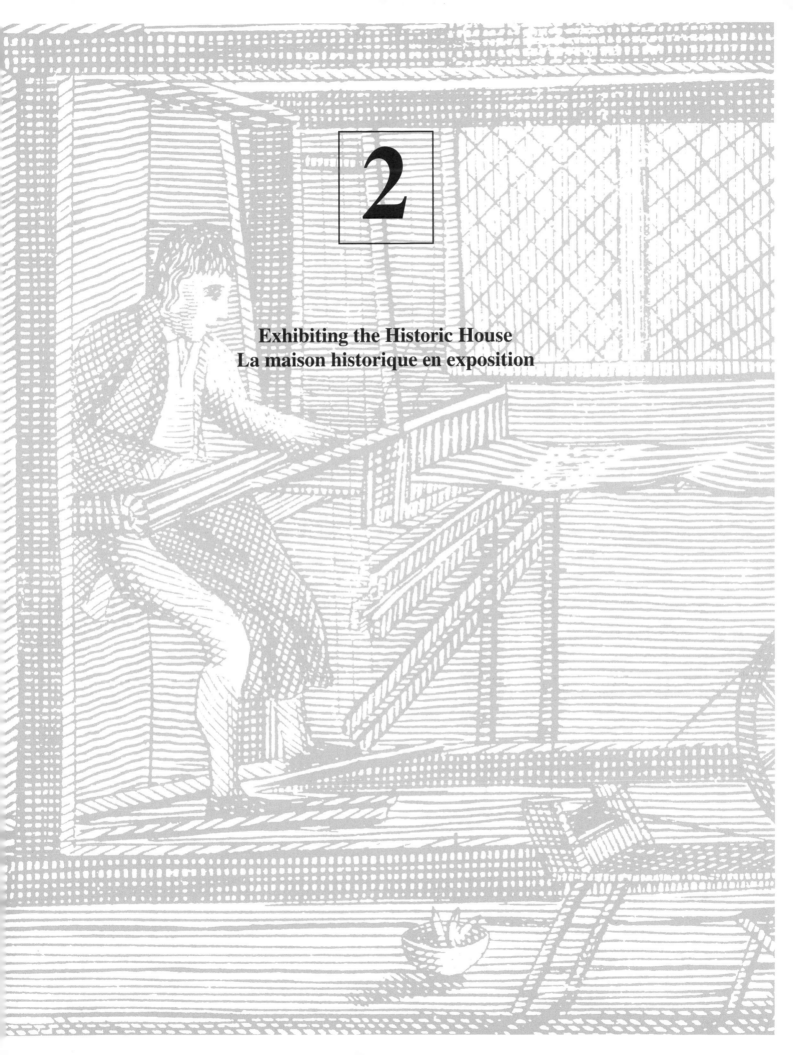

2

Exhibiting the Historic House
La maison historique en exposition

Invisible Boundaries: Searching for Common Ground Between Curators, Conservators, and Interpreters

Abby Sue Fisher

National Park Service
175 East Fifth Street
Suite 418, Box 41
St. Paul, MN 55101 USA
Tel.: (612) 290-3795
E-mail: Abby_Sue_Fisher@nps.gov

Abstract

This paper addresses the roles and interrelationships between curators, conservators, and interpreters within the framework of exhibits in historic house museums. It is a curious fact that discipline-specific specialists in the same field have subtle conflicting viewpoints and approaches. Exhibition or interpretive philosophies tend to heighten differences that often lead to frustration. While role definitions outline our specific tasks, it is how we perceive these roles, and the roles of others, that affect our ability to work collaboratively. In an examination of case studies, this paper will explore potential solutions to minimize the anxiety caused by different approaches. Ultimately, displacing the invisible boundaries between discipline-specific specialists can be achieved though open communication and education. Understanding the similarities and differences between our professions will benefit collaboration, and diminish frustrations in our efforts to exhibit material culture in historic house museums.

This paper will address the roles and interrelationships between curators, conservators, and interpreters within the framework of exhibits in historic house museums. Frequently, the preservation of vulnerable textiles is compromised by their placement in historic house exhibits. In an attempt to recreate an accurate historic period, original artifacts are often placed in the context they were used at a specific point in time. While historic house exhibits gratify visitors who glimpse an earlier time with the aid of an interpreter, the objects on display are in effect being used consumptively. Excessive light, pests, and fluctuations in temperature and relative humidity quickly take their toll on static exhibits. How can objects be protected while on display? Can curators and interpreters be sensitized to the risks foremost in the minds of textile conservators? Is it possible to work collectively toward a common ground?

It is a curious fact that discipline specific specialists in the same field have subtle conflicting viewpoints and approaches. We respect history, material culture, and decorative arts, yet the distinctive roles we play in historic house museums can lead to frustrations. An examination

of these roles will show that disciplines interface in such a way that when discussed openly, the invisible boundaries between them become blurred. By focusing on exhibit challenges, this paper will explore potential solutions to minimize the anxiety caused by different approaches. Ultimately, displacing the invisible boundaries between preservation specialists can be achieved though open communication and education.

Defining Roles

Defining the roles of conservator, curator, and interpreter is not as straightforward as one might imagine. Dictionary definitions do not take into account our relationships in facing current challenges with enthusiastic board of directors, limited funds, and high public expectations. Depending on the institution or organizational body governing a historic house museum, a curator can be fund raiser, interpreter, designer, and steward. An interpreter can be curator, and in many instances, conservators function as interpreters in the development of exhibits. A number of curators, conservators, and interpreters working in different institutions provided me with definitions of their own professions as well as those of their colleagues. The responses were similar with slight variations reflecting the mission of the host institution or agency. In addition to standard definitions located in the *American Heritage Dictionary*, the following roles were described by a textile conservator:

con•ser•va•tor *n.* **1.** One who conserves or preserves from injury, violation, or infraction; protector. **2.** *Law.* One who is responsible for the person and property or an incompetent. **-con•ser•va•to•ri•al** *adj.*

Conservators are advocates for the preservation of artifacts. They develop methods for treatment, display, and storage that enable the object to be used with minimum impact or damage. They assist curators, and scholars with research by providing information about materials.

cu•ra•tor *n.* The administrative director of a museum, library, or other similar institution. [ME *curatour*, legal guardian <Ofr. *curateur* < Lat. *curator*, overseer < *curate*, to take care of < *cura*, care.]**-cu•ra•to•rial** *adj.* -**cu•ra•tor•ship**' *n.*

Curators research and present the social and cultural importance of an artifact through exhibitions, and publications to promote understanding, appreciation, and connoisseurship for the arts. The role of a curator is to develop collections critically.

in•ter•pret•er *n.* **1.** One who translates orally from one language into another. **2.** One who gives or expounds an interpretation. **3.** *Computer Sci.* A program that translates an instruction into a machine language and executes it before proceeding to the next one.

The role of an interpreter is a support position that presents research supplied by scholars to the public in a non-scholarly way. Their associations with collections is to help the audience develop an appreciation and respect for cultural property.

In today's historic preservation community, the roles of curators, conservators, and interpreters are perceived as being distinctive. While definitions outline the specific tasks of each discipline, it is how we perceive our own roles, and the roles of others that affects our ability to work collaboratively. Defining roles too narrowly, with no room for flexibility, leads to controversy in the context of the historic house exhibit environment.

Searching for Common Ground

The collaboration needed to make planning decisions regarding the interpretation of a historic house museum exhibit is considerable, but not insurmountable. Conscious decisions need to be made during the planning process. In the best of all worlds, the professionals around the planning table might consider the following:

Historical architects will be concerned with the needs and condition of the structure, the environment it will support (temperature and relative humidity), and the effects of visitor impact. They will be well aware of the New Orleans Charter and consider joint preservation of the structure and the artifacts on exhibit.

Curators will be instrumental in selecting an interpretive theme, or historic context based on the availability and condition of artifacts. They will be concerned with historical integrity and recreating an accurate exhibit. They too will be conscious of the need for the joint preservation of the structure and collections. They will be concerned about monitoring the environment, housekeeping, preventive conservation, accessibility, security, and fire protection. They will work with the docents, or interpreters to educate them about preservation concerns.

Conservators will focus on all aspects of the environment including light, temperature, relative humidity, pest control, and air pollution. They will be concerned with the

orientation of artifacts in relation to light sources and windows. They may recommend UV filters for the windows, passive window treatments, or the integrated use of reproduction textiles. They may also suggest the possibility of rotating artifacts, or collection retirement for long-term preservation.

Interpreters and educators will focus on the story in the context of the site. They will concentrate on objects that will assist them in telling the story. It will be their mission to educate the public and include preservation as part of the visitor experience. They will also provide first line security during open hours by protecting objects and the structure from theft or damage.

Facility managers will focus on the mechanicals (if any exist), safety, security, fire protection, and accessibility.

Administrators and Boards of Trustees will want to advertise the site and bring as many visitors as possible. They will need to be reminded by curators, conservators, and historical architects of the detrimental effects too many visitors can have on their primary resource. They will be concerned with fundraising to ensure that all recommended actions are programmed accordingly.

Working together, historical architects, conservators, and curators will make decisions about the tour route visitors will take, the impact on artifacts and structure, and whether the number of visitors will be controlled. Curators and conservators will be most instrumental in deciding which artifacts can and cannot be used.

Most likely decisions will be made collectively by the professionals listed above in addition to many others. Opportunities to participate in planning for long-established historic sites occur only when a needed change in strategy is perceived. In these instances, change can be affected by gathering an interdisciplinary group of specialists together, and re-visiting the exhibit framework. The problem is convincing colleagues that change is in fact needed. This can be done by presenting factual information about existing conditions, and recommending alternatives for discussion. Negotiating a recognition for needed change is the first step toward collaboration.

Challenges in Exhibit Environments and Some Potential Solutions

While collaboration and open communication is essential to resolving challenging situations in the exhibit environment, it can also lead to controversy. The key is to work through the controversy toward accommodation. Much of the controversy between curators, conservators, and interpreters is directly related to exhibition, or interpretive philosophies. Exhibition philosophies are dependent on a number of factors including choices made by the management or governing body of the institution, the availability and condition of original artifacts, and the purpose or mission of the site. Generally the mission is to recreate and maintain a specific historical context. How an institution decides to interpret a historic house museum in one era has subsequent impact on future restorations. For example, an institution may decide to retain original textiles such as window treatments, upholstery, bedding, and floor coverings in their historic house museum. Future restorers will not have this option if the original fabrics are deteriorated beyond repair or recognition.

One exhibit philosophy commonly used is to maintain a historic house and its contents in the exact context it was turned over to a cultural institution. Endowments such as this are generally transferred out of the owner's custody when an important person is deceased. This approach tends to focus on the declining years of an individual or family, instead of representing an energetic time when the home was the center of activity. The visitor views objects worn from years of use that would have been automatically replaced in their functional context. This form of interpretation poses unique preservation problems, especially when there is no flexibility to adapt or expand interpretive themes. Textiles used in the interior of the home are generally worn and faded, and window treatments are deteriorated from years of use. What is the role of the textile conservator in this context? Recommending an integrated use of reproductions is one option, while treatment is another. A cost assessment comparing reproduction fabrics with object treatment would determine the feasibility of this approach, although both options are bound to require substantial funds. It is a well known fact that high costs can quickly dissuade historic house administrators from implementing improvements, however financial obstacles can be challenged with creative fundraising techniques. Educating friends groups, cooperating associations, and the public about the preservation needs of a historic site is one approach. Recognizing that funds are necessary for improving or changing exhibit environments, and planning for them is critical.

Deborah Trupin makes a strong case for using reproduction textiles in her paper, "Exhibiting Textiles in Historic House Furnished Rooms—Balancing Conservation and Interpretation." She cites a particular restoration approach that is using reproduction fabrics to replace original textiles that were naturally faded and worn after a century of use. Based on primary source documentation, reproduction fabrics are being integrated throughout the historic house to represent a picture of the living spaces during a specific period of occupation. A group of specialists decided that restoring color, pattern, and texture better illustrated the importance of textiles during this period than using original worn fabrics. While use of reproduction fabrics throughout a historic house museum makes preservation less of an issue, a stronger emphasis is placed on interpretation and education of a historic period.

Or, what if the historic house museum has a large collection of material in storage that could potentially be used for rotation in exhibits. Wouldn't revisiting the interpretive philosophy be prudent for long-term planning and preservation? What happens if a site does in fact have a large collection in storage but interpretive themes are set in stone, and change is viewed as a breech of tradition? The curator supports this "no-change" philosophy, meanwhile textiles left *in situ* are deteriorating. Who is the advocate for change? This kind of dilemma calls for open dialog between a team of outside specialists, and the entire staff of the museum. One possible solution is to collectively re-examine exhibit philosophies. The inherent risks of leaving exhibits unchanged need to be illustrated and communicated. High-cost treatment, collection retirement, or loss of irreplaceable fabric are the least desirable consequences. A conservator may ask, what is the impact on the integrity of the site if one tablecloth is rotated for another when both are original to the site? Will the staff consider seasonal variations in furnishings such as festive linens for holidays, and light floral linens for the springtime? The answers to these questions are dependent on the quantity and condition of textiles in storage. But if they exist, and are not being used, then this approach is viable. A textile conservator would have a strong case to support this approach if for example, they had recently treated a table linen perceived as being the only one to adequately lend historic integrity to the scene. But what table cloth was used as a replacement while the other was in the lab for treatment? Did the visitor notice the change? These are difficult questions to ask, but they will promote lively discussions that will hopefully lead to accommodation.

An exhibit philosophy that challenges the "no change" strategy is to examine how our own environments change daily in small ways. We replace soiled towels and linens with clean ones, and modify our living spaces during cold and warm seasons. Therefore, an accurate recreation of a historic house could reflect slight modifications in exhibits during the course of a year if in fact collections exist to support the changes. We should keep in mind that static exhibits are more stimulating to the public when they are perceived as being vital and alive.

Another challenging situation deals with a reconstructed National Park Service (NPS) fort, with over a dozen historically furnished structures recreating the Civil War era. Buildings are open daily for self-guided tours, but the site also has a strong living history program, and gives guided tours upon request. Only six artifacts original to the site are placed throughout the structures. All exhibit furnishings were acquired based on a Historic Furnishing Report produced by the National Park Service specifically for the site. Exhibits contain a variety of object categories that tell the story of the fort, and the people that occupied it. These distinctions include objects original to the period but not the site, reproductions, and period pieces, or antiques.

Climate control exists in some of the buildings, but for the most part, objects are subject to environmental fluctuations. The site has a part-time museum technician responsible for the collections, and a large interpretive staff to support programming.

The museum technician recognized that several textiles on exhibit were in need of repair, and programmed a collection condition survey. In my position as Regional Curator assisting the site, a decision needed to be made about how best to proceed. A general assessment of the textiles showed that several quilts were in shreds, and a small hooked rug had a sizable hole in the center. I recognized the cost of conservation treatment, and proceeded to assess each artifact to see how it was acquired, and whether it was one of a kind, or replaceable. After a careful look at the collection records, and taking the site conditions into account, a conscious decision was made not to contract a textile conservator. I consulted with the site staff, explaining the cost of treatment compared to the cost of purchasing replacements. Information about each object was also shared including acquisition data, and the fact that replacements could easily be obtained. Contact was also made with a textile conservator familiar with the site who agreed that it would be best to replace the period pieces with similar pieces in better condition. The scenario illustrates how a calculated judgment was made based on the original exhibition philosophy (the Historic Furnishings Report), the origin of the artifacts in question, and existing site conditions.

Yet, having made a measured decision, several questions can be raised about this situation. Was a new dilemma created by purchase of "sacrificial artifacts" that we know will be used consumptively in this environment? What are the thresholds of care if property is considered disposable? When does an object purchased specifically for exhibit become treatable? Do objects need to be a certain age to be considered historic? Even though none of the objects assessed in this scenario were original to the site or even the period, they are considered to be part of the NPS museum collection and need to be regarded accordingly.

Education, Communication, and Accommodation

There is a significant amount of interface that occurs between the three disciplines examined in this paper. Textile conservators are interpreters by nature of the historical research they conduct to identify fabrics, materials, and fabrication technologies. Preventive conservation bridges the roles of curators and conservators. Both educate museum personnel and the public about a holistic approach to preservation. Because conservators and curators have less contact with the public, they are often dependent on

interpreters to educate the visitors about preservation at the start of a historic house tour. Explanations about why light levels are kept to a minimum, or the hazards of touching, slamming doors, and leaning on objects set the stage for walking into an exhibit environment and give the visitor an opportunity to assist with preservation.

The common element uniting these disciplines is education. As philosophies underlying the management and interpretation of historic house museums develop, we see more emphasis on interdisciplinary approach. Narrow definitions tend to emphasize boundaries, whereas collaboration and crossing disciplines blurs them.

In an attempt to facilitate an understanding of the differences and similarities between conservators, curators, and interpreters, the following exercise may be effective to practice prior to a planning meeting. Let's assume the meeting will focus on how to interpret a particular site. Collective decisions will need to be made regarding what time period to interpret, consideration of the condition of original objects to be displayed, will reproductions be appropriate, and preservation issues such as environment and visitor accessibility will be discussed.

Pass out a blank piece of paper to each person around the planning table. Ask that the following question be considered by everyone, with a brief response written on the paper. Give a 15 minute window for the exercise. The question is: if you could decide how your home would be interpreted at some point in the future, what approach would you take? Imagine that most of your belongings will be available for interpretation. If you are met with blank expressions, you may wish to guide the participants by asking: given your knowledge of your life and achievements, how would you use artifacts to tell your story?

While this concept is simple, it will stimulate a number of responses from varying perspectives. The ultimate goal of discipline-specific specialists, and even management, in the context of a historic house, is to interface an enriching visitor experience with sound preservation policies. In this respect, understanding the similarities and differences between philosophies and approaches will enable the group to work toward their common goal.

This paper attempts to open a dialog about the challenges we face in working in historic house exhibit environments. We need to focus on arriving at measured solutions based on critical thinking and exchange among professionals. When we listen to, and understand the different viewpoints of our colleagues, we will be better equipped to move beyond controversy toward accommodation.

References

APT Bulletin: The Journal of Preservation Technology.
Special Issue: *Museums in Historic Buildings*, vol. XXVII,
no. 3 (1996).

Jessup, Wendy Claire, ed. *Conservation in Context:
Finding a Balance for the Historic House.* Washington,
D.C.: Museum, National Trust for Historic Preservation,
1995.

Résumé

La frontière invisible - à la recherche d'un terrain d'entente entre les conservateurs, les restaurateurs et les interprètes

Cet article porte sur le rôle et l'interaction des conservateurs, des restaurateurs et des interprètes dans le cadre des expositions situées dans les maisons historiques. Il est surprenant de noter que les spécialistes qui exercent des disciplines différentes dans le même domaine aient des opinions et des démarches contradictoires. Les principes directeurs des expositions et de l'interprétation tendent à accentuer les différences et de ce fait à être source de frustrations. Si la définition des rôles décrit nos tâches individuelles, c'est notre perception de ces rôles et de ceux des autres qui détermine notre aptitude à travailler en collaboration. Par l'examen d'études de cas, l'auteure explore des solutions qui permettraient de réduire au minimum l'anxiété causée par les différences dans les méthodes. En bout de ligne, on peut effacer les frontières invisibles entre les spécialistes de disciplines différentes par la bonne communication et la sensibilisation. La compréhension des similitudes et des différences entre nos professions facilitera la collaboration et réduira les frustrations qui se font sentir durant les préparatifs de l'exposition des signes de la culture matérielle dans les maisons historiques.

Exhibition and Preservation of Artifacts with Textile Components at Point Ellice House Historic Site

Jennifer Iredale

Southwestern Okanagan Region, Heritage Branch
Ministry of Small Business, Tourism and Culture
5th floor - 800 Johnson Street
Victoria, BC V8W 2Z2 Canada
Tel.: (250) 387-4696
E-mail: jennifer_iredale@tbccc01.tbc.gov.bc.ca

Abstract

This paper will present case studies of conservation techniques used in the period rooms at Point Ellice House Historic Site that allow exhibition of historic artifacts with textile components. Point Ellice, the Victoria home of the O'Reilly family from 1868 to 1974, is a rambling Italianate structure set in a beautiful, restored garden on the banks of the Selkirk waterway. Most of the household textiles pre-date the turn of the century. The preservation and exhibition *in situ* of 4,000 primary artifacts is the focus of the curatorial team at the site. The varied challenges of preservation and exhibition *in situ* ranging from moth and rodent infestations; our techniques for controlling light and humidity fluctuations; issues around unobtrusive barriers; replication of original objects; and descriptions of our new project to involve entrepreneurs in interpretation, site development and stewardship are presented.

Point Ellice was the Victoria, British Columbia, home of the O'Reilly family from 1868 to 1974. It is a rambling Italianate structure set in a beautiful, restored garden on

Figure 1. Point Ellice House and Garden, ca. 1890. Note original awnings replicated in 1995 for light conservation purposes. (British Columbia Archives and Records Service, #50121, C-3926)

the banks of the Selkirk waterway. The buildings contain the household collection of the O'Reilly's, which is complemented by a significant archival collection of household receipts, accounts, letters etc., and numerous photographs. Most of the textiles pre-date the turn of the century. The preservation and exhibition *in situ* of these 4,000 primary artifacts is the focus of the curatorial team at the site.

Textiles on exhibit at Point Ellice include curtains, tablecloths, throws, runners, carpets and 19th-century "costumes". There is also a large collection of textiles in storage — much of it inside the exhibition furniture — chests of drawers, and wardrobes. Artifacts in these include needlework pieces, linens, and a wide variety of clothing.

At historic sites, artifacts are displayed in context. In fact, the context is also an artifact. For example, the house at Point Ellice is a primary artifact, and has preservation concerns that are sometimes in conflict with preservation of the household objects inside. The display of the household objects is *in situ* — these objects still function as a bureau, as curtains, as carpets. The environment is difficult to control for light and humidity, because the doors are opened and closed, the windows let light in. In many cases, the historic buildings are required to upgrade services to current zoning, fire and health standards, often compromising the historical integrity of the structure or the original function of the artifacts. All of these factors make conservation at historic sites a real challenge, and quite different from conservation in a museum setting.

In the early 1990s, curatorial effort at Point Ellice House focused on establishing a solid program of preventative conservation at the site. We contracted with conservator Margaret Graham-Bell to co-ordinate the project and write a housekeeping manual.

It identified the main problems relating to textile damage at Point Ellice:
1. Over-exposure to light.
2. Handling.
3. Display — mounts, supports, security.
4. Storage — over-crowding, protective conditions.
5. Humidity.
6. Pest control.

Between 1990 and 1996, we have continued to undertake projects to ameliorate these and other conservation problems. I will outline a few of our solutions below.

Light Levels

Over-exposure to light causes fading and fibre embrittlement. This is a problem for curtains and original blinds at historic houses. It also affects upholstery or other textiles exhibited near windows in the period rooms. To control this damage, we have:
1. Installed ultraviolet filters on all the windows.
2. Replaced original blinds with replica blinds.
3. Installed replica exterior awnings.
4. Monitored light levels monthly.
5. Held weekly staff meetings.

Ultraviolet filters were installed on the windows at Point Ellice in the early 1990s. The project included sending samples from the actual rolls being installed back to the Canadian Conservation Institute, Ottawa, Ontario, for analysis.

We also replaced original blinds with replica blinds and try to keep the blinds drawn as much as possible, especially in the south-facing rooms. As visitors move through the house, light levels slowly drop in the hope that as they reach the south-facing rooms, their eyesight has adapted to the very low light levels of the drawing room.

The drawing room, with its extensive collection of upholstered furniture, rugs, lace and velvet curtains was a room of particular concern. It faces south, and has a large, gracious bay window. Late afternoon sun is a problem, in our time and the O'Reilly's time. The O'Reilly's solution — to install awnings on the south-facing windows — provided us with a perfect solution also. In 1995, we replicated the awnings and installed them on the bay window, complete with replicated hardware, and a somewhat complicated system of string pulleys. Not only does the house look more historically correct, but the drawing room artifacts are safer from light damage.

We have acquired light monitors and a monitoring program to record light levels on a bi-monthly basis. These records are kept in binders accessible to all staff and which can be provided as "proof" when problems occur.

Nevertheless, the dim room is a constant source of preservation/presentation conflict. Part of the preventative conservation process, to my mind, is to ensure that these issues/conflicts are discussed and aired at any time staff need to talk about it. As long as discussion continues between curatorial and interpretive staff, compromises and solutions can occur which prevent artifact and staff relations deterioration. To this end, we have weekly meetings during the summer at Point Ellice to which all "stakeholders" are invited.

Handling/Use

Many of the textiles at Point Ellice are fragile and some are further weakened by moth damage or light damage. Original carpets and upholstery would suffer from use. In the 1980s there was discussion and pressure to develop Point Ellice as a living history site and to allow visitor access to period rooms or interpretive access for demonstrations in the period rooms. The Southwestern Okanagan staff (curators, interpreters, managers, and operations people) did some strategy planning for all our sites, and decided to apply a tiered collections policy to "rationally" determine use of the collections.

Since the artifacts all have provenance to the site and to the O'Reilly family, they are in our Tier A - Point Ellice collection. We allow visitors visual access to the collections; the period rooms are behind barriers and alarm systems. Handling is by curatorial staff or conservators only. Guidelines for handling include removal of all personal jewellery that could snag the textiles, wearing of clean cotton gloves to prevent soiling from hand oils, and providing adequate support to large awkward pieces. This often means two or more people must work on artifacts such as carpets, curtains etc.

Display

Many textile pieces are on display at Point Ellice. They are not in cases but are exhibited in context — essentially they still function as they were originally intended. A table cloth is still used as a table cloth; curtains still hang as curtains. Often pieces are very fragile and require more support that they originally did.

A case study is the heavy lace and tapestry curtains in the drawing room and dining room. In March 1993, we took them down, cleaned and re-hung them. Cleaning was done by laying the pieces flat, and gently vacuuming them through a screen. This removed a great deal of dust and grit. Inspection revealed that the tapestry panels have had extensive modifications over the years. The original lining is gone and the curtain rings were modern S-hooks spiked through the fabric. There were not enough of them to adequately support the curtains. Our conservator suggested that we could improve the support for the curtains by:
1. Installing more curtain rings threaded onto the original iron cornice pole.
2. Remove the spiked S-hooks and hand sew a heavy, wide cotton tape to the top of each tapestry panel to which many small, brass (non-corrosive) curtain hooks can be sewn. The tape will distribute the weight of the panels evenly; the hooks can be attached to the curtain rings enabling the tapestry panels to be gently opened or closed if necessary.

3. Unstitch the curtain lining and hand sew on a good quality heavy cotton lining to protect the tapestry fabric from light damage, and provide some support to the tapestry curtains.

This work was undertaken during the next cleaning of the curtains, the winter/spring of 1995.

Figure 2. Christmas at Point Ellis House, 1943. Note dining room curtains.

Figure 3. Desk in dining room, 1967. Note original curtains now moved into study.

Storage

When I came to the site as curator in 1988, artifact storage at Point Ellice was in the damp attic and carriage shed. There was little shelving and no organisation. The house had recently undergone building restoration and Project Moth, and energy had not been expended on artifact storage. As part of our housekeeping manual, we asked that better solutions for artifact storage be identified.

We moved the objects stored in the attic and carriage shed off-site, but into a monitored environment with some light and humidity controls. We put them on shelves or pallets on the floor. We envisioned an on-site controlled environment storage area and curatorial workshop in a replica barn structure, but had little hope of realising this solution when priorized against necessary improvements to visitor facilities (washrooms), necessary restoration work to the buildings, etc. However, we were able to design a facility that provided for visitor facilities and artifact storage, and in 1995 initial funding for the visitor orientation centre/ artifact storage area came through! In 1996, we returned a portion of the artifacts stored off-site back to Point Ellice. The new space allowed us to undertake a comprehensive study/conservation cleaning/cataloguing of the extensive carpet collection, before rolling and hanging them. Work continues to complete the building and allow us to return all the off-site objects to Point Ellice.

Over the past five years, extensive work has been done to review all the textiles stored in the bureaus and wardrobes in the house; to vacuum or brush clean them and to repack in polyethylene to prevent/deter moth problems. These are then returned to the wardrobes, but in less compacted condition.

The large clothing collection was reviewed in 1994. We needed to either create more storage space for them or to de-accession inappropriate material. Our policy is to actively collect objects with provenance to the O'Reilly family at Point Ellice House between 1868 and 1889 and objects with later years provenance to the O'Reilly's up until they opened it as a private museum in 1966. After serious discussion, we decided to de-accession the clothing that had been collected by the family for their museum operation (post-1966). These were donated to the Canadiana Costume Museum. This provided us with much needed space and a collection that more authentically documented the O'Reilly family living at the house.

Monitoring of the environmental conditions in the rooms is an ongoing task of my curatorial assistant.

Humidity Control

Humidity control is one of the issues in a heritage house where doors are constantly opened and closed and there is little insulation. To deal with this problem, we began by monitoring the humidity using numerous hygrothermographs. This showed us which rooms were suffering from humidity fluctuations the most. Overall, the rooms remain fairly constant.

Pest Control

Project Moth
Point Ellice House suffers from infestations of moths and problems with rodents. Over the years, moths have caused major damage to curtains, carpets, upholstery and other textiles.

A major project was undertaken in 1988 to cope with a major problem with the moths. "Operation Moth", directed by Royal British Columbia Museum conservator, Colleen Wilson (described by her in a June 1988 report and subsequent *BCMA Newsletter*). She had all artifacts bagged, removed from the site and frozen. An application of 'Sevin', (a residual insecticide containing 5% Carbaryl) was used in critical areas before the artifacts were returned to the site. However, thereafter, site staff instituted a program of pest monitoring. A sticky, fly trap is attached to a small plug-in night light which is left on continuously plugged into a wall socket. The Curatorial Assistant checks these weekly and notes the number of moths found. This number is compared with previous weeks and any infestations or increase in numbers in various locations can be immediately identified and dealt with. Occasionally, we resort to Vapona-like strips to combat small infestations. A project to plastic bag each and every textile artifact stored in the numerous bureaus and cupboards in the house has recently been completed. Sawdust insulation (installed in the 1960s) was removed from the attic in 1995 because it was identified as a possible source of moths. Exhibit artifacts (such as carpets and fur rugs) are carefully vacuumed on both sides once annually, and more frequently if moths are found on the monitoring traps. Moth larvae are a cause for major alarm at Point Ellice, and we try to prevent further damage to these extraordinary textiles.

Preventative Conservation
The most important program we have in place to conserve the Southwestern Okanagan historic sites is a program of conservation cleaning. This preventative conservation measure ensures each and every period room and artifact receives attention, monitoring and cleaning (if necessary) on a frequent schedule.

Involving the Visitor

We involve the site visitors through educating them about the rarity and fragility of the artifacts, as soon as they come through the door. Interpreters and signs impart the special nature of the history, the individual artifacts and the site. The audio tour each visitor listens to welcomes the visitor as though they were a new houseboy to the site, who is being guided through his new duties by the departing servant.

Thus, cautions as to the "do's and don'ts" of the job are frequent. As in: *"The sink in here is made of wood, so we'll not crack or chip any fine china. Always take great care in your cleaning. The O'Reilly's have Minton dinner service, with 140 pieces that came around the horn from England. . . . "*

Permittee Involvement

At sites where the period room exhibits are publicly accessible (the objects are interpretive, have no provenance to the site and were collected for hands-on use), the contract conservation cleaner works with the site permittee two or three times a year to provide conservation training and to assist with cleaning of any of the more fragile objects.

Artifact security is also a role the permittee's play at our sites. There staff is trained to monitor the alarm systems and to deal with any breaches of period room barriers. They are trained at the beginning of each season in why conservation is important and what they can do to help. This is the opportunity for curatorial staff, contractor's and permittee staff to get to know one another and develop a good working relationship.

Permittee staffing of the Southwest Okanagan historic sites is a relatively recent development. Permittees are entrepreneurs (and often museum professionals) who bid to operate the sites. Their revenues are derived from charging for programs, gift shops or other ventures compatible with the historical themes and conservation policies of the site. Permittees have generally brought refreshing new energy, enthusiasm, creativity and commitment to their site. Part of their permit requires them to provide cleaning services for all public areas (including hands-on period rooms), but not for hands-off and barriered period rooms. Consequently there is frequent interaction between permittees and curatorial staff. This could lead to conflict, however, as all of us are aware of the inherent conflicts between conservation and presentation (which exist no matter what the management structure is), we work to maintain accord. We have frequent and scheduled meetings to keep lines of communication open and prevent problems from happening. At these meetings, issues of concern are raised and all players make suggestions for their solution. We can usually come up with compromises that suit all parties, and we hope, are best for the historical integrity, good interpretation and careful preservation of the site.

Major plusses of this new management structure, are such projects as the restoration of the south garden at Point Ellice House. The Heritage Branch had decided that we would be unable to restore the south garden (a kitchen garden) due to capital costs and, more importantly, maintenance costs. The permittee came to us with a proposal to undertake the capital work and then maintain the garden at her expense. In return, she could grow and sell anything in that garden, and use the area as an education centre, for which she could generate tuition. We agreed to undertake a small archaeological contract to document and reveal historic pathways and other features, much of which had been excavated previously. Our staff also undertook archival research to provide the permittee with authentic information on paths, features, plant massing, seasonal changes, and original plants. We also documented the permittee's work as it went forward. Point Ellice House now has a restored kitchen garden that grows vegetables and fruits typical of the period. Some varieties are known to have been grown by the O'Reilly's. The permittee interprets all of this, through signage and through workshops and courses offered on site. Although this story does not focus on textile conservation, I thought it might be of interest in showing the benefits and partnerships we have been able to develop through the permittee system. As we evolve in this management model, we continue to find new benefits from working with entrepreneurs who value the history of the provincial historic sites and are extremely creative and committed to finding ways to develop the sites relevance and to bring visitors and revenues through the doors. They have no trouble seeing the importance of maintaining the resource (conservation) and increasing the knowledge (research) needed to tell the site story.

Bibliography

Careless, V. A. S. *Responding to Fashion, The Clothing of the O'Reilly Family*, 1993.

Dean, P. *Research Project on the Point Ellice House Carpet Collection*, 1989.

Dix, U., B. Byers, and M. Gates. *Point Ellice House Survey Report*, 1975.

Files on the Curatorial and Conservation Activities at Point Ellice House. Maintained by Iredale, J., 1989 - 1997.

Graham Bell, M. *Point Ellice House Conservation Services Contract*, March 1993.

Graham-Bell, M. *Storage Assessment and Action Plan for Heritage Properties Branch*, 1990.

Graham-Bell, M. *Conservation Report for Point Ellice House*, 1988.

Graham- Bell, M. *Interim Report on the Current Environmental Monitoring at Point Ellice House*, 1992.

Graham-Bell, M. *Report on Work Carried Out at Point Ellice House*, 1989/90.

Graham-Bell, M. *Heritage Housekeeping Manual for Point Ellice House*, September 1988.

Stark, S. *Report and Specifications for Awnings at Point Ellice House*, 1990.

Volumes of the Annual Conservation Monitoring Program at Point Ellice House. Maintained by Molinaro, T., 1993 - 1997.

Wilson, C. *Moths, Moths, and More Moths*. From British Columbia M. A. Museum Round-Up, Feb. 1990.

Résumé

Exposition et préservation des objets comportant des éléments textiles dans la maison historique Point Ellice

Dans cet article, on présente des études de cas concernant les techniques de conservation utilisées dans les salles d'époque de la maison historique Point Ellice, en vue de l'exposition d'objets historiques comportant des éléments textiles. Point Ellice, résidence de la famille O'Reilly à Victoria de 1868 à 1974, se présente comme une construction italienne exubérante sise au milieu d'un jardin élégant restauré, sur les rives de la voie navigable Selkirk. La plupart des textiles domestiques sont antérieurs au début du siècle. La préservation et l'exposition in situ des 4 000 objets principaux est l'objectif premier de l'équipe de conservateurs du site. Les divers défis de la préservation et la présentation in situ vont des attaques des mites et des rongeurs aux techniques de régulation de la lumière et de lutte contre les fluctuations d'humidité, en passant par la recherche de barrières non gênantes, la reproduction des objets d'origine et la description de notre nouveau projet aux entrepreneurs en interprétation, en développement de site et en services d'accueil.

Exhibiting Textiles in Historic House Furnished Rooms: Balancing Conservation and Interpretation

Deborah Lee Trupin

New York State Office of Parks, Recreation and Historic Preservation
Bureau of Historic Sites
Peebles Island, P. O. Box 219
Waterford, NY 12188 USA
Tel.: (518) 237-8643, ext. 241

Abstract

This paper examines the different ways in which New York State historic sites have chosen to include textiles in their furnished room exhibits. Generally, the solutions for each house are based upon what was extant in the house upon its becoming a state historic site. At sites which retained few or no textiles original to the site's interpretive period, reproduction textiles have been introduced. Selection of the reproductions is based on information gleaned from documents; the more specific the information, the less generic the reproduction. Sites which retain many of their original furnishing fabrics present another set of issues and possible solutions. At these sites, the existing textiles are evaluated in light of their condition and the interpretive needs of the site. At times, this evaluation results in the decision to replace fragile and worn historic textiles with exact reproductions.

For centuries, textiles have been an important factor in the decoration of houses. It is nearly a cliché to note that prior to the Industrial Revolution, textiles were one of the most costly items in a house. However, if one stops and really considers this statement, the contrast between how textiles are treated in contemporary homes and those of the past is striking. Thus, incorporating textiles into historic houses is crucial for the proper understanding and interpretation of many historic houses. The significance that textiles — especially bed- and window-curtains, upholstery fabrics and floor coverings — had in earlier houses must be respected and conveyed in their use in historic houses.

This paper will examine the different ways in which New York State Historic Sites have chosen to include textiles in their furnished room exhibits. Generally, the solutions for each house are based upon what was extant in the house upon its becoming a state historic site. One group of sites retained few, if any, textiles that were original to the site's interpretive period. At these sites, reproduction textiles have been introduced.

Schuyler Mansion State Historic Site, in Albany, New York, was the late-18th century home of General Philip Schuyler.

Schuyler and his family were one of the most wealthy and powerful in the Albany area and Schuyler built and decorated his home to reflect this status. The house passed out of the family just after Schuyler's death in 1804, was owned by several other families and served as an orphanage before becoming a New York State Historic Site in 1911. By that time, no original fabrics remained on site. In the intervening years, Schuyler descendants have donated some of Schuyler's furniture, but none of this retained its original upholstery fabrics either.

Schuyler Mansion was first restored between 1912 and 1917; work at this time concentrated on the building and acquiring collections. There does not seem to be any documentation for fabrics used in this restoration. Between 1947 and 1950, the house was again restored, under the auspices of the New York State Education Department. This restoration resulted in: installing new window sash with smaller panes, restoring the original colors of the interior woodwork and replacing all draperies for windows and furniture with reproductions of eighteenth-century originals. All of the reproductions of eighteenth-century textiles made especially for Schuyler Mansion were produced and donated by Franco Scalamandre.[1]

By the late-1980s, the 1950 restoration looked dated and worn. Working from the Schuyler papers,[2] in conjunction with standard sources and a new paint analysis, staff wrote a furnishing plan. Using a combination of public and private funds, the site is being re-interpreted.

New reproduction textiles played a key role in this reinterpretation. Where in the 1950s restoration there had been Oriental carpets in Colonial Revival fashion, there are now Brussels carpets, in documented period weave and patterns. Furniture that was previously upholstered in a generic damask has been recovered (using non-interventive methods) in a yellow worsted moreen. The moreen is still somewhat of a compromise, as the receipts in the Schuyler papers list "yellow worsted damask". However, no appropriate damask was available and the budget precluded commissioning a custom reproduction.[3] The suite of yellow-covered furniture was placed in the room that paint analysis showed was originally yellow; yellow flocked wall paper was also used in that room.

The results of the current restoration are so striking and so pleasing to staff and visitors, that it is tempting to feel superior to the last generation of restorers. However, to read about the 1950 decoration in Anna Cunningham's book is sobering. She and her colleagues also had access to the Schuyler papers; they simply made other decisions about what to do with a reference to "yallow worsted damask". Describing these decisions, Miss Cunningham wrote that after searching for fragments of the original damask, she decided to use a damask loaned by descendants of Chancellor Robert E. Livingston as the model for the reproduction fabrics.[4]

It has been said that restorers of Miss Cunningham's and earlier generations were trying to show houses as they should have been: In a sense, like the great French 19th-century restoration architect and theoretician Viollet-le-Duc, the Board was improving on history, restoring the mansion, if not to what it was then to what in (the Board's) eyes it should have been.[5]

Present-day historic house staff must recognize that past generations were doing what they felt best with the information they had available. Essentially, this continues to be the goal. The attitude today is one of strict adherence to sources; tolerance for deviation from the sources seems smaller today than it was a generation or two ago. Another key difference is in the emphasis on leaving evidence for decision-making about restorations. This evidence may be in the form of written, and even published, furnishing plans and/or in-house documents. Present-day restorations (or re-restorations) have the advantage of access to greater scholarship than did previous restoration efforts.

This progression in the restoration and interpretation of an historic house can also be seen at John Jay Homestead State Historic Site in Katonah, New York, where, in recent years, restoration efforts have been paralleling the developments at Schuyler Mansion. The Homestead is the family farm that John Jay, first Chief Justice of the US Supreme Court, developed as his retirement home at the close of the 18th century. Unlike Schuyler Mansion, John Jay Homestead remained in the family until the 1950s. Of course, during 150 years, its appearance had changed significantly, as subsequent generations enlarged, remodelled and redecorated in accordance with changing fashions. During its early years as a State Historic Site, John Jay Homestead depicted the life of several Jay generations, with different rooms decorated in the styles of different generations. On the whole, however, John Jay Homestead, like Schuyler Mansion, had a faded Colonial Revival look. In the late 1980s staff re-evaluated the interpretation of John Jay Homestead and decided that the different rooms for different generations approach was no longer meaningful. Instead, they decided to interpret the house for the time period when John Jay was in residence, from 1801 to 1829.

Many pieces of family furniture (from all of the generations) remained in the house, but no original textiles remained. The total loss of textiles is attributed to an attic fire in 1926 as well as to the expected amount of replacement and change. Thus, as at Schuyler Mansion, for information about the textiles used in the Homestead, site staff was limited to documentary evidence, both primary and secondary. Among the primary sources available to John Jay Homestead staff are a (household) account book kept by Jay from 1813 until 1829 and family diaries and letters; several letters record Jay asking one son or another to order items from New York City. Using this information, a new furnishing plan has been written and is being implemented.

New textiles have been introduced: window and bed hangings, carpeting, upholstery, and slipcovers. The changes are extraordinary. The house has gone from a fairly dull, generic historic house to one where the staff can use the furnished rooms to discuss Jay's life, his family and the socio-political era. Particularly successful at John Jay Homestead are the use of "scenarios," or room interpretations which present a given moment in time. For instance, the house can be set up for a house party of forty-eight people, based on the diary of Maria Jay Banyer (Jay's widowed daughter), who wrote, "Our guests their domestics & our family amounted to 48."[6]

As at Schuyler Mansion, a combination of public and private funds has helped to implement the reinterpretation. The Friends of John Jay Homestead have funded most of the reproductions. The Friends' House Committee, which works closely with the staff, is chaired by a decorator who negotiates with vendors and fabricators. Elizabeth Leckie, John Jay Homestead's curator, has worked to educate the House Committee; they now see the Homestead from a historic perspective and do not try to "decorate" it in late-20th century styles.

For a textile conservator, these sorts of reinterpretations, with their heavy use of reproduction fabrics, can be liberating. The perpetual conflict between exhibition and preservation is essentially nonexistent. Instead, the conservator works with curatorial staff on selection of fabrics, contract specifications for reproductions and advises on preservation of the new reproductions. Visiting these houses, a conservator can be as absorbed by the history as a nonspecialist visitor, free from the painful distractions of fading and deteriorating valuable historic fabrics.

Other New York State historic sites retain many or all of their original furnishing fabrics. These fabrics, all in various stages of deterioration, present another set of questions and possible answers. At these sites the conservator must confront all of the issues inherent to the preservation versus interpretation dilemma.

Mills Mansion State Historic Site, in Staatsburg, New York, is one such site. This Beaux Arts mansion was designed and decorated by Stanford White and Jules Allard et Fils in 1895 for Ogden and Ruth Livingston Mills. It was donated to New York State in 1938, with 95% of its furnishings and furnishing fabrics still *in situ* (the furnishings were on loan from the family until 1970, but remained in the house in the intervening years). Although the Mansion has been open to the public since 1938, it was not until 1986, with the hiring of the current director, that New York State committed to fully restoring Mills Mansion as a house museum. The interpretive period for the Mansion is 1895 - 1920, which corresponds to the period when the Mills family most actively used the house; it served annually as their fall and holiday residence. An inventory taken in 1938, when the property was first turned over to the state, provided the outline for the furnishing plan. A small number of historic photographs supplemented the inventory.

From 1987 to 1988, site staff worked from these documents to recreate the room settings, putting as much furniture as could be identified into its appropriate locations. One of the biggest questions staff then had to confront was that of the textiles. Furnishing fabrics, used as window treatments, wall coverings and upholstery, were the one of the key decorative elements in the house. Mills Mansion was fortunate to retain almost all of its original furnishing fabrics, but, as can be imagined, after ninety-odd years, their condition and appearance were poor.

To begin to answer some of the questions raised by the fabrics, in 1988 Mills Mansion invited ten museum colleagues to a two-day symposium on the Mansion's textile and upholstery conservation issues. The symposium participants confirmed the importance of the furnishing fabrics and upholstery to the interiors of Mills Mansion — both to the interpretation of the house and as a collection of late-19th century furnishing fabrics. To preserve the interpretation of each room, participants felt it would be crucial to approach the restoration in an integrated way. To preserve the furnishing fabrics themselves, participants recognized that many would have to be removed from furniture and windows and replaced with reproduction fabrics.

That two-day symposium, followed by ongoing research into the site's history and fabric availability, has set the direction for the restoration of the interior of Mills Mansion. To date, Mills Mansion has commissioned the custom, exact reproduction of several fabrics, which have been used to recover upholstered furniture and create exact reproductions of draperies and bedcovers. Some less important fabrics, such as the velvet for the squabs on the dining room chairs, have been replaced by similar, but not identical fabrics. Original fabrics have been preserved in storage.

This approach is working fairly well. The rooms which have been fully restored present a far more accurate picture of how they were used and seen by the Mills family and their guests than do the unrestored rooms, with their

shredded, faded fabrics. For the site staff, this is the key issue. As at John Jay Homestead, the restored rooms can be used to educate visitors about the social history of the site.

The process and results are not without compromise, however. Not all of the fabrics in a given room have been replaced with reproductions. In Mr. Mills's bedroom, for instance, the carpet was conserved, while the bedcover, drapery, and upholstery fabric was reproduced. The balance between conserved and reproduced is not quite right; the colors, brightness and "patinas" are noticeably different.

The other issue that remains, and will probably always remain, is that of what people are looking at — and what people want to look at. Is it more valuable to see the tattered remains of a late-19th century damask or a reproduction of this fabric which fully shows its pattern, color and texture? In the case of Mills Mansion, it has been decided that the overall appearance of the house is more important in context than retaining the worn originals in place. Reproduction fabrics help to convey the image, the social status, that was such an important force behind the decoration of Mills Mansion. However, it is the goal of staff to create an exhibition of the original fabrics in a future visitors center. In that setting, visitors will be able to study and appreciate the historic textiles for themselves. In the furnished rooms, they will be able to appreciate the mansion as its architect, decorator and owners intended.

Olana State Historic Site, the home of Hudson River School painter, Frederic E. Church, was built between 1870 and 1874, with a studio addition dating to 1889-91. Olana is today understood by Church scholars to be his last, great work. Although he worked with architect Calvert Vaux, Church provided most of the design for the exterior, interior and landscape of Olana. The house was much visited and admired during Church's life.

Like Mills Mansion, Olana also retains most of its original fabrics. Most of these fabrics too are in fair to poor condition. The issue of original versus reproduction is even more poignant at Olana than at Mills Mansion.

Logically, one would follow the precedent of Mills Mansion and begin to replace the historic fabrics with exact reproductions. However, this solution is not necessarily appropriate or possible for Olana. After his death in 1900, Olana was inherited by Church's son Louis and daughter-in-law, Sally. Because of her admiration for her father-in-law, Sally changed relatively little in the house. Thus, when the property was taken over by the State of New York in 1967, it retained many of its original furnishings and interior wall treatments. This, combined with the extraordinary amount of documentation — letters from visitors, family diaries, newspaper accounts, professional and amateur period photographs — permits Olana to be preserved in an almost shrine-like manner.

This shrine quality makes it more difficult to introduce new materials into Olana. The question of balance is also a tricky one here. The interiors retain original stencilled decoration as well as original furniture, household and decorative arts objects and textiles. Thus, much of the house presents a muted, faded appearance. Introduction of new reproduction fabrics could be quite jarring.

On the other hand, many of the textiles are quite important individual artifacts — Church travelled in the Near East and in Mexico and collected fabrics and objects in his travels. Many of these textiles are in poor condition from years of use and display. Site staff attempt to rotate which textiles are displayed each year, but the number of pieces that are in condition to be displayed, or can be put in condition to be displayed, limits their choices severely.

The significance and variety of the textiles at Olana presents a further complication. Unlike the other historic sites discussed, many of the textiles at Olana are not the typical European furnishing fabrics that can be easily reproduced. Olana features Resht work pieces, suzanis and serapes used as table covers and wall hangings and kilims used as portieres. In typical Victorian style, shawls are draped over chairs and sofa. One chair was originally covered in Resht-work, while another featured leopard skin. Draperies featured Resht-work appliqued onto Western textiles. Currently no original draperies are hanging and most of the fabrics on upholstered furniture primarily date to the 1930s.

The solution for textiles at Olana has not yet been fully articulated. The interpretive goal of the site is to present it as much as possible as it was between 1891, when Church completed most of his work on the property, and his death in 1900. Site staff recognize that the faded textiles do not look as they did in Church's day, yet for the reasons outlined above, there is hesitation to introduce new fabrics. Some of this hesitation may stem from practical and financial reasons. In 1994, Olana's curator Karen Zukowski described her vision for the site, in the keynote lecture at the symposium, "Conservation in Context: Finding a Balance for the Historic House Museum." Zukowski used the metaphor of a "web" to stress the importance of context in the understanding the property and its significance: If we were to re-create the web, this entire physical plant should reflect one point in time. To carry out such a restoration we would have to have hundreds of people working together. Some would be embroidering fabric to replicate middle-Eastern textiles used as upholstery, ...others would be stencilling our cornices in the five patterns designed by Church. Then to get all those things patinated identically, we would have to have people sitting on the newly-embroidered seat cushions, and to weather the cornices we would need people up at the cornices with blow-dryers.[7]

Clearly, Zukowski was describing an impossible, indeed absurd, situation, but she did this to stress the importance of the goal of exact recreation at historic houses. In her lecture, she noted that this goal is a key factor distinguishing historic houses from Disneyland and other theme parks.[7]

Realistically and practically then, how can the display of textiles at Olana be approached? Following the precedent established at Mills Mansion, the first step will be to continue to study the textiles and documentation for the room presentations in the interpretive period, with the goal of obtaining a comprehensive listing of what textiles were used in what rooms. From that point, a list of what textiles are needed will be developed, and from there, staff will explore how to obtain these textiles. It seems likely that the solution will be multi-faceted, using a mixture of reproduction fabrics, original collection fabrics and possibly, newly acquired historic fabrics similar to those collected by Church. Historic fabrics would be used in rotation to supplement those owned by Church. The newly acquired textiles would be treated as historic (collection) fabrics, i.e., they would be displayed as safely as possible (as is now done with Church's textiles). The trickier issues of draperies and upholstery that incorporate both Western and Near Eastern textiles has not yet been resolved. By working closely with fabric houses, it should be possible to obtain good reproductions of the more typical late-nineteenth-century fabrics, although the issues of color and brightness may still be difficult.

In conclusion, then, exhibiting textiles in the New York State historic houses becomes largely a question of exhibiting reproduction fabrics. The question of conservation versus preservation has, in many cases, been answered by the lack of original textiles or by the poor condition of these textiles. While there is some remorse about using so many reproductions, this is tempered by the realization that, where they exist, the originals are protected for future generations. The reproductions become more acceptable too when one returns to the concept of the importance of textiles in the historic periods being interpreted. Because textiles were such a significant part of the statement of the house, it is essential that they convey that status now. Faded and deteriorated fabrics, while historical and original, do not let the public understand how important these originals were. Reproductions that are as accurate as possible actually come closer to presenting the house in its "original" state.

Acknowledgements

The author would like to thank Abby Sue Fisher, Susan May Haswell, Elizabeth Leckie, Jane Merritt, Melodye Moore and Karen Zukowski for their comments on drafts of this paper.

Endnotes

1 Anna K. Cunningham. *Schuyler Mansion: A Critical Catalogue of the Furnishings and Decorations.* Albany, New York: New York State Education Department, 1955.

2 The Schuyler papers provide rich documentation for how Schuyler's house looked in the last quarter of the 18th century and the very early 19th. Schuyler Papers, Manuscripts and Archives Division, The New York Public Library, Astor, Lenox and Tilden Foundation, New York City.

3 Currently accurate reproduction fabrics cost $300.00 and up per yard of (generally) narrow goods, i.e., 27 in. loom widths. Commissioning a custom reproduction fabric entails similar or greater costs per yard plus additional charges for design and/or set-up charges, typically in the thousands of dollars. Thus, costs always play a role in the decisions about purchasing reproduction fabrics. The cost must be weighed against the quantity needed, the significance of the fabric in the room and the degree of knowledge of the original fabric.

4 Cunningham, op.cit. pp. 9-10.

5 Gibbons, Kristin. *Schuyler Mansion: A Historic Structure Report.* Albany, New York: New York State Office of Parks, Recreation and Historic Preservation, 1977, p. 63.

6 Diary of Maria Jay Banyer, September 29, 1824 (unpublished). John Jay Homestead State Historic Site Archives, Katonah, New York.

7 Zukowski, Karen. "The Importance of Context," *Conservation in Context: Finding a Balance for the Historic House Museum,* Wendy Claire Jessup, ed. Washington, D.C.: National Trust for Historic Preservation, 1995, p. 11.

8 Ibid., p. 9.

Résumé

Exposition de textiles dans les pièces meublées d'une maison historique - Équilibrer conservation et interprétation

Dans cet article, on examine les différentes méthodes que des sites historiques de l'État de New York ont choisies pour intégrer des textiles dans leurs expositions de pièces meublées. Dans le domaine des maisons historiques, les solutions choisies sont généralement fondées sur ce qui se trouvait dans la demeure au moment ou elle a été classée monument historique. Dans les maisons où il ne reste que peu ou pas de textiles d'origine de la période d'interprétation choisie, on fait appel à des reproductions. La sélection des reproductions est fondée sur les renseignements tirés de la documentation; plus les renseignements sont précis, plus on s'éloigne des reproductions génériques. Les maisons qui ont conservé une grande partie de leur textiles d'ameublement d'origine se caractérisent par d'autres problèmes et solutions. Dans ces demeures, les textiles existants sont évalués à la lumière de leur état et des besoins d'interprétation du site. À certains moments, les résultats de l'évaluation orientent la décision de remplacer les textiles historiques fragiles et usés par des reproductions exactes.

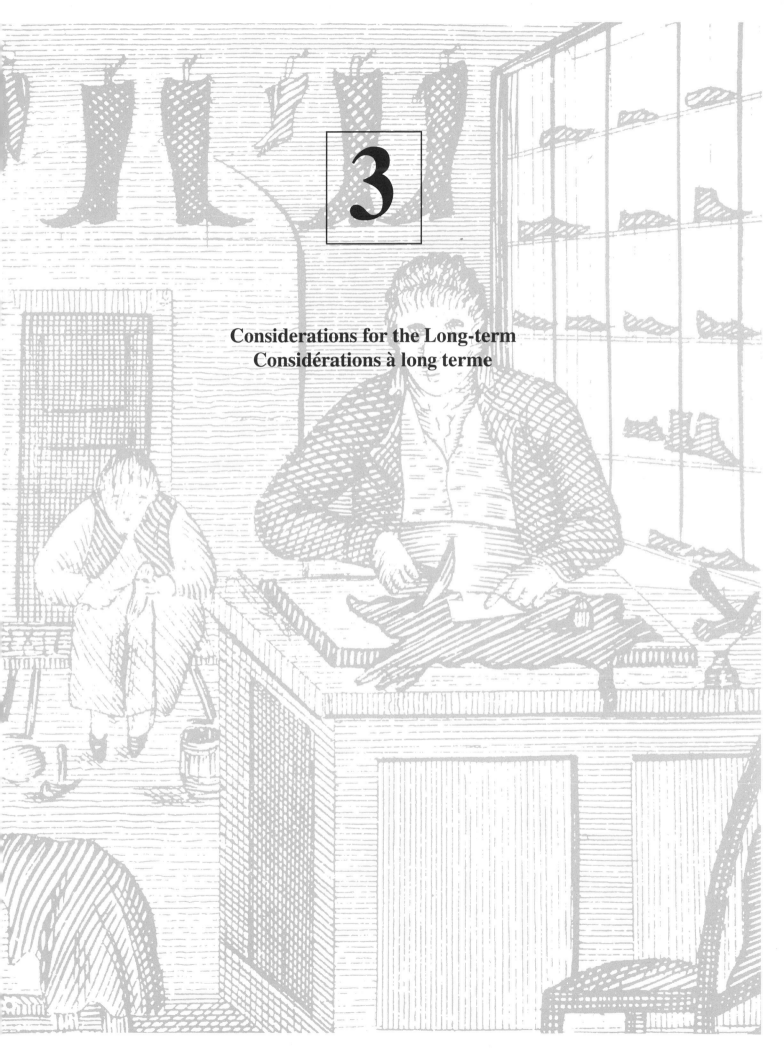

3

Considerations for the Long-term
Considérations à long terme

Balancing Long-term Display with Preservation: The Treatment of the Fort Sumter Garrison Flag

Jane L. Merritt

National Park Service
Division of Conservation, Harpers Ferry Center
P. O. Box 50, Harpers Ferry, WV 25425-0050 USA
Tel.: (304) 535-6142 – Fax: (304) 535-6055
E-mail: jane_merritt@nps.gov

Rita Kauneckas

914 Fifth Avenue
Helena, MT 59601 USA
Tel.: (406) 442-7183

Abstract

Fort Sumter National Monument in South Carolina request-ed the American garrison flag associated with the 1861 opening battle of the Civil War be prepared for long-term display at a new museum under development. Extremely deteriorated, the oversized flag presents a number of chal-lenges in its treatment, including the construction of a stable and tightly sealed permanent storage and exhibition contain-er. The two-year long project in the Division of Conserva-tion, Harpers Ferry Center required the collaboration of conservators, conservation scientists, exhibit designers, engineers, and cabinet manufacturers to resolve the numer-ous questions that arose with each phase of the project.

Introduction

The long-term display of a textile is contrary to all of the principles that conservators try to follow. Light, relative humidity, temperature, pests, atmospheric pollutants, and dusts which contribute to deterioration of textile materials are most difficult to control in a gallery setting. Conserva-tors routinely work with administrators and curators to rotate textiles off display and allow them to "rest" in a well-maintained storage environment.

There are textiles that, for a variety of reasons, are displayed for decades with no chance for rotation. Over time, their installation is modified and improved, but the textiles remain on display. Conservators regularly balance the competing needs for accessibility to the viewing public with concerns for preservation by carefully researching and selecting mate-rials that come in contact with a textile, and by providing a tightly controlled environment with low levels of light.

This paper will review the history and condition of the 6.1 x 7.3 m (20 x 24 ft.) Fort Sumter garrison flag and briefly discuss its conservation treatment. The size, extreme significance, physical state, and planned exhibition location drove the treatment decision-making process.

The flag could be rolled, but the powdering hoist end need-ed to be positioned flat. The selection of compatible mate-rials for rolling and the development of a container that would serve as both storage and exhibit housing and permit safe display was integral to the treatment. Costs to treat and prepare the flag for exhibition had to fall within a tightly controlled budget. Eventually a new building incorporating a museum, visitor center, and tour boat facility will be built in Charleston, South Carolina. The flag will permanently reside in the museum exhibition portion of this building.

A powder-coated aluminum container was eventually developed and fabricated for the flag. The process was complicated and required the assistance of numerous spe-cialists. The large size alone made most fabricators reluc-tant to consider construction of such a case. Therefore, the project was broken down into phases. A design for the con-tainer was developed, and a scale prototype built and tested before constructing the final container.

Figure 1. Fort Sumter Garrison Flag, Catalogue Number 8, Fort Sumter National Monument, Charleston, South Carolina. Before treatment. Photograph taken in 1982 of flag supported on muslin.

Brief History of the Flag

The Fort Sumter garrison flag is made of wool bunting with thirteen red and white horizontal stripes. Thirty-three white cotton stars are sewn to the blue background of the union. It is handsewn with flat felled seams, extremely worn, and in very fragile condition. This flag is extremely significant because it was flown at the time of and figured into the surrender terms of the opening battle of the American Civil War at Fort Sumter, South Carolina in April 1861.

The provenance of the Fort Sumter garrison flag is well established. Its history is documented from the time of surrender in 1861 to its 75-years of continuous display in wooden and glass cases by the War Department and by the National Park Service. Problematically, the owner, Fort Sumter National Monument, is planning to build a new tour-boat facility, visitor center, and museum in Charleston, South Carolina, and requests that this historically significant textile be on long-term display in this building. Concept drawings depict the flag mounted flat and installed vertically against a wall. Its sheer size and powerful image ensured that the flag would be the focal point of the installation.

Condition of the Flag

The flag is very weak and deteriorated. From historical research and photo documentation, we know that approximately half of the length along the stripes is missing. The flag contains patches and repairs, and there is evidence that holes were repaired with sections from the original fly end. It suffered from exposure to ultraviolet rays from the sun, mechanical stresses from flying in the wind, and contamination from salt spray. It was stored and displayed under a variety of unstable conditions for the past 135 years. The flag contains all original material, significant in terms of a historic textile, and has not received any previous adhesive or stitching treatments.

Wool Bunting
The red, white, and blue wool fibers are desiccated and friable. The bunting is thin, very weak, distorted, and creased. The white wool has discolored considerably and has a greenish brown cast. The blue union however, is almost intact, the color remains strong, and the fabric has retained its integrity. The pH of the wool fibers taken from fiber dust measured between four and three.

Hemp Hoist
The hoist is formed from a hemp sleeve and an extant plied hemp rope runs its length. The hemp fibers are very fragile, deteriorated, and near the end of their life expectancy. They no longer flex but split and become detached. The incompatibility of the weight and bulk of the rope within the hemp sleeve seriously compromises the hoist by fracturing the fabric with every movement.

Cotton Stars
The cotton fabric that makes up the stars is intact, although the fibers are yellowed and darkened with discoloration. Traces of fugitive blue dye from the union stain the cotton, a result of exposure to excessive levels of humidity or moisture.

Treatment Proposal

Given the deteriorated condition of the flag, vertical installation for long-term display was impossible. Traditionally, a flag in such condition would be burned. However, the importance of this flag required that significant resources be expended in order to preserve and eventually prepare it for exhibition. An image-based condition report was instrumental in informing the park staff about the current state of the flag and the treatment options that existed. The flag could be safely rolled, but the fracturing hoist would have to be maintained flat at all times. Among the treatment options offered was to build a custom storage container and use a photomural reproduction of the flag for vertical installation in the tour-boat facility. The park agreed to allow us to roll the flag, but requested that the storage container have viewing windows so at least a small portion of the artifact could be viewed. The container would serve as a permanent storage and display housing, eventually going into the museum portion of the tour-boat facility.

Treatment

Goals
The goals of treatment were to retard the degradation process of a very thin, creased, and distorted wool fabric and prepare it for long-term display. Fractured areas of the hoist were stabilized with stitching, distorted areas relaxed using humidification techniques, and a tightly sealed, stable, permanent storage/display container constructed. For 15 years, the garrison flag was stored rolled between two layers of muslin in the Division of Conservation. A move to new and larger laboratories in 1993 meant that the flag could now be worked on. Microscopic examination showed that there were few soil particulates, but shedding wool fibers adhered to the surface. Surface vacuum cleaning was not deemed appropriate since it would take hundreds of hours with a micro-pipette and low suction and would remove large amounts of the flag in the form of fiber dust.

Stabilization Techniques
The very desiccated and brittle hoist needed physical protection for the hemp fibers. It was sandwiched between two layers of Stabiltex, a sheer polyester fabric. This portion of the flag would be kept flat at all times.

Humidification
Several humidification techniques were tested. Acid-free blotter paper slightly dampened with de-ionized water and applied with a mister was selected as most effective. All areas of the flag were accessible from the perimeter and from voids in the

stripes, making a bridge unnecessary. Straightening and realigning the flag was possible by gently manipulating the seams of the stripes, which are the strongest area of the textile.

Rolling the Flag

All materials that would be in contact with the flag and used to construct its container were carefully considered and researched. Storage materials consisted of a rolling tube with an inner pipe to support the 6.6 m (22 ft.) length, fabrics to cover the tube, and an interleaving fabric for the flag itself. The criteria for selecting materials included: 1) stability, 2) lack of residual particles, antioxidants, or finishes that release acids or staining materials, and 3) acceptable aging properties. Discussions with conservation scientists and the manufacturers of the individual materials considered were essential to our selection process.

The flag was rolled between two layers of fabric to reduce friction and support its weight. This support material needed to be lightweight, have a gentle tooth or grab, not compress the flag, be dimensionally stable, and be non-reactive. Lighter weights of superfine pima cotton, acid-free tissue, Tyvek, Gor-Tex, and Nomex were considered.

Cotton-based materials were eliminated as they would degrade and accumulate contaminants and would not be replaced. Therefore, material selection focused on synthetic fabrics. Gor-Tex, a polyester non-woven and polytetrafluoroethylene laminate was eliminated due to a high price per yard. Tyvek, a high density fiber of spun-bonded olefin had many positive attributes including a neutral pH, smooth surface, and some moisture regain. It was rejected because of an incompatible hand and an unnecessary anti-static coating and corona treatment which allows printing on its surface.

Nomex Soft Wrap made by Dupont was selected to roll with the flag and to cover the tube. Nomex is in the nylon family. It is known primarily for its inherent flame retardant properties. It has a very slight moisture regain, is thermally stable, and has a neutral pH. It has a soft hand with a small amount of tooth. It is fungus and mildew resistant due to the nature of the fiber and is dimensionally stable. Since it is in the nylon family, it will yellow when exposed to ultraviolet rays. However, the flag will be in a dark storage container and, when on display light at low levels will be passed through ultraviolet filtering glazing.

The flag is rolled on an acid-free cardboard tube. Tubes made from carbon fiber, aluminum, polyethylene, and polypropylene were considered but rejected because of cost, weight, or deflection amounts. A powder-coated aluminum pipe inside the tube provides support and functions to attach the tube to a platform inside the container. The acid-free tube was covered with a layer of Mylar and padded with high-loft needle punched polyester batting to a diameter of 20 cm (8 in.). The flag is now safely rolled, and the hoist is laid flat on a support.

Container Requirements

The container is intended to be the permanent storage and display housing for the flag. The flag should not need to be removed for treatment or maintenance again. Therefore, the container had to be fabricated with tight seals and from stable materials. A constant relative humidity is controlled passively through the use of desiccants. A side or back access door permits installation of the flag on an internal platform support. Viewing windows with covers and an exterior fiber optic lighting system satisfy display requirements. Ultraviolet wavelengths 370 nanometers and above are filtered out.

The stable materials required for the container included the construction materials, finishes, and gasketing around doors and windows. The *NASA Outgassing Data for Selected Spacecraft Materials* was used for reference. Any outgassing had to be within acceptable museum standards. The container had to be tightly sealed against moisture, pests, and airborne pollutants inherent to a tour-boat facility with a museum exhibition space. Materials that are water and corrosion resistant, especially to atmospheric salt, received the most consideration. They also had to be durable, lightweight, and maintain integrity when the container is moved, lifted, or transported. All seams need to be flat. Corners and edges need to be smooth and rounded to facilitate handling and prevent injury. However, the container would ultimately have exhibit furniture installed around it, coordinated to exhibition designs still years away from planning.

Long-term display would require visibility into the container through shatterproof and scratch-resistant glazing with ultraviolet protection, a controllable lighting system, and a comfortable height for viewing. Security would need to be integrated into the design. An internal support that would accommodate the combination rolled and flat configuration of the flag needed to glide effortlessly into the container through a door. Portholes for desiccant maintenance and environmental monitoring were essential for long-term preservation. Wheels would facilitate moving. Costs needed to be carefully considered with every design and material selection decision so that the project did not exceed the budget.

Container Design

A design began to evolve once the conservation and display criteria were developed. A sketch made by Harpers Ferry Center exhibit designer Donald Branch was used in discussions with potential fabricators.

None of the fabricators contacted had ever built anything so large and complex. It became apparent during discussions with fabricators that the expertise of an engineer would be required for the design due to size and structural integrity requirements. Those vendors who worked in wood were willing to try to build the container, all others asked for detailed blueprints. Since wood was not an acceptable

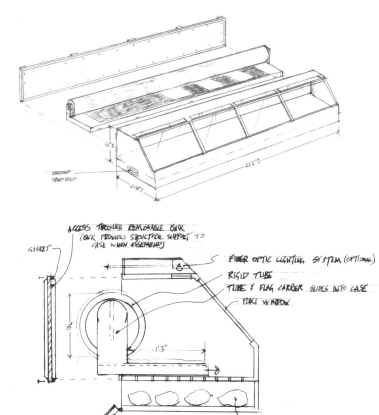

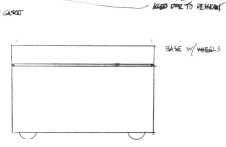

Figure 2 a, b. Concept drawing of the container as sketched by Don Branch.

material, and there was no in-house expertise to develop the requested blueprints, a design contract was developed. Drawings for the full-sized container and construction of a scale prototype became an unanticipated but vital phase of the project.

Fabrication Materials Investigated

Carbon fiber, polyethylene laminates, aluminum honey comb panels, stainless steel, ABS or acrylonitrile butadiene styrene (high impact styrene), anodized aluminum, high-density plastic laminates over plywood, and powder-coated aluminum were among materials considered for the flag container. We narrowed the list of possible materials to carbon fiber and powder-coated aluminum honeycomb panels or sheets. The other materials were rejected due to offgassing of volatile materials, corrosion potential, excessive weight, and lack of experienced fabricators to build a museum-quality container.

A carbon fiber container was initially looked at very closely. Carbon fibers are formed from Orlon scorched at high temperatures and become carbonized in a resin matrix. This material is used where water resistance, strength, stiffness, and light weight are important, such as for sailboats. Eventually, the idea of a carbon fiber container was not pursued due to high cost and the unwillingness of the fabricator to provide a prototype for testing and examination. It became evident that by choosing a powder-coated metal container, companies already existed who were experienced in building museum cabinetry and were familiar with our requirements. Therefore, aluminum sheet (inherently lightweight and strong) with a polyester powder-coated finish was selected to fabricate the container and coat all interior metal parts.

The park requested that scratch- and shatter-resistant glass be used for the viewing windows. Laminated architectural glass from Globe Amerda Glass Company with some ultraviolet filtering properties was used. For additional ultraviolet filtration, a layer of Polycast acrylic glazing where transmission of ultraviolet wavelengths in the 370 nanometer range is 0 percent, and transmission of wavelengths at 400 nanometers is 4 percent was set just below the glass. Six windows with easily attachable blackout covers are angled along the front side of the container.

Desiccants will be used to maintain relative humidity at 50 percent. Three small access doors are equally spaced along the front to facilitate exchange and maintenance. A porthole in the top of the container is available for a relative humidity sensor and alarm and will allow a light meter to be inserted when it becomes a display case. Activated charcoal is used in the case to absorb contaminants given off by the flag itself. The access doors are also used to replace the charcoal as required.

The engineer designed a side entry door for the flag, determined necessary in order to maintain the structural stability of the container. The internal platform support glides into the case on rails that are faced with UHMW (ultra high molecular weight) polyethylene strips for an effortless installation. A tight seal was ensured by Volara (crosslinked polyethylene foam) gasketing, held in place with 3M pressure-sensitive adhesive transfer film. Concerns about Volara maintaining its compression were evaluated on the prototype using an ultrasonic leak detector. Performance of this material was acceptable. The container has two lockable swivel (360 degree rotation) wheels at each end.

The process of developing construction plans and building a scale prototype took more than nine months. It was extremely valuable to have the prototype for testing. It also meant that the park understood completely how the container would look and function. Modifications did have to be made to the drawings in order for the container to perform as desired. With the drawings modified,

Figure 3. Scale prototype of container showing flag entry, platform, tube support, and viewing window.

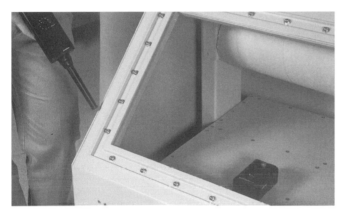

Figure 4. Testing seals of prototype using an ultrasonic leak detector. Transmitter inserted in container and receiver scans exterior surface.

contracting the fabrication of the container was not the challenge it was the year before.

SmallCorp of Greenfield, Massachusetts, built the container. They worked from the drawings (hard and disc copies) and the prototype. They also used parts from the prototype for the container to reduce costs.

The container needed to be built in three sections and then joined together. These joins are sealed with a neutral curing caulking, Number 2501 manufactured by General Electric.

Conclusion

The flag is permanently rolled with its hoist laid flat on the inner support within the powder coated storage and exhibition container. The container performs as required and will reside in a museum storage facility at Fort Sumter National Monument until needed for display. At that time, an exhibit box will be constructed so that the look and color of the container will conform to the overall exhibit design. A fiber-optic lighting system will be purchased and attached to the outside windows so that the flag will be lighted

Figure 5. Full-sized container in the offices of SmallCorp.

safely. A reproduction of the flag will line the wall directly behind the preserved garrison flag.

Bibliography

Campbell, Wm. *Outgassing Data for Selecting Spacecraft Materials.* Revision 3. September 1993. NASA-RP-1124. Scientific and Technical Information Branch.

Cooper, Grace Rogers. *Thirteen Star Flags, Keys to Identification.* Washington D.C.: Smithsonian Institution Press, 1973.

Gohl, E.P.G., and Vilensky. *Textile Science, An Explanation of Fibre Properties.* 2nd edition. L.D. Melbourne, Longman Cheshire, 1983.

Greene, Jerome A. (Foreword by). *U.S. Army Uniforms and Equipment, 1889.* University of Nebraska Press, Reprint 1986.

Joseph, Marjory L. *Introductory Textile Science.* 3rd edition, Holt Rinehart and Winston, 1977, pp. 130-131.

Lafontaine, Raymond H. "Silica Gel," *CCI Technical Bulletin 10*, Ottawa: Canadian Conservation Institute, 1984.

Padfield, T., D. Erhardt, and W. Hopwood. "Trouble in Store," *Science and Technology in the Service of Conservation*, IIC Preprint, London: 1982, pp. 24-27.

Macleod, K.J. "Relative Humidity: Its Importance, Measurement and Control in Museums," *CCI Technical Bulletin*, Ottawa: Canadian Conservation Institute, May 1978.

Richards, E. "Non-Woven Textiles for Conservation Use," *ICOM Committee for Conservation. 7th Triennial Meeting.* Copenhagen: September 1984, pp. 84.9.42-45.

Rose, Carolyn L., Catharine A. Hawks, and Hugh Genoways, eds. *Storage of Natural History Collections: A Preventive Conservation Approach.* Society for the Preservation of Natural History Collections, 1995.

Rose, Carolyn L., and Amparo R. De Torres, eds. "Materials Table," *Storage of Natural History Collections: Ideas and Practical Solutions*, Society for the Preservation of Natural History Collections, 1992.

Tétreault, Jean. "Display Materials: The Good, the Bad and the Ugly," *Scottish Society for the Conservation and Restoration Preprint*, 21-22 April, 1994, pp. 79 -87.

Thomson, Garry. *The Museum Environment.* 2nd Edition, London: Butterworths, 1986.

Wick, Charles, and Raymond Veilleux, eds. *Tool and Manufacturing Engineers Handbook.* Volume 3, Materials, Finishing and Coating, Dearborn, Michigan: Society of Manufacturing Engineers Publication Committee, 1980, Chapter 27, pp. 12 -17.

Williams, R.S. "Conservation Material Report Summary, Tyvek 14," ARS Number 2475, p.1. CCI Analytical Research Services.

Suppliers

Powder-coated aluminum container
SmallCorp
P. O. Box 948,
Greenfield, Massachusetts 01302 USA

Nomex Soft Wrap
E.I. DuPont de Nemours and Company
1000 Market Street
Wilmington, Delaware 19898 USA

Volara Type A foam
Dow Chemical USA
2020 Willard H. Dow Center
Midland, Michigan 48674 USA

Acid-free cardboard tube
Archivart, Division of Heller and Usdan
P. O. Box 428, 7 Caesar Place
Moonachie, New Jersey 07074 USA

TGIC-Polyester powder coating
O'Brian Powder Products, Inc.
9800 Genard
Houston, Texas 77041 USA

Ultrasonic leak detector
Ultra Probe 500 STG
UE Systems
14 Hays Street
Elmsford, New York 10523 USA

Silicone caulking Number 2501
General Electric Company, Silicone Sales
6803 W 64th, Suite 330
Shawnee, Kansas 66202 USA

Laminated architectural glass
Globe Amerada Glass Company
2001 Greenleaf Avenue
Elk Grove Village, Illinois 60007 USA

Polycast acrylic glazing
Polycast Technology Corporation
70 Carlisle Place
Stamford, Connecticut 06902 USA

Stabiltex polyester fabric
Talas
586 Broadway
New York, New York 10012 USA

Résumé

Faire l'équilibre entre l'exposition à long terme et la préservation : le traitement du drapeau de la garnison du fort Sumter

Le Fort Sumter National Monument en Caroline du Sud a demandé à ce que le drapeau américain associé à la bataille d'ouverture de la Guerre civile, en 1861, soit préparé en vue d'une présentation à long terme dans un nouveau musée en cours de conception. Extrêmement détérioré, le drapeau de grandes dimensions présente plusieurs défis au chapitre du traitement, notamment la construction d'une vitrine permanente stable et hermétique pour la mise en réserve et l'exposition. D'une durée de deux ans, le projet mené par la Division de la conservation du Harpers Ferry Center a nécessité la collaboration de conservateurs, de scientifiques en conservation, de concepteurs d'exposition, d'ingénieurs et d'ébénistes pour résoudre les nombreux problèmes qui se sont présentés à chaque étape.

Working With Long-term Exhibits Containing Textiles

Deborah Bede

Minnesota Historical Society
345 Kellogg Boulevard West
St. Paul, MN 55102 USA
Tel.: (612) 297-5490

Abstract

Exhibits at the Minnesota Historical Society are scheduled to last from one to ten years or more. The Conservation Department has developed several systems to allow the use and protection of light-sensitive materials in these long-term exhibits. These include gallery lighting which incorporates motion sensors, dimmers and timers, an exposure tracking system which accurately predicts when a target exposure will be reached, and plans for the rotation of sensitive artifacts.

Introduction

The Minnesota Historical Society (MHS) displays artifacts from its collections in three large galleries at the Minnesota History Center, a new $70 million building in St. Paul. While the Society also has exhibits in period rooms and visitor centers at its historic sites throughout the state, this paper will focus on the History Center. Exhibits are intended to last from one year to ten years or more, and each exhibit contains artifacts incorporating organic materials. The Conservation Department has developed some ways to reduce the damage to light-sensitive materials while working with this schedule of long-term exhibits. These methods include measures taken to reduce the amount of time an artifact is displayed as well as to protect it while on display. Some of these systems are in place and operating successfully, while others are still in the process of implementation.

The primary goal of the Society is to effectively serve the people of Minnesota, and making its collections accessible to the public is central to this service. The Society's Mission Statement declares that "the Society must be a creative and dynamic institution, documenting life in Minnesota and offering programs that are at once educational, engaging and entertaining." These principles permeate the exhibits at the History Center.

These exhibits are somewhat different from those in an art museum. Exhibits are developed not to showcase MHS collections, but rather to illustrate broad themes, such as in the "Families" and "Communities" exhibits. While Minnesota history is the central motif, an important aim of our exhibits is to ensure that the visitor is entertained. The exhibits are complex and engaging, and contain many interactive components including flip books and games, costumed interpreters giving presentations in the galleries at regular intervals, and various educational programs built around the exhibits. The exhibits have elaborate installations with complex furniture built specifically for each exhibit. Design is a predominant element of these exhibits; in some cases the historic artifacts are overshadowed by the exhibit furniture, graphics and interactives. Exhibits at the History Center are very expensive to produce: the "Families" exhibit alone cost over $1.5 million.

These exhibits are long-term by intent and also as a result of the very high cost of producing them. The Society cannot support the financial and human resources necessary to keep the $13,500 \text{ m}^2$ (45,000 ft.^{2}) of gallery space in the History Center filled with continually changing exhibits of this type. Exhibit schedules are constantly in flux; "Minnesota A to Z" was originally intended to be on display for five years and is currently scheduled for ten or more.

The Conservation Department works to maintain museum standards in all aspects of the Society's work as well as to preserve the collections, while supporting the Society's mission and the goals of other departments. From the initial design of this building, techniques and systems have been developed to reduce the impact of display on the artifacts in the collection. Because the climate, exhibit materials and display methods at the History Center all conform to professional standards, the control of light exposure is the focus of preservation efforts.

Setting Exposure Limits

During examination of each artifact, a light-exposure limit is set by the conservator. This is expressed as the number of lux hours of illumination the artifact can receive before it must be removed from display. In this way, the lighting designer can light the artifact at a desired level. It is the total exposure received, not the display duration that determines when an object is taken off display. While properties of materials and their degradation by light are considered when setting the targets, the basis for their calculation lies in display duration. For example, for many textile and paper objects the target is 156,000 lux hours. This figure was originally calculated from the number of hours the galleries are illuminated per year, and the assumption of 50 lux illumination. Thus, a target of 156,000 lux hours is based on a display duration of one year at 50 lux rather than on the amount of damage that exposure will cause. MHS conservators are currently in the process of developing a policy that will give guidelines for target lux hours and subsequent storage periods for different classes of materials. To the extent possible, this will be based on published research on the rate and amount of damage and fading due to exposure to light. For some materials such as birchbark, however, there is no published data and further research may be necessary.

Tracking Exposure

Low light levels have been established throughout the exhibit areas. Motion sensors positioned throughout the galleries control the light levels for each section of the exhibits. Lights are kept at a very low level until the motion of a visitor trips the sensor and the lights are raised to a preset display level. The higher level is still quite low, usually below 100 lux, and has been set by the appropriate conservator in consultation with the lighting designer. The lights are automatically dimmed after a period in which no motion is sensed.

When the History Center was built, a system was designed by the head of Conservation and the lighting designer to record the number of lux hours of illumination any individual object receives on exhibit. This system combines the manual measurement of light levels with computer technology. The high and low light levels for each sensitive artifact are measured with a light meter at the time of gallery installation, and this information is entered into a Microsoft Excel spreadsheet. Also entered into the spreadsheet is the target number of lux hours of total illumination the artifact can receive before it is removed from exhibit and replaced with a rotation. The motion sensors in the galleries each control a group of lights referred to as a "room". A programmable logic controller in the lighting system records the number of hours each room is at the high level and at the low level and the information is then downloaded into a laptop computer. A macro transfers this data into the spreadsheet and performs a number of simple calculations. The spreadsheet, known as the "Luxlog", contains the results of these calculations, which include cumulative total lux hours to date, and a projected date when the target number of lux hours will have been reached. This projected date is calculated from the average weekly exposure for each object.

Rotation of Sensitive Artifacts

Once an artifact's target exposure has been reached, the intention is that it be removed from exhibit and replaced

with another object. With periodic refinements, the system for recommending rotation of sensitive artifacts has been in place from the opening of the History Center. The implementation of this policy has not been without problems, however.

While a number of artifacts have been rotated in the past, at the moment, rotations at the History Center are currently at a standstill. There are a number of reasons for this. One is that a large number of different people and departments are involved in the process, and there is no one person who has responsibility for rotations with authority to direct the assorted departments involved in the process. The exhibit curator must select the rotation object, the Museum Collections Department catalogues it and has it photographed, Conservation conserves it, Exhibits prepares mounts for it, an exhibit researcher writes text for a new label, the exhibit designer works out how the object will fit into the case, a graphic designer creates the label, and Conservation and Exhibits staff actually perform the exchange of objects. The situation is also complicated by the fact that the Exhibits Department works on the team principle. Exhibit teams are formed to develop and produce an exhibit, but the teams are disbanded and members are given other assignments as soon as the exhibit opens. Financial resources for rotations are also problematic because the Exhibits Department is funded on a project basis; money is almost exclusively restricted to exhibit development and production. Another factor that is affecting this situation is that the duration of several exhibits is being extended beyond the original intention.

The Luxlog is used to accurately calculate projected rotation dates to aid in the planning and implementation of this process. But with 13,500 m^2 (45,000 ft.^{2}) of exhibits, it is not practical to plan rotation of single objects. For optimal efficiency and cost-effectiveness, at least 15 objects or one exhibit section at a time should be rotated. Rotation of groups of objects will be scheduled based on exposure of the most sensitive artifacts in the group, and other artifacts may need to be rotated before their projected rotation date. The amount of work involved in rotating artifacts in the complex exhibits at MHS dictates that rotations be scheduled at least six months ahead of time. Because of this lead time requirement, in some cases it may become more practical to assign a rotation date rather than an exposure limit when an artifact is installed.

A Rotations Work Group was formed to look at the rotations situation and make recommendations for catching up with the backlog and continuing to keep up with rotations in the future. The work group concentrated on defining the scope of the current situation by quantifying the number of objects in need of rotation and the resources needed to rotate them. They found that over 700 artifacts currently on display in the History Center are due to be rotated by the end of 1997, and that many of these objects are already years beyond their planned rotation dates. The Work Group produced the Rotations Process Analysis, which is a step-by-step listing of every task in the rotations process. The process was broken up into eight sections incorporating 63 separate steps, and a time estimate for each participant was included for each step. Eleven or more staff members are involved in the rotation of a single artifact, and the rotation of this one object would take an estimated 105.75 hours of staff time. The work group also examined how to reduce the time and costs involved by rotating objects in batches.

The recommendations of the work group include the assignment of a project manager and the formation of a rotations team. They also recommended that future exhibit teams plan for rotations, and facilitate them by simplifying case design and layout, choosing rotation objects while the team is still in place, and including costs for rotations in exhibit budgets.

The final report of the Rotations Task Force was distributed to department and division heads in November 1996. As of January 1997, the first steps are being taken by MHS management to evaluate and implement the work group's recommendations.

Displaying Non-collection Materials

In addition to artifacts, exhibits at the History Center include reproductions and props. Color photocopies of paper artifacts are fairly routinely displayed in place of the real thing because they can be exhibited for an unlimited length of time. In one exhibit a color photocopy of a textile artifact, a printed silk campaign ribbon, is used. If an exhibit designer or curator wishes to use an object in a way that would be inappropriate for a collection item, a similar object or prop can be purchased at an antique store. Because these are not collection objects, they are not restricted in terms of light exposure or mounting techniques. In some cases a prop is purchased to fill a specific need in an exhibit. Some of these objects will be accessioned into the collection after the exhibit, but until then there are no restrictions on their display. There are also purchased props used in hands-on interactives; in the "Families" exhibit a crazy quilt is provided for visitors to touch. Because props are so popular with the Exhibits Department, there are fewer collections artifacts on display than there might be and the light exposure of items from MHS collections is thereby reduced. The impetus for using props comes from the Exhibits Department rather than

Conservation, however. The Conservation Department is in the unusual position of actively encouraging Exhibits to use more artifacts from the collection in exhibits.

Conclusion

After a period of very rapid growth in space and in staff, the Minnesota Historical Society is making an institution-wide effort to address the question of preservation of the sensitive artifacts it displays. Some preliminary work has been done to achieve this goal, and several new initiatives are in process. One new development that promises to have positive results is that a conservator is now assigned to each exhibit team. The result of this has been that teams now consider rotations at an early stage in the development of an exhibit, and conservators can also have some input into the design and contents of exhibits. At the moment there is some movement away from the use of textiles and other sensitive materials because prompt rotation is not likely. In other cases, these materials are being included and plans for rotations are being made from the very beginning of an exhibit. There is some promise that a Rotations Team or other mechanism for accomplishing rotations will be in place soon. Conservators are working to develop a policy recommending exposure limits for various classes of sensitive materials. While the predilection for long-term exhibits at MHS is not likely to change, the institution is working to develop new systems to protect its collections on display.

Résumé

Les expositions à long terme comprenant des textiles

Les expositions de la Minnesota Historical Society sont prévues pour une durée d'un à dix ans ou plus. La section de conservation a mis au point plusieurs systèmes qui permettent d'utiliser et de protéger les matériaux photosensibles pour les fins de l'exposition à long terme. On compte notamment un éclairage à détecteurs de mouvement, des gradateurs et des minuteries, un système de suivi de l'exposition à la lumière qui calcule avec précision le moment où le niveau d'exposition cible sera atteint, et des plans de rotation des objets photosensibles.

Mechanical Aspects of Lining 'Loose Hung' Textiles

Thomas Bilson

Department of Conservation and Technology
Courtauld Institute of Art
Somerset House, Strand
London WC2R ORN United Kingdom
E-mail: t.bilson@courtauld.ac.uk

David Howell

Historic Royal Palaces
Hampton Court Palace
Surrey KT8 9AU United Kingdom
E-mail: davidathcp@intonet.co.uk

Bill Cooke

Textile Design and Design Management
Department of Textiles
UMIST, P.O. Box 88
Manchester M60 1QD United Kingdom
E-mail: bill.cooke@umist.ac.uk

Abstract

This paper critically examines lining practices within textile conservation. A brief review of current techniques is presented against the perceived need to support what is judged to be a fragile weave structure. The relationship between the maximum exposed stress and the maximum sustainable stress is summarised and predicted in a mathematical model of the hanging textile. The actual effects of hanging on the yarns and weave structure of a tapestry are illustrated by three-dimensional computer modelling. A series of condition reports on real objects is used to identify types of damage and to suggest causes for that damage that may or may not benefit from lining. An experimental section uses data from an Instron tensile strength tester to compare the forces exerted on individual yarns and fibres within the weave to their individual breaking strains. The conclusion summarises the perceived and real benefits of lining a variety of loose hung textiles.

Introduction

Current techniques for the conservation of large, "loose hung" textiles, described at the recent Lining and Backing conference, all include the application of some sort of physical support; both to reduce the stresses caused by gravity whilst hanging, and to protect the textile during handling or storage.[1, 2, 3] Of all the types of large textile perceived as requiring some sort of support, the most prevalent is tapestry. However, whilst there is widespread consensus that protection in the form of either a full support, patch support, or straps is necessary, there is very little data upon which to estimate the actual forces that an object is subjected to whilst on display.

For instance, at Hampton Court Palace there are only three tapestries for which the weight is known, whilst the number of fibres in a cross section of a typical weft yarn has seldom been calculated. Without such information, the stress-strain graphs of individual fibres carry little meaning in the context of what is essentially a woven, three-dimensional, and highly variable structure. Traditional forms of treatments have hitherto addressed this uncertainty by incorporating a high and generalised margin of safety, rather than being tailored to the specific, even localised, condition of any one object.

Of course, we all recognise the marked degree to which a tapestry that has been supported onto another textile feels and behaves as though it is stronger. But this "feel good" factor must be weighed against the real benefits to the object. Does the tapestry need to be strengthened to such an extent? Will the support stitching really be reversible? Is the life of the tapestry extended to any significant degree? And what is the most cost-effective approach? (This is not simple as, for instance, it can be far more time-consuming to apply many small patches than applying a full support!) It is in an attempt to answer some of these questions that the following theoretical and practical research has been carried out.

A Simple Model of a Hanging Tapestry

In order to examine and predict the effects of hanging on a large historic textile such as a tapestry, it is useful to consider the structure in terms of a simple mathematical model. Typical values are given in Figure 1. Let us assume therefore that our model tapestry is 4 m high, and 6 m long and weighs 24 kg. The warp is 100%, 2/90 tex wool with an initial tensile strength of 2.7 kg force/end, sett with 9 ends/cm, whilst the weft is 100%, 150 tex wool with an initial tensile strength of 2.25 kg force/end, sett with 20 ends/cm. [4]

	Typical range of values	Values used in this model
Size	3 m x 2 m - 5 m x 12 m	4 m x 6 m
Warp sett	5 - 12 ends/cm	9 ends/cm
Weft sett	very variable: 12 - 40 ends/cm	20 ends/cm
Warp count	80 - 220 tex	180 tex
Weft count	100 - 200 tex	150 tex
Weight *	500 - 2000 g/m^2	1000 g/m^2
Wool tenacity (new)	15 g/tex	15 g/tex
Silk tenacity (new)	38 g /tex	38 g/tex

*Figure 1. Data for a model of a hanging tapestry. * Tapestries containing metal thread may weigh as much as 0.25 g/cm^2 in the metal areas of the design.*

The slits are closed with a 50 tex. linen thread with a tenacity of 55 g.force/tex, and a tensile strength of 2.75 kg force. This is worked at 5 stitches/cm and, in order to take into account the damage that has accumulated in the tapestry during its extended lifetime, we will assume that it is hung vertically from a horizontal row of rings sewn at 25 cm intervals along the upper selvedge.

The Effects of Hanging

In order to understand and calculate the magnitude of the forces acting on individual elements it is convenient to focus on a vertical strip, 25 cm wide placed near the centre of the tapestry with one holding ring in the centre of the upper edge. The weight of this strip is 1.0 kg. As the weft is sett at 20 ends/cm this strip contains on average 20 x 25 = 500 weft threads across its width. As each weft is assumed to have a tensile strength of 2.25 kg force, our strip is therefore capable of supporting a load of 1125 kg force; a considerable strength to weight ratio of 1125/1. However in normal hanging conditions the strip has nothing to support but its own weight. If we assume that this weight is shared equally by the 500 weft yarns, each yarn at the top of the strip will carry 1000/500 g.force = 2 g.force. Dividing this figure by the tex value for the wool wefts (assumed here to be 150) gives 2/150 = 0.011 g.force/tex. A specific stress of such a small value will produce no measurable immediate extension in the strip, and will of course be the maximum mean load applied to the top of the strip that bears the whole weight. Naturally the lower down the strip this force analysis is applied, the lower the specific stress. Any extension that docs occur upon immediate loading is therefore due to rearrangement of the structural elements within the weave rather than extension of the textile fibres themselves.

This re-arrangement of the internal structure is shown using three-dimensional modelling in Figures 2 and 3. Whereas the resistance of the unloaded weft to bending causes it to follow a semi-circular path between adjacent warps (Figure 2), the stresses of hanging tend to deform this path towards that of a straight line, thereby producing the slight increase in length (Figure 3).[5] Finding evidence for such changes within the structure of a real tapestry is, of course, complicated by an inherent and extremely high level of structural variability. Such changes however can be detected in cross sections of the weave embedded before and during the application of load equal to that experienced by the wefts along the upper edge during normal hanging conditions. The transition from a circular to a straight line geometry is clearly visible, as is the slight compression of the transverse warp section from round to elliptical.

Figure 2. Computer generated model of tapestry showing a cross section parallel to the weft direction before hanging.

Figure 3. The same section after the application of a load equal to that experienced by the wefts along the upper edge of the tapestry as a result of hanging.

Clearly stress levels of 0.011 g.force/tex pose no threat to the integrity of the weft either in the short term, or even after the effect of very long-term creep deformation. However, within the 25 cm strip, there are three potential stress concentration situations: the slits, the effects of a significant proportion of the wefts being of silk or metal thread, and the single supporting ring.

The Effects of Slits

If we assume the worst situation where a slit extends across the whole 25 cm width close to the top, then the 1.0 kg force will be carried by 5 x 25 = 125 linen stitches. Assuming that the stitching has a strength of 125 x 2.75 kg force, the slit is capable of carrying 343 kg force for short periods: a figure approximately one-third of the 1125 kg force that the wefts alone are capable of supporting. We must however remember that the stitching used to close the slit is worked at 5/cm. Each individual stitch used to close the slit will therefore carry 1000/125 g.force, i.e., 8 g.force with a specific stress of 8/50 or 0.16 g.force/tex. Although this stress level is 14 times that imposed on the weft, it is still so low as to pose no threat to the new tapestry. However, this differential weakness may become apparent in aged tapestries as the slits tend to open up. This is not only due to the extra stress, but also to the materials (linen or cotton) commonly used to close slits which tend to deteriorate and lose their strength faster than wool.

The Effects of Silk or Metal Wefts

A more serious problem arises if some of the weft threads are replaced with a fibre with a significantly higher initial modulus, for example silk or metal-covered silk. In the case of a new tapestry, the modulus of silk is approximately 3.5 times that of wool, therefore during the initial stages of loading, the silk will require 3.5 times the load of the wool for approximately the same extension. If the silk is mixed with the wool fairly evenly on a yarn-for-yarn basis, then the structure will remain stable, however if the tapestry contains areas which are largely wool and areas which are largely silk, then the difference in modulus will cause the weave to stretch more in the wool areas than the silk areas and thus throw the structure out of balance, causing localised bowing and sagging. However in an old tapestry, the situation is reversed as the silk yarns lose their strength and become more fragile. Rather than the silk supporting the wool, it may now be a case of the relatively strong areas of wool providing a framework within which to support the degraded silk.

The Effects of a Ring Support

The final potential risk exists at the point of support, in this case a ring sewn to the top selvedge; a typical hanging method until ca. 1900. Experiments with fragments of tapestries taken from the reference collection at the textile Conservation Studio, Hampton Court Palace have shown that load sharing in the tightly crammed structure of the tapestry spreads the weight of the 25 cm strip across 30 - 40 wefts and 5 - 15 warps. Ultimately of course, the weight of the strip must resolve into stress in the warp. In this case the weight of 1000 g will be shared by approximately 10 warps which will produce a stress of 1000/10 g.force/end, i.e., 100 g.force. In terms of specific stress, this gives 100/180 g.force/tex or 0.55 g.force/tex; a figure which could be increased to 1.35 g.force/tex if a substantial proportion of the wool weft was replaced with metal-covered silk.

This level of stress is certainly sufficient to produce some creep deformation in the warp with time. Such creep will cause more warp ends to take part in load sharing, and so

it is unlikely to be destructive per se. However, it is known that stress leads to stress-induced degradation; leading ultimately to reductions in strength of the warps around the stitching securing the ring. These stresses will be reduced by a system where the weight is evenly distributed along the top, as is the case with Velcro support. Nevertheless, the damage associated with an earlier ring support will persist, and may eventually precipitate further localised degradation.

Complications

The "model" described above is simple and homogenous. In practice the combination of wool, silk and metal threads in the weft multiplies the number of variables considerably as each fibre has different stress-strain characteristics, differing responses to heat and moisture, different rates of degradation and different densities. Yet the interpretative value of the simple model is demonstrated when compared to the almost inscrutable complexity of real tapestry which, like any other textile object, does not exist primarily as a single unit or physical structure, but rather as a huge number of tiny units (fibres) held together with nothing but friction.

To illustrate this division, we can consider one tapestry in Hampton Court Palace which (like our model) measures approximately 6 m wide by 4 m high, but (unlike our model) weighs 43.5 kg. The total volume of wool can be calculated by dividing this weight by the density of wool (1.32) giving 32,954 cm^3. By dividing the volume by the cross-sectional area of wool (0.000005 cm^2), one can calculate the total length of fibre to be in the region of 70,000,000 meters. Assuming an average wool fibre to be about 10 cm long, then this one tapestry contains in the region of 700,000,000 individual units or fibres - a figure that may be useful if we are ever assessed by counting the number of objects conserved in a year! Whilst the apparent surface area of this tapestry can be calculated by multiplying the height with the width (giving a figure of 24 m^2), the sum of all the surface areas of all of the fibres is actually 2,700 m^2; over a hundred times greater.[6] How so many individual elements will behave together mechanically when hung is not easy to visualise, even in a simple model. Furthermore, most real tapestries have been repaired, patched, re-woven and subject to differing environmental conditions during their early lives, as well as benefiting from carefully thought-out modern conservation methods. The mechanics of such an object will be complex, and will form the subject of a further study.

Case Studies

It is clear that initially the elements of the tapestry are not at risk due to the tensile loads resulting from supporting it along its upper edge. It could be argued however that the low tensile loads with time will cause accelerated stress-induced degradation. If this were to be the case, then the majority of the long-term damage should be present in the upper quarter of the tapestry where the highest loads are generated. A great many tapestry condition reports have been written at the Textile Conservation Studios over many years. To test this hypothesis, a selection of these were inspected to see what types of damage had been noted. Also, a number of tapestries and other hangings were inspected *in situ* and a note made of the type and position of damage.

The types of damage encountered, in order of frequency, were: the opening of slits due to the failure of the threads (which had in some cases resulted in splitting of the weave at the edge of the slits), the degradation of silk areas, and insect damage. There was little or no evidence that there was any more damage at the top of the tapestries, and indeed in many cases there seemed to be more damage in the lower regions. Figure 4 shows a detail of an early sixteenth century Flemish tapestry, *The Triumph of Time Over Fame* from the series *The Triumphs of Petrarch*, which hangs in the Great Hall at Hampton Court Palace.

The areas of damage are spread throughout the tapestry and correlate principally with areas of silk, rather than showing a tendency to occur along the upper edge. Although there was some indication that areas of silk which had lost all of their strength along the top edge were opening up a little more than similar areas further down, this was not universally the case.

Experimental — Tensile Testing

To investigate the validity of the simple model described above, the loading behaviours of samples taken from three

Figure 5. The type of slit under investigation is shown toward the lower edge of the photograph.

different tapestries were characterised using an Instron 1026 tensile tester.[7] Each sample of tapestry included clearly defined areas of uninterrupted wool and silk wefts, as well as similar areas interspersed with slits. The slits were divided into two groups: those which had been sewn up with linen thread and remained closed, and those which had begun to open up as the linen deteriorated (Figure 5). "Lazy lines," shown in the upper left of the photograph were not tested as they are usually as strong, if not stronger than the surrounding weave on account of stresses being directed between each slit through the adjacent warps. It was possible to test each piece of tapestry destructively as they were all fragments of unidentified works that had been used previously as repair patches.

Initial tests were carried out to establish the width of sample best suited to the loading capabilities of the Instron, and to identify possible trends in the data. From these tests it was decided to measure the breaking loads in the weft (longest) direction and percentage extension at break for samples of blue wool, yellow wool and cream silk wefts in four sets of experiments:

- Yarns only - six samples of blue wool, yellow wool and silk from each of the three tapestries (54 tests). Each sample 20 mm long.
- Weave without slits[8] - six samples of blue wool, yellow wool and silk wefts from each of the three tapestries (54 tests). Each sample 20 mm x 10 mm.
- Weave with sewn-up slits[9] - four samples of blue wool, yellow wool and silk wefts from each of the three tapestries (36 tests). Each sample 20 mm x 10 mm.
- Weave with opened-up slits extending across approximately 60% of the sample width[10] - four samples of blue wool, yellow wool and silk wefts from each of the three tapestries (36 tests). Each sample 30 mm x 20 mm.

Figure 4. Detail from The Triumph of Time Over Fame, *Flemish, early sixteenth century. The degraded areas have been shaded.*

For reference purposes measurements were also taken of:

- Number of fibres per transverse cross section of weft yarn 11 - seven measurements of wool (not colour specific) and silk from each of the three samples (42 measurements).
- Weft sett - seven measurements of wool (not colour specific) and silk from each of the three samples (42 measurements).

Results

To ensure that the tensile behaviour, weave and yarn structure of three different tapestries was measured fully, each set of tests was subdivided, as described above, according to weft type and colour, and each measurement replicated either four or six times (determined by the availability of material) to confer statistical reliability. However, as this resulted in the measurement of 264 separate samples, a clear interpretation of the data could only be made by grouping similar or dissimilar results. Analysis of variance (ANOVA) was therefore carried out at the 95% level of significance on each related set measurements to determine whether variation within sets of samples from the same tapestry was significantly greater or lesser that the variation between samples from different tapestries. From these tests we hoped to see whether we could legitimately group our data on the basis of fibre type and colour alone, or whether we would still have to link our measurements to the particular tapestry from which the samples were taken. In other words, did the significant differences in tensile behaviour lie principally at the level of the object, or at a lower, common level of the constituent yarns and fibres - regardless from which tapestry they originated?

In summary, it was found that there was no significant difference between similar samples taken from different tapestries. In other words, a blue wool weft from one tapestry exhibited tensile behaviour similar to that of a blue weft from another tapestry, but that these measurements did differ significantly from those of the yellow wool and cream silk wefts. It was therefore decided to group the data solely on the basis of weft fibre type and colour. No distinction was made between the three individual tapestries from which the samples of yarn or weave were taken. The results of the tests are summarised in Figure 6. Data for all the weave samples is based on the tensile strength of a 1 cm wide strip (data for weave samples with "gaping" slits has been adjusted to take account of the larger width of sample needed to perform the tests).

Discussion

Considering that the simple model accounts for neither the effects of aging on all elements of the tapestry, nor the influence of yarn colour and fibre type, the correlation with the experimental data is very good.

	2 ply wool yarn		Single ply silk yarn
Weft yarn breaking load (kg)	1.09 [b]	0.45 [y]	0.16
Weft yarn elongation break (%)	19.48 [b]	6.84 [y]	4.15at
Weave without slits - breaking load (kg)	32.49 [b]	25.24 [y]	12.41
Weave without slits - elongation at break (%)	42.13 [b]	23.72 [y]	9.30
Weave with sewn-up slit - breaking load (kg)	31.53 [b]	18.84 [y]	8.49
Weave with sewn-up slit - elongation at break (%)	36.46 [b]	21.63 [y]	9.56
Weave with "gaping" slit - breaking load (kg)	5.05 [b]	4.82 [y]	2.81
Weave with "gaping" slit - elongation at break (%)	3.92 [b]	3.79 [y]	3.51
Fibre counts/cross section of yarn	140.52		252.00
Weft sett (/cm)	20.14		28.43

Figure 6. Weft yarn fibre count, weft sett and tensile testing data ([b] denotes blue yarn, [y] denotes yellow yarn).

In summary:

- The simple model assumes that each weft yarn has a tensile strength of 2.25 kg force. The experimental data shows that in reality this figure decreases to just under one half (1.09 kg force) for a blue wool yarn, to one fifth (0.45 kg force) for a yellow wool yarn, and to one fourteenth (0.16 kg force) for a silk yarn. The precise reasons for such a clear difference in strength between wool fibres on the basis of colour will form part of a forthcoming paper, although the results seem to dispel the notion that dark colours are more susceptible to light-induced degradation.

- Using this weft yarn tensile strength value of 2.25 kg force, the simple model predicted that a 25 cm wide strip of tapestry (containing 20 weft ends/cm) could support a load of 1125 kg force. Multiplying the experimental data for the tensile strength of a one cm wide strip by 25 to give an equivalent figure again gives slightly lower tensile strengths of 812.25 kg force for areas woven with blue wool wefts 631 kg force for areas woven with yellow wool wefts, and 310 kg force for areas woven with silk wefts.

- The presence of slits in which the linen stitching used to close them remained intact had little effect on reducing the tensile strength of the surrounding textile, however the presence of "gaping" slits in which the stitching had become loose reduced the strength of the tapestry dramatically.

The simplest method of understanding the implications of this data for the treatment of large, loose-hung textiles is to compare the actual maximum tensile forces that the various yarn and weave elements, which make up a tapestry, are subjected to under normal hanging conditions, against the maximum tensile forces that they have been shown capable of withstanding under experimental tensile testing. The following calculations are based on the 6 m x 4 m tapestry at Hampton Court Palace which weighs 43.5 kg:

For an estimate of the maximum tensile forces experienced by each yarn we can take the average values for weft set given in Figure 6 as 20.14 ends/cm for wool and 28.43 ends/cm for silk. If the tapestry were made wholly of wool, then each weft along the uppermost edge would support a load of 0.0036 kg, whereas if it were made wholly of silk, each weft would support a load of 0.0026 kg The considerable differences between these figures and the experimental loads under which the wefts have been shown to break are shown in the graph, Figure 7.

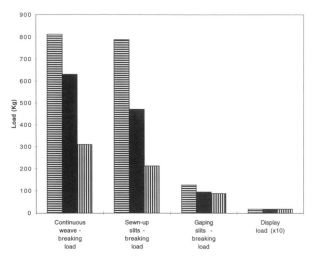

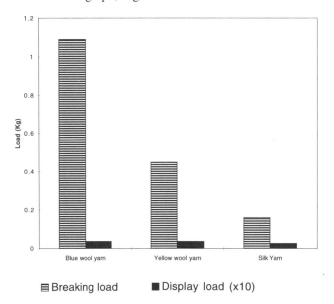

Figure 7. Breaking loads of historic weft yarns compared to the loads experienced by the same yarns during normal hanging conditions. Note: Display loads have been multiplied by a factor of 10 simply to register on the graph.

In the case of the weave, the 25 cm strip in our model supports the structure which hangs below it; a load of 1.81 kg. Again, the considerable differences between this figure and the maximum loads that the same widths of blue and yellow wool wefts, and cream silk wefts are capable of supporting - either as continuous areas or interspersed by slits - is shown in the graph, Figure 8.

Put simply, on the basis of these tensile tests, the whole of a tapestry weighing 43.5 kg could be supported by either a 1.3 cm wide strip of blue wefts, a 1.7 cm wide strip of yellow wefts, or a 3.5 cm wide strip of silk wefts. However, it would be overly simplistic to use such generalised data as

Figure 8. Breaking loads of historic samples of woven tapestry compared to the loads experienced by the areas of weave during normal hanging conditions. Note: Display loads have been multiplied by a factor of 10 simply to register on the graph.

a means of directing the conservation treatment of any one object. Although it appears that tapestries are generally far stronger than we may at first recognise, the presence of discrete areas of degradation and almost total loss of strength (which are not accounted for in these models or experiments) will always make the provision of some means of support the single most important factor in their conservation. Furthermore Figure 8 shows that in the samples tested, the most dramatic reduction in strength of the weave is caused by the opening up of slits. It would therefore seem that conservation treatments that include the reinforcement of such areas will produce significant improvements in the overall strength of the tapestry.

Conclusions

The full support of fragile textiles will almost certainly remain a mainstay in the repertoire of conservation techniques for loose-hung textiles. The discussion here concentrates on the mechanical aspects of a lined textile when hanging, but lining may, of course, be carried out for a variety of reasons. The mechanical needs of a hanging textile are simply to be stronger than the forces it is subjected to. In most textiles of good to moderate condition, the overall strength is much greater than the force it experiences by hanging under its own weight, and indeed the forces are usually so small as to suggest that stress degradation is not an issue.

The vulnerability of aged silk is obvious, especially in areas where it has deteriorated to such a poor condition that it cannot survive even the smallest of stresses. The stress in these areas requires reducing if the silk is not to pull apart. This is also true of slits which have started to open up due to failed stitches. The most obvious treatment would be to repair the slits, and the support of the damaged silk areas onto localised backing material (patches). These patches should act as bridges between sound areas, and if applied with regular and even stitching should not put these sound areas under any more tension than when the object was made. If the surrounding sound areas are actually made of silk, then it is to be assumed that these areas will eventually degrade, and that the re-applied stress will tend to pull these areas apart with time. Such an approach based on the minimum intervention required to stabilise a hanging object could be regarded as the starting point from which other conservation decisions could be made. In this way objects can be made safe with minimum time and budget while at the same time allowing for further work in the future if deemed necessary.

Acknowledgements

The detail of the *Triumph of Time over Fame* is reproduced by kind permission of The Royal Collection © Her Majesty the Queen.

Endnotes

1 Brooks, M., D. Eastop, L. Hillyer, and L. Lister. "Supporting fragile textiles: the evolution of choice," *Lining and Backing*, London: United Kingdom Institute for Conservation, 1995, pp. 5 - 13.

2 Ballard, M.W. "How backings work: the effect of textile properties on appearance," *Lining and Backing*, London: United Kingdom Institute for Conservation, 1995, pp. 34 - 39.

3 Marko, K. "Tapestry conservation: a confusion of ideas," *Lining and Backing*, London: United Kingdom Institute for Conservation, 1995.

4 Tex is a direct unit of measurement equalling the weight in grams of 1,000 metres of the staple fibre.

5 In more exact terms, the changes in structure reflect a movement from a circular arc model to a straight line model of weave geometry. For more information see: Peirce, F.T. "The geometry of cloth structure," *Journal of the Textile Institute*, vol. 28 (1937). Ellis, P., and D.L. Munden. "A theoretical analysis and experimental study of the plain square weave: parts I, II and III," *Journal of the Textile Institute*, vol. 64 (1973).

6 All of the fibres in the 6 m x 4 m woollen tapestry would, if laid end to end, stretch around the world 1.5 times, and the same tapestry would have a surface area approx. 1/4 that of a full-size football pitch!

7 Instron Ltd., Coronation Road, High Wycombe Buckinghamshire, HP12 3SY, UK.

8 All weave samples were cut slightly wide and then wefts removed from the edges to reduce them to the required width. This technique ensured that the edges of the samples were not damaged as a result of cutting, whilst the protruding, warp ends reduced the tendency for the samples to fraying during testing.

9 In each sample, the loose ends of the linen thread used to close the slit were secured to adjacent warp with a small bead of epoxy resin so as to prevent the stitching working loose as a consequence of preparing the sample.

10 The increase in sample width and length reflected the difficulty in finding representative areas containing opened-up slits bounded by intact wefts.

11 Taken from the cross sections illustrated in Figures 4 and 5 after digitising onto Kodak Photo CD and measured at 3072 x 2048 pixel resolution using Optilab image analysis software on an Apple Power PC 8100. Optilab is available from Graftek, le Moulin de l'Image, 26270 Mirmande, France. (Distributed and supported in the UK by ME Electronics, 4 Weighbridge Row, Cardiff Road, Reading, Berkshire RG1 8LX).

Résumé

Considérations physiques au sujet du doublage des textiles suspendus

Dans cet article, on porte un regard critique sur les pratiques de doublage employées en conservation des textiles. Un bref survol des techniques actuelles est présenté en regard du besoin perçu de soutenir une armure jugée fragile. La relation entre la tension maximale réelle et la tension maximale admissible est résumée et calculée à l'aide d'un modèle mathématique du textile suspendu. Les effets réels de la suspension sur les fils et l'armure d'une tapisserie sont illustrés par la modélisation informatique. À partir d'une série de constats d'état sur des objets réels, on recense les catégories de dommages pour ensuite en suggérer les causes probables et déterminer si le doublage serait susceptible de remédier à la situation. Dans la section expérimentale, les données recueillies à l'aide d'un dynamomètre Instron sont utilisées pour comparer les forces exercées sur certains fils et sur certaines fibres du tissu avec leurs tensions de ruptures respectives. La conclusion résume les avantages réels et supposés du doublage de plusieurs variétés de textiles suspendus.

Treatment Decisions for the Exhibition of a 1697 English State Bed

Nancy Britton

Sherman Fairchild Center for Objects Conservation
Metropolitan Museum of Art
1000 Fifth Ave.
New York, NY 10028-0198 USA
Tel.: (212) 570-3858
Fax: (212) 570-3859

Abstract

The conservation of a 17th-century English state bed in the collection of the Metropolitan Museum of Art demonstrated the many constraints encountered when a complex object is placed on long-term exhibition. Institutional exhibition planning and decision-making procedures, the history and condition of the object, the curatorial interpretation goals, time frame, and skills and resources available are some of the many factors that determine the course of a conservation treatment. Conservation as a profession provides both information and concrete treatment skills. Optimal decisions are not always able to be made, and the treatment plan often must compensate for these less-than-ideal factors. The sooner conservation can be involved in the planning process, the greater the positive impact for the object, particularly for maintenance. The highly successful treatment of the state bed provides a vehicle for examining the multiple factors that had to be addressed and resolved.

Introduction

The 17th-century English state bed demonstrated the many constraints that bear on a treatment plan for a complicated object. Institutional exhibition planning and decision-making procedures, the history and condition of the object, the curatorial interpretation goals, lead time, and skills and resources available are some of the many factors that determine the course of a conservation treatment. Conservation as a profession provides both information as well as treatment plans and the hand skills to complete the treatment. The information provided is wide ranging and includes recommendations for optimal environmental and exhibition conditions, storage, handling and maintenance procedures. The lead time, points of informational input during the planning stages, and the skills and resources available, all contribute to the development of a treatment plan for an artifact. Rarely in this long process are optimal decisions consistently made. The state bed project provides a vehicle for looking at the impact exhibition planning has when entwined with the many other complexities in getting and keeping an object on exhibition.

In a large and diverse institution such as the Metropolitan Museum of Art (MMA), the points of informational input for conservation issues during the planning stage are often minimal. The result is a treatment proposal that must compensate for many less-than-ideal factors. The state bed (see Figure 1 for an explanation of the parts) took over eight years of staff time, many skills and resources, a clearly proscribed sequence of treatment, and working with many factors beyond the conservator's control.

The Aitken Galleries

The Aitken Galleries, where the bed is now exhibited, are the European Sculpture and Decorative Arts (ESDA) permanent English decorative arts galleries. The first installation had been done over 40 years previously. A similar time frame should be anticipated for any artifact being installed in the Aitken Galleries' renovation.

Over 40 pieces of upholstered furniture, the blue state bed, and the Croome Court Tapestry Room were on the object list and scheduled for treatment. The bed would be the

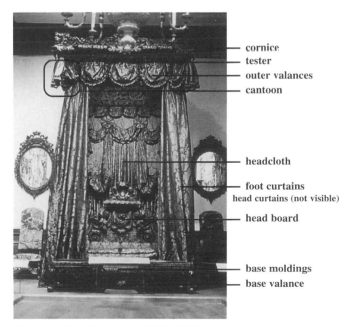

Figure 1. Blue State Bed. MMA 68.217.1

— cornice
— tester
— outer valances
— cantoon

— headcloth

— foot curtains
head curtains (not visible)

— head board

— base moldings
— base valance

largest and most time-consuming project on my roster. The conservators were contacted only when the final object list was nearly completed by the curatorial department approximately two years into the process of planning the exhibition and gallery space. The conservators then had approximately three years to submit budgets, to plan and complete the conservation work prior to the opening of the exhibition.

The Exhibition Space

The exhibition space was conceptualized by the curatorial department and designed by an out-of-house design consultant. The state bed's exhibition space was designed to approximate the size of a 17th-century English room. The room has three doors: the main entry from a larger exhibition area; and two doors in the contiguous walls, one leading into a silver gallery and the other a 16th-century period room. The bed would be placed against the opposite wall to the main entry door in the dead-end portion of the room. The location was chosen so that the viewer standing in the larger exhibition room, would see the state bed framed by the doorway, and obtain a long-distance view.

The ambiance of a 17th-century English room would be further enhanced by the placement of chairs and furniture around the perimeter of the room and the use of low, visually unobtrusive platforms. No barriers were to be used between the visitor and the objects. On the exhibition space blueprint, the distance between the foot of the bed and the end of the platform was 60 cm, resulting in large portions of the textiles being within easy reach of an outstretched arm.

The general lighting in the room would be from the ceiling using a low UV, halogen/incandescent bulb run at a lower wattage, resulting in a slightly warmer color temperature. In the initial planning stages, the tester was anticipated as creating a deep shadow in the interior of the bed since spotlights would not be used. During the installation, fiber optics were incorporated into the tester for localized illumination.

The above explains the exhibition parameters that the treatment plan for the state bed had to accommodate. The positive impact on the treatment plan when conservation issues such as a consideration of traffic flow, barriers for the protection of objects, and rotation of objects, are addressed in the exhibition planning stages had to later be compensated for. The earlier involvement would have better served the institutional and curatorial goals. The issues of most concern for the state bed were visitor proximity, lack of traffic barriers, environmental controls for airborne particulates, and the proximity of the lighting source to the tester. As a result, conservation treatment decisions and long-term maintenance of the object became more complex.

The English State Bed

History

The four-poster blue state bed was a gift from the Randolph Hearst family to the Museum in 1968, along with a second state bed: a red silk damask flying tester bed (see Figure 2, the flying tester lacks foot posts and is hung from the ceiling). Both were made for Thomas, Baron Coningsby, about 1698 for Hampton Court in Herefordshire, outside London. The house was renovated three times, most recently in the 1830s. During the last renovation, the blue bed was disassembled and removed to an attic, while the red bed had remained *in situ*. In 1911, H. Avray Tipping discovered the blue state bed and reinstalled it in the brew house at Hampton Court. The bed was subsequently disassembled and moved when the contents of Hampton Court were auctioned in March 1925. Photographs of the bed from both 1911 and 1925 provided valuable documentation and extant components and their condition from that period were useful in preparing the conservation proposal. Shortly after the 1925 auction, the beds were purchased from Permaine's by Randolph Hearst. Hearst may have stored them in New York prior to his bequest to the MMA in 1968.[1]

The beds were never packed for long-term storage during their tenure at the MMA. The subsequent relocation to

Figure 2. Red damask flying tester bed.

various storerooms as gallery configurations changed almost certainly resulted in damage to the object. Finally, in 1986, the first conservation examination of the blue bed and condition assessment for possible display took place. Aside from this conservation report and accompanying notes, the only museum records were the acquisition information in the Catalogue Department and in the object files in the Department of European Sculpture and Decorative Arts.

Condition and Treatment

The bed stands nearly 370 cm tall, with the base measuring 207 cm wide and 219 cm long. The viewer sees only textiles with wood serving as a support structure. In 1968, the bed had been accessioned as an item of furniture, but due to the prevalence of textiles, the bed was re-classified as a textile object. During the examination and condition process, it became apparent that the bed's components could be sorted into three categories for treatment: textile-only elements, wood-only elements, and textile-on-wood elements.

Examination of the textile-only silk damask components revealed that the coverlet and foot curtains were missing. The base valances and head curtains had been remade, probably from some of the now missing curtains. The remaining textiles were remarkably intact and had little restoration work. The PR corner of the bed had sustained some water damage and there were uneven color shifts throughout, but for the most part the damask was intact and in fair-to-good condition.

The textile-only elements presented several problems both as an artifact and in terms of exhibition issues. Since the coverlet and curtains were needed for this presentation the decision was finally made to reproduce the damask and trims. It was further decided to reproduce to the specifications of the original damask. The nine trims present on various parts of the bed were analyzed and also reproduced to the original's specifications.

The wood-only elements composed the bed frame and were the supporting structure of the bed. Some structural work and fabrication of some missing parts was needed. The construction of the bed dictated a strict protocol for treatment; the wood structure needed to be treated first.

The original textile-on-wood components would be treated and incorporated into the original structure. The wood needed consolidation, removal of damaging restoration work and some fabrication of missing elements. The wood substrate provided support for the textiles, so the loose fragments were readhered and the losses infilled.

The treatment plan began to fall into two main sections: the exhibition space constraints and the object-specific issues. Some treatment decisions bridged both sections. For object-specific issues, comparable objects were sought.

In England, several state beds have been put on exhibit since the beginning at the turn of the century.

The two beds that were the most informative were the companion red bed in the MMA's collection and the Melville bed that is currently undergoing treatment at the Victoria and Albert (V&A) in London. The Melville bed dates to 1696 and has all of its original textiles, including the coverlet.[2] The treatment goal of the Melville bed is to exhibit the bed with all of its original textiles in a newly renovated and protective gallery space.

Object Interpretation

The curatorial interpretation goals were defined and incorporated into the treatment plan. The curator, William Rieder, wanted to return the bed to its original configuration as closely as possible. The loss of significant parts of the object (coverlet, curtains and base valances) would significantly alter the interpretation of the object and meant that some reproduction fabric would need to be incorporated into the treatment.

Several object-specific factors indicated using reproduction textiles: the vulnerability of the original textiles to visitors; the fragile condition of the textiles and their need of support; and the length of the exhibition. A practical decision for use of time was also considered; the missing parts dictated that some reproduction fabric would have to be purchased. The process of replicating a fabric is time-consuming and expensive, but is the same for 90 cm of fabric or 180 meters. The preparation of a system to support the fragile free-hanging textiles would have been immensely labor intensive and highly skilled work. Both could not be accomplished in the three-year time frame. These factors framed the decision to use reproductions for all of the silk damask textile-only elements. The original textile-only elements would be packed for long-term storage.

To replicate the original textiles, a detailed examination and documentation of two aspects of the artifact were required: the fabric itself with its weave and design structure; and the sewing construction and techniques. The damask was the most complex aspect encompassing the weave structure, yarn construction, fabric hand and color. Detailed documentation of the sewing techniques and materials for the seams and trim attachment, and the damask pattern placement within each of the stitched components were required for the cutting and sewing of the damask fabric.

Since visitor proximity was an issue and the exhibit was long-term, extra fabric and trims were ordered in anticipation of having to eventually replace components that are vulnerable to damage, particularly the foot curtains and coverlet. Within a week of the gallery opening pinch marks could be seen in the foot curtains at chest height, indicating that a considerable amount of handling by visitors had taken place, despite a security guard and a sound alarm. Occasionally, even body impressions appear nestled in the feather mattress.

Compensation and Loss

Compensation and loss issues occurred on two levels in this object. On a large scale entire textile-only elements were missing and had to be fabricated (the coverlet, base valances, etc.). The second level was the perception of the details within the object and concerned the loss of small areas of the damask and trims within the textile-on-wood elements.

An aspect of the large-scale compensation and loss issue was the fabrication of the coverlet. The coverlet encompassed both visual and financial considerations as a compensation of loss issue. A coverlet for the blue bed had not been photographed or written about and probably was not in existence by 1911 when Tipping found the bed. The head curtains and base valances appeared to have been remade from other curtain parts, since the curtain ring tape appeared on one end of the base valances, which were also cut with the warp running parallel to the floor (the damask was even reversed back for front on one of the base valances).

The design and coverlet trims on the blue bed would undoubtedly have varied from the tester as well, but how the blue bed trims were allocated within the design would only have been guesswork on our part. The cost of the labor and materials for the reproduction trims would have been exceedingly expensive, although at the MMA the money could probably have been raised to support such a project.

In addition, the coverlet was at high risk for damage. Visitor proximity, in conjunction with an horizontal surface and dust-catching tassels and trims, presented significant long-term maintenance problems. The fact that the blue bed is rather less fancy than the Melville, and consists of a single color that is dark in value, meant that the absence of an elaborate coverlet had less of a visual impact than if the colors had been different hues or more contrasting in value. The above factors resulted in the decision to leave the coverlet unadorned.

On the second level, both the trims and damask suffered small losses throughout the textiles-on-wood. The damask losses occurred in two forms: small areas of the original damask that were missing, resulting in exposure of the wooden substrate; and carved wooden elements that had detached and become lost resulting in a recarved replacement that would need to be covered with the textile. Three factors guided the use of infills: whether the contrast between the loss and the surrounding area was visually disturbing; whether the loss contributed to a lack of coherence within the object; and how confused the original

materials and the added conservation materials within the object were likely to become over time.

The losses in the damask were compensated first, since that was the original sequence of fabrication. Two methods were used depending on whether the damask losses had wood underneath or an entire wood element needed to be carved and covered. The first form of loss represented relatively small areas, usually under 2.5 cm in either direction. For these areas, a plain silk satin weave was dyed in a variety of shades of blue. The reflectance and depth of shade varied with the weave structure on the satin-face and the plain weave backside, similar to the weave structures in the figure/ground of the damask, so both the satin face and plain-weave backside were used. The satin face was used in the event the loss was in the satin ground, and the plain back in the event the loss was in the plain weave figure of the damask.

When the carved element was missing and had to be remade, the area needing a damask replacement was large. The weave structure and color difference between the ground/figure in the reproduction damask was visually necessary to disguise the loss and help to visually integrate the recarved element into its surrounding original elements. In these cases, the reproduction damask was used.

In the case of the trims on the textile-on-wood elements, the losses did not interfere with the interpretation of the object by the viewer or with the cohesiveness of the design. In addition, the reproduction textiles were so precise in weave and yarn structure, and fiber content that even with good documentation, scattered small infills risked confusion of original and later infill materials over time. An absence of reproduction trims meant that all of the trims remaining would be known to be original to the object and resulted in a consistency of treatment.

Mattress and Sack Cloth Supports

Since the exhibition had initially been conceived as allowing the visitor close proximity to the object, accidental and/or unauthorized use of the object had to be considered throughout the treatment as a highly likely (and possibly frequent) occurrence. The mattress area contained original textiles vulnerable to inadvertent use. The original mattress sack cloth remained in place in the frame of the bed and its attachment to the bed rails was considered to be original and therefore was to be left in place. The sack cloth position meant that it needed to be both supported and buffered from the environment underneath, but also had to be shielded from the additional weight of a feather mattress and coverlet placed on top.

A support system was designed composed of two freestanding platforms which were built by the carpentry shop. The first frame was stretched with polyester filament filter cloth (Tetko) and supported the sack cloth from underneath. The size of the interstices of the weave would allow ventilation, yet block airborne particulates. A second solid platform was built in two parts and put on top of the sack cloth, protecting it from above, as well as supporting the feather mattress and coverlet.

Visitor proximity, past experiences in the galleries with vandalism, and the long-term nature of the exhibition also suggested that we should prepare for the eventual replacement of some of the reproduction textile-only elements, such as the foot curtains or coverlet. Since the damask was made to our specifications and included one-time expenses, set-up charges and custom dyeing, it would be difficult to have it rewoven later. Extra reproduction fabric was ordered and put in storage.

Accommodating Long-term Maintenance in the Galleries

ESDA, like many other departments within the MMA, has its own housekeeping staff that is supervised and trained by that department. Routine maintenance tasks are appropriate for the housekeeping staff, while more complex tasks fall to the conservation staff. The design of the exhibition space can reduce or increase the time and skill needed to maintain objects, particularly a large object that is so vulnerable to the environment. Considering the limited accessibility of many of the parts and the objects complexity, the majority of the maintenance of the state bed cannot be done on a routine basis.

The maintenance of such a large object, that once installed cannot be moved, had to be taken into consideration in designing the assembly of the reproduction textile-only parts. When in place, the most inaccessible area for routine maintenance was the headcloth. Originally the headcloth was tacked to the tester frame and the sides were wrapped around and tacked to the back of the headposts. Although the headcloth is not particularly heavy, the weight was considered significant when attached to the tester frame. For these reasons, weight reduction and maintenance, the headcloth was subsequently built on a separate frame that stands behind the headboard. The edges of the reproduction headcloth were wrapped around the headposts and fastened to the back of the frame with hook and loop tape. The frame can easily be detached from the headposts and slipped out from behind the bed for vacuum cleaning and maintenance.

In examining the original textiles from the bed, the observation was made that the coarse linen lining of the tester textile which was the uppermost portion of the bed, was the most soiled component. Anticipating that the tester cloth would accumulate the most airborne soil once again, and it also being inaccessible for maintenance, a broadcloth tester fabric was constructed and placed over the attached tester cloth. This can be removed, laundered and replaced.

The tester cloth was originally tacked in place to the tester frame. The reproduction tester cloth was attached in a manner that made it removable without having to take the entire tester frame off the head and foot posts. Strips of Velcro attached to a nylon strip (Velstick) were clamped in place on top of the tester frame.[3] The tester cloth had the loop tape sewn to the edges, making the tester cloth detachable. This was important to allow access behind the carved shells and cartouche of the tester without requiring a major disassembling should maintenance or another problem arise during its long exhibition.

Conclusion

Object-specific factors already narrow the treatment options and when the conservator is able to participate during the initial planning stages, more treatment options will be available. Exhibition and environmental conditions contribute to the frequency and skill level involved in the maintenance of the object. Reducing the routine and complex maintenance procedures is beneficial to the object over time and frees staff time for other responsibilities. The treatment of large objects is time-consuming, requiring supervision, management and coordination of resources and staff, which in turn reduces the availability for accomplishing other projects and responsibilities.

The treatment of the state bed successfully resolved many of the issues that arose during the planning stages. Involved treatments of large objects with defined time parameters always present unanticipated challenges during the course of treatment. All of these issues were addressed with highly satisfactory results. The act of exact reproduction of the textiles - woven and stitched - produced insights into the original manufacture and assembly process, as well as a highly successful interpretation.

Endnotes

1 White, Lisa. "Two English State Beds in the Metropolitan Museum of Art," *Apollo*, August 1992.

2 Clinton (White), Lisa. "The State Bed from Melville House," Victoria and Albert Museum Masterpieces, Sheet 21, 1979. The Melville bed was originally installed in Scotland and has its original coverlet. The Melvilles and the Coningsbys were contemporaries in the Royal court and the beds were executed about a year apart. Nicola Gentle, then on the conservation staff at the V & A, was in charge of the Melville bed treatment and was of immense help in guiding the initial object treatment decisions. At the time that I was planning the conservation of the blue bed, the treatment for the Melville bed had been underway for nearly seven years, with many hands working on the bed (students, interns, fellows and permanent staff).

3 Velcro U.S.A., Inc., 406 Brown Ave., Manchester, NH 03108 USA.

Résumé

Décisions quant au traitement d'un lit d'apparat anglais de 1697

La restauration d'un lit d'apparat anglais du XVIIe siècle appartenant à la collection du Metropolitan Museum of Art révèle les nombreuses contraintes qui se posent lorsqu'il faut intégrer un objet complexe dans une exposition à long terme. Les procédures fixées par l'établissement pour la planification d'exposition et la prise de décision, l'histoire et l'état de l'objet, les objectifs d'interprétation, les échéanciers ainsi que les compétences et les ressources disponibles ne sont que quelques exemples des nombreux facteurs qui décident de l'orientation du traitement. La restauration est une profession où doivent s'équilibrer l'information et les compétences concrètes. Il n'est pas toujours possible de prendre la décision qui semble la meilleure, et il faut alors s'efforcer de compenser les lacunes dans le plan de traitement. Plus tôt la restauration est incluse dans le processus de planification, plus les avantages pour l'objet concerné sont importants, surtout en ce qui a trait à l'entretien. Le traitement couronné de succès du lit d'apparat constitue un excellent exemple pour examiner les multiples facteurs dont il faut tenir compte dans les travaux de restauration.

Comprehensive Approach to Textile Problems in the Hermitage

Elena Mikolaychuk and Nina Pinyagina

State Hermitage Museum
St. Petersburg, Russia 191065
Tel.: 7-812-1 10-96-32
Fax: 7-X 1 2-3 1 1 -90-09

Abstract

This article covers all the stages of preparation of textiles for exhibition. We carry out a careful investigation of the textile's physical condition, which makes it possible to choose the optimal method for its cleaning and conservation, and minimizing invasive techniques. We investigate all auxiliary materials, which come in contact with the exhibit. The method of artificial aging is often used. Textile exhibition also envisages a number of requirements aimed at the exhibits' safety. This paper describes the methods of eliminating consequences of previous conservations and incorrect storage, as well as the methods of conducting a new conservation treatment of the clothes of the 1814 Dutchwoman Doll.

The Hermitage possesses rich collections of textiles from different eras. The largest are the Russian, West European and Oriental textiles collections. A special place is given to textile artifacts, the oldest exhibits dating back to 6th century B.C. The diversity of fabrics in different degrees of condition requires a varied approach to their conservation, storage and exhibition. These decisions are made in a comprehensive manner, taking into consideration all characteristic features of the exhibit.

A textile exposition is preceded by a period of careful preparation. The process starts with an estimation of the textile's physical condition.

1. The article is examined for having dirt, spots, cuts or losses. If the nature of dirt and spots is not clear, it is established by means of a chemical analysis. Cuts and losses and the degree of the fabric's damage sometimes determine the choice of a conservation method. Thus, for example, there are alternative methods of preventive conservation and conservation with the use of wet or dry duplication.

2. The effects of previous conservation are traced. Sometimes, a wrong conservation method aggravates the fabric's condition over the course of time. In such cases the effects of such conservation treatment are removed, if possible. Regretfully, not all substances previously used in the conservation of museum textiles can be removed. In some of the fabrics, irreversible changes took place and the removal process became practically impossible.

3. The microscopic research of the textile's structure and composition, i.e., practically its technological analysis, is conducted. Its results are taken into account when choosing restorative fabric for filling in losses, or lining fabric for the textile's strengthening or replication. Knowing the textile's structure and composition is also important for choosing the appropriate concentration of a finishing agent or adhesive.

4. The composition of all components of the textile is identified. This is taken into account when choosing washing and bleaching agents, and also when establishing the bath's temperature. This test is important when, for example, there are golden threads, especially on textile artifacts. It is a known fact that during the production of golden threads in different periods, apart from the metal, an imitation was used: rice paper, a serous intestinal membrane, or simply an animal glue as a base for gilding. If the article has imitation golden threads, cleaning the fabric with water is limited.

5. The degree of damage to the textile is established by the degree of damage to the threads and fibres in the threads. Cracks, breaks or ruptures in the fibres mean that the fabric has lost, to a large extent, its mechanical strength. If the fibres in the threads do not have visible mechanical damage, while the fabric feels flabby, the reason of the loss of mechanical strength lies in the fibres' natural aging, and in such sources of influence on the fabric as, for example, the exposure to ultraviolet light or the fabric's heightened acidity. Of course, there can be other reasons as well, but these two are the most common ones.

6. One of the determining indicators of the fabric's condition is its acidity. There are quite a lot of reasons that lead to a heightened acidity. The main ones are the fabric's exposure to ultraviolet light and also dyes on the fabric, which have acidic mordants. Cellulose fibres are especially deterioration-prone in the case of heightened

acidity. Protein fibres, because of their chemical composition, are not as susceptible to acids, but, since they have both acidic and amino groups, they too are better if they are not exposed to heightened acidity. In order to halt the destroying effect of heightened acidity the fabric is usually, if it is possible, cleaned with distilled water or a neutralizing agent.

7. The nature of the fabric's dyes is established, and the dyes' solubility is also tested. Dyes with high solubility sometimes exclude the use of water treatment and make us turn to other methods of cleaning and conservation.

The totality of the information received during the estimation of the textile's physical condition, normally gathered according to the above system, allow us to choose the optimal ways of cleaning and treating, and minimize the invasion into the exhibit. Sometimes we use various agents in these processes: cleaning, bleaching and strengthening substances. If necessary, modern materials are also used: fabrics, threads, paper, cardboard, metal cords and fittings. All auxiliary substances and materials undergo a careful inspection at the Hermitage's chemical laboratory, and testing for their suitability and safety towards the exhibit. They should have no negative effect on the exhibit's physical, mechanical, chemical and colour characteristics both during the process of conservation and over the course of time, if such auxiliary substances remain in contact with the exhibit. The selection is based on the establishment of the above characteristics. The artificial aging of the examined material is done, if necessary.

There are a lot of examples from the international practice of textile conservation with uninvestigated materials, the effect of which was only visually and organoleptically estimated immediately after the treatment of fabric. Thus, for example, the treatment of fabrics with hydroxypropyl cellulose (Klucel J.) does strengthen the fabric without making it too stiff and without changing the fabric's colour and texture. However, the research of the preparation's properties we have conducted with the use of artificial aging showed that the whiteness of the samples' silk fabric decreased from 72% to 49% - the fabric became yellowish, the mechanical strength decreased, and undesirable stiffness increased. The term of artificial aging corresponds to approximately 50 years of natural aging of silk fabric. After careful research, this preparation was rejected as a strengthening agent for old fabrics and is not applied in the Hermitage.

Another example is illustrated by the restoration process of the coronation coach of Catherine the Great of Russia. The embroidery, created with golden threads on the coach's roof, needed to be restored. Synthetic golden threads were supplied by an American company. Regretfully, that company could not present any technical characteristics for these threads. The analysis that we did showed that the main constituent element of the thread is a

polyethyleneterephthalate film. Inside the threads, there were various fillers: cotton fibres, viscose fibres and softwood sulphate cellulose fibres. The composition of the threads was of no danger to the main materials of the coach, and the embroidery was restored. In that case there was no need to test the materials' properties with the method of artificial aging, since their properties and behaviour over the course of time were known.

When the textile is ready for exposition the next stage of work starts. The textile exposition plans, in particular, a decorative design of the showcase. For this purpose, designers use various fabrics — often used are cardboard or wall painting. All auxiliary materials, including the mannequin's surface covering, also undergo a test for stability of the materials used in the exhibit. Thus, for example, the Hermitage designers prefer to use voluminous, woven woollen fabric to decorate showcases. Each fabric is tested for the composition of its fibres, since modern woollen fabrics often contain other fibres as well. The fabric's acidity and the type of its dye are also established.

The conditions of the exhibit's display at the exhibition are stipulated in each case, taking into consideration:

1. The textile's general physical condition. Thus, for example, historical carpets or tapestries are better hung horizontally or with a slight inclination, but not vertically.

2. Temperature and humidity. In principle, these parameters are known by all museum staff, but changes are possible in some special cases, depending on the article's individual features.

3. Illumination of the showcase. It should be installed taking into consideration the textile's physical condition, the nature of its fibres and of its dyes. Also, the nature of materials introduced into the exhibit during conservation should be reckoned with.

4. The showcase materials should have no negative effect on the exhibit. Thus, for example, if a dress contains a silver embroidery the walls of the showcase should not be covered with a woollen or viscose fabric. The sulfur contained in woollen and viscose fibres leads to darkening of the silver over the course of time.

5. The nature of exhibits displayed in the same showcase. The objects must be compatible by their chemical nature and should not have any adverse influence on one or another.

6. Biological protection of the exhibit should be planned for. This is achieved either by the showcase's construction or by the introduction of special substances into it, which, in turn, should not exert any adverse influence on the exhibit on the whole.

7. The showcase construction should protect all textile exhibits from dust, dirt, ultraviolet light, etc.

8. Designers' wishes. The designers' task, at the same time, is to take into consideration all the above requirements.

Because the approach is so comprehensive, everyone involved in solving these difficult tasks constantly searches for new solutions or improves the existing ones, however, one condition always remains unalterable - the exhibit's safety.

Unfortunately, such a comprehensive approach to textile problems did not always exist in the Hermitage. Here is one example. In 1814, a doll was presented to Emperor Alexander I to commemorate Emperor Peter I's visit to Holland. The doll is dressed in late 17th century clothes, like the ones worn by the hostess of the house where Peter I lived at that time. The house's model was presented along with the doll. The doll's figure is made of wood. The head, neck, arms and legs are covered with an oil paint. The chest is sewn with white kidskin, and the waist with thick chamois leather. The doll is 76 cm tall. It is dressed in the following order: a chemise of fine linen, a bodice of pink silk with a lacing. The doll has drawers, then a white skirt of diaper-cloth, then a padded skirt, above it there is a hoop-skirt of yellow satin with two hoops, then above it, there is one more white padded skirt, then a pinkish-yellow pleated silk skirt, and the last upper skirt of goldish-brown fabric with many deep pleats. Over all the skirts, there is a corset of pink silk with a fine linen lining. Over the corset, the doll wears an overcoat of greenish-golden silk lined with a yellow wool cloth. The doll also wears cuffs, a collar, a neckscarf, an apron, headgear, stockings and shoes.

The first conservation of the doll's clothes was done in 1912, which was accompanied by detailed documentation.

Figure 1. Doll's dress fragment before conservation.

It says that the drawers, the skirts, the cuffs, the collar and the apron were completely darkened with dirt. They were washed by the restorer in warm water. The other pieces of the dress were wiped with soft terry towels. The apron, which had torn, was sewn up.

The next restoration of the doll's clothes was conducted in 1948. The photographs of that time show that the overcoat, the skirts and the headgear were soiled, the fabric was very damaged, had cuts and big losses. In those years, the Hermitage restorers mostly used an adhesive method of gluing fabrics to a new substrate with flour glue prepared to a specially developed formula. That method was justified and technologically developed for restoring silk banners, which saved a lot of unique artifacts. Unfortunately, that method was also applied to the restoration of the doll's clothes, namely, the overcoat, the skirts, the cuffs and the collar were pasted on a hued cotton tulle with a 3% flour glue. Before gluing, the fabrics were not subjected to any cleaning. In the process of conservation, seams were removed. Then the doll was displayed for more than 40 years in a badly equipped showcase, which did not properly protect it from dust, humidity and temperature fluctuations, and exposure to the rays of the sun.

Two years ago, the textile restoration laboratory received the doll in a very miserable state. The paint on the doll's face was peeling off. The costume fabrics were dirty, brittle, frail and had a lot of losses. The fabrics glued on with the flour glue generally became yellowish. This cast doubts on the possibility of restoring the clothes. The curator's first decision was to sew a new dress for the doll according to the original patterns. However, it is the Hermitage tradition to preserve originals, therefore it was then decided to carry out a careful investigation with the goal of developing methods to reverse previous conservation and incorrect storage, and to develop a new conservation treatment.

It was discovered as a result of the investigation that the flour glue became stiff, brittle and acquired a yellow colour. The cotton tulle lost its mechanical strength to a large extent and could not perform its function as a strengthening material any more. The tulle had a heightened acidity of 4.3. It became obvious that first of all the

Figure 2. Doll's pleated skirt before conservation.

substrate tulle and the flour glue should be removed. With that aim, a structural analysis of the glued fabrics was made. Practically all silk fabrics of the clothes are smooth and have a dense structure thanks to the lack of twisting of the threads, a high linear density and no interstices between the threads. During the process of gluing, the high density of these fabrics prevented the glue from penetrating into the fabric's structure and all the glue remained on the fabrics' reverse side, having strongly united with the cellular structure of the tulle, which had twisted threads. The tulle was rather easily removed by a mechanical method with the help of a thin knife. After the fabric's moistening in a 10% water solution of glycerin at the temperature of 40°C, the clothes were washed with an addition of a detergent, and then with water. Then the fabrics were dried and ironed. The silk clothes became soft and bright.

During further work, we faced the problems of aesthetic and technological changes in the doll's clothing connected with previous replacement and destruction or alteration of costume parts. Thus, for example, the overcoat's shape and size were changed during the restoration of 1948, its lower part was lost, the lining was cut down and the waist was shortened. The sizes of some of the skirts at the waist were changed. As a result of the present restoration, we managed to establish the overcoat's original size, and renewed the missing parts and parts of the yellow woollen lining with the help of fabrics similar in texture and using natural dyes. The numerous losses of the silk fabrics were restored in the same way, the restoration fabrics being deliberately slightly different from the original in colour and texture. The fabrics were sewn up with silk threads. The pleated skirt had so many losses that it was decided to strengthen it all with a thin silk cloth, sewing the skirt to it with a thin silk thread, and then to re-pleat it, which somewhat disguised the losses.

The restoration of the doll's headgear turned out to be more problematic, because in 1948 a flour glue of higher concentration was used for the headgear in order to preserve its stiff shape.

Upon the completion of all restoration works, the Dutchwoman Doll will be displayed in the exposition

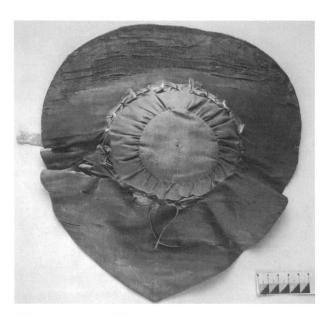

Figure 4. Doll's hat before conservation.

in its restored conditions, taking into consideration all the characteristic needs of the costume.

Bibliography

Agnes Geljer. *A History of Textile Art*. Stockholm: 1979, p. 317.

Sheila Landi. *The Textile Conservators Manual*. England: 1985, p. 202.

N.N. Semenovich. *Restoration of Museum Fabrics*. Leningrad: State Hermitage, 1961, p. 78.

Résumé

Approche globale des problèmes relatifs aux textiles de l'Ermitage

Cet article couvre toutes les étapes de la préparation des textiles en vue d'une exposition. On examine en détails l'état physique du textile, afin de choisir la méthode optimale de nettoyage et de restauration, et on tente d'éviter dans la mesure du possible les techniques «envahissantes». On étudie tous les matériaux auxiliaires qui entrent en contact avec la pièce exposée. On utilise souvent la méthode de vieillissement artificiel. L'inclusion de textiles dans une exposition suppose aussi plusieurs exigences au chapitre de la sécurité des pièces exposées. Dans l'article, on décrit les façons d'éviter les conséquences des traitements antérieurs et d'une mise en réserve déficiente, ainsi que les méthodes employées pour restaurer des vêtements d'une poupée néerlandaise de 1814.

Figure 3. Doll's dress fragment during conservation.

4

The Exhibition Environment
Les facteurs ambiants d'une exposition

Conservation Guidelines for Museum Exhibition Cases

Toby J. Raphael

Division of Conservation
U.S. National Park Service
Harpers Ferry, WV 25425 USA
Tel.: (304) 535-6139
E-mail: toby_raphael@nps.gov

Abstract

This paper proposes guidelines for the planning and design of exhibition cases and introduces a more comprehensive work on the subject being published this year by the National Park Service. The paper is aimed at assisting institutions, involved in the exhibit planning process, to achieve maximum preservation of their collections. The larger work is a three-part handbook including narrative guidelines, technical notes and technical illustrations aimed at incorporating conservation into the entire exhibition planning and design process. Both works identify key conservation issues critical to long-term preservation. The lack of comprehensive and practical guidelines has constituted a serious deficiency within our field. Here, the benefits of numerous case designs are discussed and a methodical approach is recommended. Thoughtful exhibit case design can be one of the most cost-effective methods of preventing deterioration. Well-designed and carefully fabricated cases can successfully mitigate unnecessary damage resulting from nearly all mechanisms of deterioration.

Introduction

Ten years ago I developed a set of exhibition guidelines that I hoped would help integrate conservation concerns into exhibits produced by the National Park Service. This year, I have revisited those guidelines, with the goal of revising and expanding them into a more comprehensive publication called *Conservation and Exhibits: A Handbook. Incorporating Conservation into the Museum Process*. The Handbook seeks to reflect the exponential increase in our knowledge of preservation over the past decade. The following paper, which focuses on the preservation-responsible planning and design of exhibit cases, derives much of its content from the Handbook.

Museum exhibitions have not, in my view, received the same methodical attention from conservators as have museum storage systems. Therefore, in the Handbook I recommend a systematic decision-making process that incorporates conservation concerns at all stages of exhibition development. Because each museum and its collections are unique, the Handbook offers guidelines—rather than definitive standards—that are to be custom-tailored for the safe display of objects. I strongly urge that each exhibit project involve a qualified specialist in the area of exhibit conservation.

The Handbook draws upon the experience and research of many individuals in the conservation and exhibition communities, but no one person more than conservator Nancy Davis. Experience and considerable trial and error have helped us better understand how objects interact with—and can be protected by—their exhibition environments. The Handbook, composed of an issue-oriented text along with supplementary technical information sheets and drawings, will be available in paper and electronic formats.

Incorporating Conservation Into Exhibit Case Planning and Design

If the dual responsibilities of preservation and exhibition are to be met successfully by a museum, conservation must be integrated into the planning, design, and production of display cases; however, variables in an exhibit's design, location, and budget (among other things) make it impossible to provide absolute standards for case design and fabrication.

When To Use Exhibit Enclosures

Any group of objects displayed without protective enclosures can be defined as an "open" exhibit. Given the inherent problems for collections care and preservation, open display is rare for long-term museum exhibits, except those in historic buildings. In general, open displays should be limited to temporary exhibits and the display of reproductions or oversized artifacts.

For exhibit periods of less than six months, enclosed cases for all display objects are sometimes considered unrealistic and cost-prohibitive. The ultimate decision to use enclosed cases must, however, take into consideration all of the following:

- the length of the proposed exhibit
- the sensitivity and condition of the proposed exhibit objects

- the environmental condition of the exhibit space
- the age and nature of the targeted exhibit visitor
- the likelihood of vandalism and theft
- the availability of curatorial maintenance resources

In instances where cases are not used, special security arrangements and maintenance procedures and schedules will be required. Additionally, every effort should be made to limit dust infiltration into the exhibit hall or gallery and to moderate the environmental conditions of the entire area.

Benefits of Enclosed Cases

Although enclosed cases are the norm for the majority of museum exhibits, the benefits of enclosure are rarely calculated methodically. If designed appropriately, an exhibit case can protect its contents from physical damage and deterioration caused by inappropriate environmental and biological conditions. In sum, the exhibit case can:

- prevent handling and incidental touch
- decrease the threat of theft and vandalism
- stop insect and rodent ingress
- block out dust and foreign substances
- buffer collections from rapid changes in temperature and relative humidity
- remove or limit harmful radiation (if filtered)
- allow for the introduction of environment modifying agents (such as absorbers and scavengers for atmospheric pollutants, relative humidity, and oxygen)

The benefits of displaying objects in exhibit enclosures cannot be overstated. Experience and research have consistently shown that the way in which collections are housed while on exhibit has a profound impact on their long-term condition. Furthermore, over the past decade a wide variety of case designs, with varying degrees of enclosure, have provided protective environments for objects while supporting or even enhancing the aesthetics and informative content of exhibits.

Early Inclusion of Preservation Requirements

The importance of considering conservation design features during the earliest stages of exhibition planning cannot be overemphasized. It is costly and difficult (if not impossible) to retrofit a case design later in the process. Discussion and cooperation between the designer, curator, and conservator at the beginning of a project will help achieve a successful balance among the conservation needs of the objects, the academic, education, and aesthetic exhibit requirements, and the practical constraints of tight budgets and demanding schedules.

The exhibit team must understand the key issues affecting object preservation in order to design and implement a preservation-responsible case (see Figure 1). Early in the planning, specific conservation criteria should be developed (and written) for each object proposed for exhibition.

Specifically, these criteria should address temperature, relative humidity, pollutants, exhibit lighting, biological infestation, visitor contact, exhibit rotation, and maintenance issues. A thorough discussion is required to establish whether the environmental conditions and conservation features identified as part of the criteria can be more efficiently achieved at the exhibit room level or within the exhibit enclosure itself. Exhibit cases should then be engineered to meet the criteria.

A successful end-product will demand a close and constructive working relationship between qualified exhibition

---

Key Preservation Input: Planning

- Selection of Exhibit Objects
- Development of Conservation Criteria for Objects
- Identification of Criteria to be met by Exhibit Case

Key Preservation Input: Design

Case Construction Features
- Physical Security Requirements
- Characteristics of Case Frame and Shell
- Characteristics of Inner Chambers
- Design of Chamber Entry Systems

Air Exchange Features
- Degree of Seal of Exhibit Case
- Moisture Permeability of Shell
- Passive Design Ventilation System
- Active Design Ventilation System

Climate Control Features
- Passive Low-tech Designs
- Active Mechanical Systems
- Air Purification Systems
- Environmental Monitoring Systems

Exhibit Object Lighting
- Room vs. Case-mounted Fixtures
- Isolation and Venting of Fixture and Lamp Heat
- Conventional vs. Fiber Optic Systems
- Control of Radiant Energy Levels

Figure 1.

---

and preservation specialists, as well as a sense that all team members share equal responsibility for collections preservation.

Multiple Levels of Conservation Response

Preservation-responsible case design can be a multileveled process rather than an all-or-nothing proposition. The level of exhibit case technology and environmental conditioning required depends upon the sensitivity of the objects to damage and the ambient environment of the geographical location and the exhibition space.

Once the conservation criteria for safe display of the objects are established, the exhibit team can work together toward the most practical and cost-effective way of providing appropriate protection. One approach to conservation decision making is to identify clearly the multiple levels or categories of features available to meet specific requirements (see Figure 2). In such a strategy, the team should first define the lowest level or baseline scenario (i.e., in which no conservation features are included), and the highest level (in which ALL possible conservation features are included); the team can then establish interim levels, representing various options between the two.

Team members must understand that preservation-responsible design requires conscious choices and trade-offs. Decisions should fulfill the established conservation criteria while taking into account the risks that are deemed acceptable to the materials going on display. Since a completely "risk-free" situation is probably unrealistic, if not impossible, the team should perform a thorough risk assessment to determine what constitutes acceptable or minimally tolerable levels of risk.

Summary Conservation Guidelines: Exhibit Case Planning and Design

1. Use an enclosed exhibit format whenever possible.
2. Avoid open display, except when in historic building museums or when the object's size makes enclosure impractical. Open display should never be a routine exhibition option or a choice made solely for financial reasons.
3. Initiate the discussion of required conservation features early in the exhibition planning process after establishing the specific conservation criteria for the selected exhibit objects.
4. Develop an effective working relationship between the exhibit team members sharing responsibility for collections preservation.
5. Incorporate specific conservation concerns into the case's technical design, taking into account both the available technology and the limitations of the project's budget.

Exhibit Case Construction

Exterior Case Styles and Interior Compartments

Exhibition designers have created tremendous variation in exhibit case styles within the basic categories of wall cases and free-standing cases. Each one presents slightly different preservation challenges. Issues such as how the display objects and lighting are accessed; how cases can be sealed or ventilated; where environmental modifying agents are housed and how they are serviced, all are effected by design style.

In view of the considerable variations, it is less intimidating to know that preservation concerns need to remain focused on only a few of the key components of a case:

- the display chamber, also referred to as the object compartment
- the lighting chamber, also referred to as an attic
- the curatorial maintenance compartment

Exterior case features and aesthetics are of relatively little concern if the objects are safely housed within a protective display chamber. The design of the display chamber and the materials from which it is constructed are of key importance to a successful, preservation responsible design.

Exhibit lighting that originates at the case is conventionally attached to the case structure and should be housed in a separate chamber with its own entry and adequate venting. Environmental manipulation of the interior atmosphere is done with equipment located in a compartment which communicates with or is located within the display chamber. Here, auxiliary materials such as pollutant absorbers and moisture absorbers are housed.

Curatorial Access to Exhibit Objects

A primary performance feature of any case is its ability to discourage unofficial access without blocking or encumbering legitimate access. The design of the curatorial entry system should allow for the following activities without unduly compromising security:

- cleaning of the case interior
- maintenance of environmental control equipment located within the case
- periodic object inspection and routine collections care procedures
- retrieval of objects for period rotation or during emergencies

Each object in an exhibit should be accessible without major disruption to adjacent objects. Object layout within the case should take into account installation and object removal procedures; for example, interior walkways can be provided.

Exhibit Case Design and Fabrication
Multilevel Preservation Features*

Feature	Level 1	Level 2	Level 3	Level 4
1. Physical Security Features	1.1 Level: no security features	1.2 Level: minimal security Example Features: conventional construction materials; tamper resistant screws and fasteners or locks.	1.3 Level: moderate security Example Features: materials with higher resistance; concealed screws; tamper resistant fasteners; locks; low-level alarms.	1.4 Level: high security Example Features: level 1.3 plus highest rated construction materials, high level sensors and alarms.
2. Construction Material VOC ** **Restrictions**	2.1 Level: no restrictions	2.2 Level: minimal restrictions Example Features: conventional museum case construction; sealed wood products.	2.3 Level: moderate restrictions Example Features: high quality materials and finishes; low VOC emitters, sealed wood products.	2.4 Level: high restrictions Example Features: inert materials, no wood products or potential VOC emitters.
3. Degree of Air Seal (airtightness)	3.1 Level: unsealed	3.2 Level: minimally sealed Example Features: conventional construction; standard backstop design for panels, doors and glazing; standard tolerances for joined materials	3.3 Level: tightly sealed Example Features: gasketed panels, doors and glazing; strict tolerances for joined materials and use of sealants; increased frequency of fasteners.	3.4 Level: hermetically sealed Example Features: level 3.3 plus airtight design and construction; specialized sealants, gasketry and fasteners.
4. Interior Environmental Control Features	4.1 Level: no control features	4.2 Level: minimal passive control Example Features: control based on passive case design, construction material selection and case seal.	4.3 Level: moderate passive control Example Features: control based on case design, material selection; inclusion of passive environmental modifying agents — absorbers, scavengers.	4.4 Level: maximum active control Example Features: control based on active mechanical system; very limited environmental deviation.
5. Exhibit Lighting Control Features	5.1 Level: no controls	5.2 Level: minimal controls Example Features: separate lighting compartment with own entry; minimal restrictions on visible light range.	5.3 Level: moderate controls Example Features: separate lighting chamber; visitor activated lighting; moderate restricted range of visible light, ultraviolet and infrared radiation.	5.4 Level: maximum controls Example Features: level 5.3 plus highly restricted range of visible light, ultraviolet and infrared radiation; no heating of interior case.

* Levels for different features usually vary within a single exhibit case.
** VOC refers to volatile organic compounds.

Figure 2.

The overall door design, weight, and location should be thoughtfully engineered with curatorial input. Rollers and temporary opening supports can be added to assist in the entry of oversized doors. Some cases may be configured in such a way that the entire vitrine above displayed objects can be removed. In these instances, the glazing material's size and weight must be calculated and taken into consideration. Whenever possible, design criteria should assume that the case will be opened and serviced by a single individual—even though, in exhibits with high security risk, two persons may be obligatory.

Selection of Stable Construction Materials
Various Hazards
Exhibition designers have a wide range of materials to choose from for constructing exhibit cabinetry and finishing case interiors. From a preservation standpoint, however, it is crucial that only non-hazardous materials be used for the construction and decoration of cases. Damage can result when exhibit objects are in direct contact with unsuitable and unstable substances, such as acidic materials, fugitive paints, soluble dyes and oils. Damage can also occur with the "out-gassing" of vapors from volatile organic substances, including acids, formaldehyde, and solvents.

It is always necessary to evaluate every material proposed for use within a case's primary chambers. Consider the following:

- The deleterious effects of acidity in low-quality mat boards are well-known; less recognized is the fact that a wide range of materials, including many wood products, fabrics, paints, and adhesives, can also emit chemical substances in the form of gases.

- Out-gassing often occurs when such materials are new, but may continue throughout the life of the material and can sometimes increase in rate over time.

- Un-reacted monomers and solvents from otherwise stable compounds can become interior pollutants. Case construction materials often contain unsuspected additive materials and unannounced chemical reagents as well.

- Many plastic products contain ingredients that improve handling characteristics but that may, over time, migrate out of the plastic and deposit onto the objects it contacts.

- Other additives include surface finishers and fire-retardant products in textiles and ultraviolet radiation absorbers in plastics. It is common, for example, for cotton fabric to be treated with a permanent press finish that can corrode metal objects.

Experience has revealed that control of volatile materials becomes a serious concern when objects known to be particularly sensitive to out-gassing are displayed. These include items with high acid vulnerability; metals such as lead and its alloys; silver and its alloys; solder; and shell or other objects containing calcium carbonate. Additionally, well-sealed or hermetically sealed exhibit cases can pose dangers, because even a small amount of volatiles can build up to hazardous levels in such a confined space.

A Two-Tiered Approach to Materials
The most successful approach to protecting objects from out-gassing and acidity involves the careful selection of construction materials, followed by the isolation of problematic materials away from contact with objects.

- There is enough information on the stability of general material classes to aid in an informed choice. Exhibition conservators are also generally willing to share information about previously tested and accepted exhibit materials.

- A manufacturer's product literature should be reviewed for clues. It will often include a material safety data sheet (MSDS) that lists basic components and safety precautions for the product's use. Additional concerns can be addressed by talking to the technical department of the manufacturer, or through independent testing.

It should be noted that companies can change the exact composition of their commercial products over time, so it is possible that a product used in a previous application will no longer be conservation approved. It is therefore wise to test each batch of a product before use. Testing services are available commercially, and conservation laboratories can perform some less complex testing. Exhibit conservators can assist in this process.

Even once the research phase is complete, it will not always be possible to choose inert, non-hazardous materials that do not out-gas. When practicality dictates that less-than-ideal materials be employed, or when collection objects are particularly sensitive to out-gassing, the materials in question must be sealed to inhibit the release of undesirable volatile substances. Specially formulated barrier layers of metal or plastic foils, as well as specialized paint and sealant systems, can be used to seal problematic substrates, such as wood-based products, used within the display chamber.

Finally, it should be emphasized that before objects are installed in the exhibition space or case, all surfaces and construction materials must be absolutely dry and fully cured. Objects should never be placed immediately into newly constructed cases. Paints, adhesives, and caulks generally require a minimum of three weeks.

Physical Security Features
Although appropriate security measures for the institution will begin with the building itself, museum staff cannot be

expected to monitor all spaces within an exhibition at all times. Therefore, exhibit case design itself must resolve basic security issues. A risk assessment should be performed early in the planning process to establish the level of security required and to determine whether the room or the case will provide such security.

- Cases can be designed to offer different levels of security (see Figure 2) which can vary according to the specific requirements of a collection. (For instance, objects of moderate to high monetary value—as well as particular types of objects such as firearms, jewelry, precious metals, and coins—are often the target of theft.)

- The highest level of secure case design—necessary when the exhibit includes "national treasures" or objects of extraordinarily high monetary value—can include such features as dual locking systems, movement sensors and alarms, and shatter-proof security glazing.

- Special glazing can also provide stringent protection against forced entry, ballistic attack, and bomb blast. This glazing can be ordered with specific ratings for intrusion resistance, and the materials comprising the case shell should be selected with a comparable physical strength.

Given the tremendous range in features and costs of security items, the exhibit team should gather preliminary estimates early in the planning process before proceeding with case design.

Summary Conservation Guidelines: Case Construction

1. Focus preservation concerns primarily at features within the three main case design factors: display, maintenance, and lighting.
2. Design cases to discourage unofficial access while facilitating curatorial access.
3. Allow for case entry and artifact removal by a single individual wherever possible.
4. Select materials wisely, after consulting the available research, talking with other museum professionals, and testing new and unknown materials.
5. Develop a risk assessment to determine the level of physical security a case must provide.

Climate Control

Exhibit Cases Designed as Microclimates
In addition or as an alternative to controlling climate within the entire exhibit space, exhibit cases can be designed to provide a specific microclimate for the objects on display. A tightly controlled case environment can either moderate or buffer the effect of relative humidity changes coming from outside the case, or maintain a specific relative

humidity level inside the case at all times. This type of case requires careful design and high-quality construction, and will include either a mechanical (active) or a passive (static) system. Mechanical systems are comprised of small, commercially made heating, air conditioning, and humidifier units, while passive systems, developed over the years by museum staffs, use silica gel, saturated salts, or hygroscopic materials to affect the relative humidity within a sealed case.

Case microclimates are particularly useful when tight control of the entire macroclimate is financially or technically impractical, or when a few objects require a different climate than the rest of the exhibit.

Sealing of Exhibit Cases
Air Exchange, Relative Humidity, and Foreign Matter
By reducing air exchange, sealed cases can simultaneously reduce dust, atmospheric pollutants, and insect infiltration, while stabilizing the relative humidity inside the case.

There are several factors that change relative humidity within a case, but the chief one is air exchange through loosely constructed case materials. In a tightly sealed case, the rate at which air exchanges between the interior and the exterior can be reduced to as little as one complete change per 72 hours or longer. An unsealed or leaky case, by comparison, can experience several exchanges per hour.

In the design of sealed cases, there are different levels of airtightness achievable, corresponding with different preservation requirements (see fig. 2). Most such cases provide a minimal to tight, rather than hermetic, seal. To maximize case performance, the design team must consider:

- the precise fitting of, and use of gaskets and conservation-approved caulk on, all construction joints and seams
- the use of less permeable construction materials

Natural convection is a driving force behind the air exchange through a case, as it forces large quantities of air out of one small gap or hole and into another. Thus, if a case is to be well-sealed, convection must be limited by effectively sealing all gaps with gaskets or caulk. Gaskets are necessary around any access door into the case, and doors must be designed to provide the pressure needed to compress the gasket.

Moisture Permeation
Moisture migration occurs as a result of differences in relative humidity between conditions inside and outside the case, but it is also dependent on the permeability of the specific materials used. For example, moisture migrates through low-fired earthenware or wood relatively quickly as compared with porcelain or glass. Moisture diffusion occurs very slowly in a well-sealed case, but it is still a

design concern. Acrylic and glass both have rates of diffusion low enough to be suitable for a sealed, environmentally controlled case. Cases made of metals such as aluminum will eliminate moisture diffusion, but are very expensive to build. For most applications, a wood product can be used to construct cases, but will require a sealant to lower permeability. Laminates, such as resin-based high pressure laminates and moisture barrier sheet materials, coatings and films can be used.

Deliberately Ventilated Cases

Most conventional case designs in the past allowed for ventilation through unsealed joints and gaps, but this uncontrolled ventilation did not protect display objects from dust, insects, or rapid climate changes. It is preferable, therefore, to construct a relatively sealed case and to ventilate it through controlled portholes (also called vents).

A ventilated case mirrors the temperature and relative humidity of the ambient exhibition space, but filters the incoming air to exclude dust, gaseous pollutants, and/or insects. Ventilated cases are therefore appropriate only when climatic conditions throughout the entire museum or exhibition space meet the established conservation criteria for the displayed collections. It is common that most display cases in an exhibition be ventilated, while a few well-sealed cases are used for objects that require microclimates.

Mechanical ventilation systems—those using a fan to force air through the case—are usually unnecessary except in very large cases. A passive system is usually sufficient, since it will use natural laws of convection to direct airflow through filtered portholes or vents.

In certain circumstances where dust and airborne particulate infiltration is a problem, exhibit cases can be designed to maintain a positive pressure. In these ventilated enclosures an electric-powered fan is used to force air into the case through a series of filters. Seams of the case are left unsealed and the air rushes out precluding any ingress of foreign material.

Filtration is a critical design feature for any ventilated case. Three methods are common:

- The porthole or vent can be covered with a fabric containing a pollution absorber, usually activated carbon or a manganese permanganate-based product.
- Prefabricated filters, such as a commercial respirator filter, can be fitted into a porthole equipped with a matching screw thread.
- Natural cotton wool has even been used as a cost-effective alternative to such pollution-absorbent products.

Portholes do not need to be large; a hole of 0.6 cm (1/4 in.) in diameter can allow for an airflow of 120 cm^3 (4 ft.^{3}) per minute. A series of portholes functions best when located laterally (i.e., along intervals at the same height) on the exhibit case, thereby reducing the "chimney effect." Two portholes are usually sufficient, and work best when located on opposite ends of the same case wall, or on two opposing case walls.

As with a sealed case, the careful choice of non-hazardous construction and finishing materials is an imperative, however, the increased airflow of ventilated cases considerably reduces the risk of a build-up of hazardous volatiles within the case.

Summary Conservation Guidelines: Sealed and Ventilated Cases

1. Determine which objects, if any, require microclimates, and design cases accordingly.
2. Choose construction materials that limit air exchange and moisture migration.
3. Design and construct tight joints and entries. It is now commonplace to design well-sealed cases which allow no more than one (1) air exchange every three (3) days.
4. Use conservation-approved gaskets and caulk to minimize leaks. Wherever possible, choose materials that minimize out-gassing and isolate any problematic or hazardous materials.
5. For ventilated cases, first design sealed cases, then provide portholes; filter the portholes to prevent dust, insects, and chemical pollutants from being sucked into the case.

Further Conservation Issues in Case Production

Case Vibration and Movement

Cases need to be designed to limit vibration and unintentional movement of the objects. This means, for example, that cases should not be physically connected to walls or ceilings that experience vibration due to HVAC vents or other equipment. Likewise, the case and floor interface should be designed in such a way that cleaning equipment does not jar the case interior. Free-standing cases generally require anchors, and top-heavy pedestal cases require some type of weighting method. Specialized fasteners are required for exhibition cases located in areas at higher risk for earthquakes and natural disasters.

Case Lighting and Overheating Concerns

The display chamber of an exhibit case is particularly vulnerable to overheating due to inappropriate, integral lighting (case lighting systems which are attached to the exhibit structure itself). Exhibit lighting is frequently found to be the source of artifact heating and can be responsible for irreversible damage. Improperly designed exhibit lighting can raise the temperature of display objects through radiation heating, convection heating and conduction heating.

A glazed display enclosure within an exhibit case can be heated by the greenhouse effect: amplification of the heat of any light passing into the chamber, particularly in tight or hermetically sealed cases. If allowed to build up, heat from incandescent lamps, transformers used in low-voltage lighting systems, and the ballasts of fluorescent lighting systems can excessively raise the temperature of the display objects, as well as the air in the case, which changes the case's level of relative humidity.

Lighting fixtures and lamps must therefore be isolated in well-designed, separate lighting chambers (or attics) to allow for their control. The following features should be considered when designing a lighting chamber:

* a transparent separation panel which is gasketed or sealed in place — no air, insects or dust should be able to enter display chamber from the lighting area;
* an independent entry system — for maintenance and security reasons the door should be independent with a separate locking device other than that used for the case;
* a well-designed ventilation system — one that utilizes natural air convection design for exhausting rising heat, and where necessary, appropriately sized electric fans;
* a sufficient chamber height — to allow for placing the lights at a sufficient distance from the case and the addition of light directing devices and radiation filters.

A secondary effect of overheating is that elevated temperatures within a case create a pressure differential that can draw air into the case as it cools during non-lit hours. This results in large amounts of unconditioned air and dust to flow into the case. The lighting plan, therefore, must be carefully considered to minimize this effect. Similarly, locating a sealed case near heating or air-conditioning ducts or return air vents can have an adverse impact on the climate inside the case.

Testing and Prototype Production

Complete drawings and specifications for either sealed or ventilated cases should ensure that the fabricator understands all case construction details. Different case styles, however, present special challenges to preservation and require different levels of assessment and involvement during the production and installation phases. Issues such as how objects are accessed, how lighting fixtures are safely serviced, how environmental modifying agents are housed and serviced, can be practically evaluated during the case's final design and construction. The actual function and performance of the display chamber design and the materials from which it is constructed are of key importance to a successful case.

A pre-production meeting should be held to clarify that construction parameters must be controlled within tight specifications. In some instances, a mid-production inspection is necessary, and often final phase testing is recommended to test the case for overall function and make any final alterations. Whenever possible, it is advised to first fabricate a prototype that can be fully tested. Inspection examinations can include:

* air leak location and exchange rate determination;
* performance of environmental control functions;
* temperature gradients within the case due to lighting;
* transmission of visible, ultraviolet and infrared radiation;
* construction material off-gassing;
* case entry time for emergency object retrieval.

Summary Conservation Guidelines: Further Issues in Case Design

1. Construct a physically stable case, limiting movement and vibration.
2. Separate exhibit lighting from the display chamber; use fixtures and lamps that produce little heat, and case designs that dissipate heat from lighting.
3. Provide detailed drawings and specifications. Construct exhibit cases to strict tolerances to insure that conservation parameters are fully met.
4. Test and monitor the case to determine whether or not it meets design objectives and performance is acceptable.

Résumé

Lignes directrices pour les vitrines d'exposition

Cet article propose des lignes directrices pour orienter la planification et la conception de vitrines d'exposition. On y présente aussi un ouvrage traitant du sujet plus en détails, qui sera publié cette année par le National Park Service. L'article vise à aider les établissements qui se consacrent à la planification d'expositions à préserver au maximum leurs collections. L'ouvrage annoncé est un manuel en trois parties comprenant des lignes directrices narratives, des notes techniques et des illustrations techniques; il vise l'intégration de la conservation dans le processus global de planification et de conception. Dans l'article et dans le manuel, on dresse la liste des questions clés de la préservation à long terme. Le manque de directives pratiques et complètes sur le sujet est une grande lacune dans le domaine de la conservation. Dans le cas présent, on traite des avantages des nombreux types de vitrines d'exposition et on propose une méthodologie. La conception de vitrines d'exposition adaptées peut constituer l'un des moyens les plus efficaces et les plus économiques de prévenir la détérioration. Une vitrine bien conçue et bien fabriquée peut atténuer efficacement les effets dommageables de pratiquement tous les mécanismes de détérioration.

Concerns About Plastics During Exhibition and Transport of Textile Objects

R. Scott Williams

Canadian Conservation Institute
1030 Innes Road
Ottawa, Ontario, K1A 0M5 Canada
Tel.: (613) 998-3721
E-mail: scott_williams@pch.gc.ca

Abstract

Many textile objects (including flat textiles, costumes, and costume accessories) made in the 20th century contain plastic components. These plastics may react with other textile and non-textile components in the textile objects. The reactions that may occur during exhibition and transport will be discussed in terms of the initial inherent properties of the plastics and the properties they acquire upon aging. Modern plastic products are also used extensively to construct exhibition and transport appliances for travelling exhibitions. Inappropriate plastics can react with textile objects to cause physical (e.g., staining, abrasion), chemical (e.g., disintegration by acid hydrolysis), and mechanical (e.g., breaking and tearing) damage. The chemical and physical properties and the aging characteristics of selected plastic products will be discussed in a general way, and guidelines for selecting appropriate plastic products for use with textile objects will be given.

Introduction

Plastics are associated with textiles either as part of the textile object such as buttons and foam padding, or as auxiliary materials used to construct mounts, exhibit cases and packing crates. In both cases, the plastics can damage the textiles. Plastics or components from the plastics can react with textiles either directly at points of contact, or remotely where the plastic and textile are not in contact. In the latter case, the active agent from the plastic is almost always a gas, and, since a gas is the active agent, the airtightness and ventilation of the enclosure around the plastic and the textile are important.

Thus when plastics and textiles are together, we must know whether they are in direct contact and whether they are in an airtight or ventilated enclosure. Since the physical and chemical properties of plastics change with age we should monitor plastics used in auxiliary materials to ensure that they are still performing the specific function as intended.

Problems with Plastics

As can be seen in Table 1, many plastics suffer or create problems as they age. Some are prone to breakage because they are inherently fragile or brittle or because they become so as they age by reaction with environmental agents. Some plastics exude or emit hazardous products, either substances that are initially present in the plastic, or degradation products that are produced as the plastic ages.

Damage to Textiles Caused by Plastics

Damage to textiles from plastics usually takes three forms:

1) mechanical damage such as breakage, abrasion or cutting;
2) physical damage such a staining or discolouration; and
3) chemical damage such as acid catalyzed decomposition.

Mechanical Damage (Breakage, Abrasion, Cutting)

Mechanical damage to objects occurs when plastic components break. Some plastics are inherently brittle and easily fractured, like general purpose crystalline polystyrene. Others increase in brittleness and fragility with age due to chemical reactions like oxidation, crosslinking, and chain scission (e.g., polyethylene), to physical changes like loss of plasticizer by evaporation or extraction (cellulose nitrate, cellulose acetate, poly(vinyl chloride)), or to gradual mechanical deterioration from crazing or microcracking caused by environmental agents such as extreme temperature values or variations, relative humidity fluctuations, or to exposure to chemicals such as aqueous washing solution, dry cleaning fluids, and repair materials such as adhesives (acrylics).

Some plastics are inherently weak or prone to tear, and may be used in applications not suited to their properties. Designers of haute couture costumes have used plastic components for their visual appearance without regard for their mechanical or structural properties. Garments have been made by sewing together metallized Mylar sheets or by sewing metallized Mylar attachments onto garments. Mylar has the property of being very tear resistant until it is notched, then, once a tear starts it runs very easily in a generally random direction. A good example of this is the potato chip bag that you cannot open until you bite it to create a notch, after which it tears too easily in all directions. Sewing introduces, into the Mylar, needle holes with a thread in the hole. The hole is a notch and the thread is a saw. The slightest stress on the sewn seam causes the Mylar to tear at the needle hole, usually

Table 1
Problems with Plastics

Plastics that are initially fragile or become fragile as they age

Plastic	Problem
cellulose nitrate	brittle
cellulose acetate	brittle
casein formaldehyde	brittle
rubber, ebonite, vulcanite	brittle or sticky
polyurethane	brittle, sometimes sticky
clear polystyrene	may become brittle due to stress crazing
any plastic component in a stressed state (stretched, compressed, bent, etc.)	may embrittle
any plastic in a constant state of motion (vibrating, rotating, etc.)	may suffer fatigue fracture

Plastics that are prone to damage by environmental agents
(including UV and excess light, high or low temperature, high relative humidity)

Especially UV and light:

polystyrene	yellowed
poly(vinyl chloride)	yellowed, brittle
rubber, ebonite, vulcanite	brittle
all plastics (and organics)	should be considered as prone to damage by UV radiation

Especially high and/or fluctuating relative humidity:

protein (gelatin, casein formaldehyde)	moldy, brittle
phenol formaldehyde (phenolics, Bakelite)	discoloured and more matte

Plastics that produce hazardous products as they age

cellulose nitrate	acidic and oxidizing nitrogen oxide gases
cellulose acetate	acetic acid gas, oily plasticizer liquids
casein formaldehyde	formaldehyde gas
rubber, ebonite, vulcanite	hydrogen sulfide and other sulfur containing gases
poly(vinyl chloride)	oily plasticizer liquids, maybe hydrochloric acid gas
polyurethane	organic acid gases and liquids, nitrogenous organic gases and liquids

resulting in opening the seam or separating the attachment from the garment.

Many fabrics used in the past decade have shimmery, metallic, holographic, iridescent, or similar optical effects. These effects are achieved by a variety of techniques such as by weaving with fibres that have very particular surface characteristics, by using ribbon-shaped fibres and/or mixtures of fibres with different shapes oriented in different, but in very specific, directions in the fabric, and by using fibres that have delicate coatings, often less than a micrometer thick, to obtain optical effects by subtle optical phenomena such as interference and holography.

Often, because the optical characteristics of the material are the reason for the material's inclusion in the garment, rather than its mechanical properties, many of these special materials are very weak. Handling that would be considered as normal for traditional fabrics, may be too rough for these. The example of tearing Mylar has been given above.

Damage to the optical appearance of these textiles occurs by subtle means. Very light abrasion can scuff off the coating or disrupt fibre orientation; exposure to liquids can etch or dissolve coatings; creasing or crushing disrupts fibre orientations; thin delicate optical coatings may be tarnished, etched or even removed completely by very small amounts of pollutant gases because they are so thin. Although it may be easy enough to repair the mechanical damage by conventional methods such as sewing, gluing, patching, etc., it may be impossible to repair the optical damage. This is somewhat akin to the problems faced by painting conservators in repairing damage to colour field paintings — a tear in the middle of a metres square area of absolutely feature less, slightly matte, slightly off-white paint can be patched, but the appearance of the paint can never be matched.

Mechanical damage to textile objects caused by plastics in auxiliary exhibit and transport materials are usually caused by sharp, pointed or other shaped features of the plastics that cut, puncture, snag, pull, or abrade fibres and fabrics. For example, the cut surfaces of polyethylene foams have a coarse structure that can snag textile fibres. These hazardous features may be inherent to the object (abrasive surfaces of cut coarse foams), or may be created by damage or deterioration of the auxiliary material, such as breakage which produces sharp edges and points. Because these problems can develop over time due to aging, auxiliary materials should be examined and monitored to ensure that they are still doing the job intended.

Physical Damage (Staining, Discolouration)
Physical damage like staining most often occurs when there is direct contact between the plastic and the textile and some material transfers from the plastic to the textile. The plastic may be a part of the object, such as buttons and foam pads, or an auxiliary exhibit and packing material.

The main culprits that cause stains are the additives in the plastics, including plasticizers, antioxidants, heat stabilizers, UV absorbers and stabilizers, antistatic agents, and fire retardants. Of all the additives in plastics, plasticizers are usually the most abundant, comprising as much as 50 percent by weight of some poly(vinyl chloride) products, and are responsible for most staining. Plasticizers are particularly troublesome, because by their very nature, they are usually oily organic liquids with very strong solvent properties. Other additives are generally used at much lower concentrations than plasticizers (0.1% to less than 10%), and therefore, do not pose so much of a threat.

But, problems have been reported. The antioxidant butylated hydroxytoluene, BHT, is quite volatile and has transferred from polyethylene laundry bags to enclosed textiles, eventually leading to yellow stains on the textiles. Some fire retardant and antistatic agents are applied to plastic products by dipping the products into aqueous solutions of the agent or spraying these solutions onto the products. This produces plastic surfaces that are coated with salt or surfactants that could absorb water and promote hydrolytic degradation or corrosion of objects in contact. Fire retardants and antistatic agents can be incorporated into plastics by dissolving them into molten plastic before fabrication of the products. Products made this way have no significant surface coatings, and do not have the problems inherent to dipped or sprayed products.

Chemical Damage
(Acid Decomposition, Tarnishing of Metallic Threads)
Chemical damage occurs when there is a reaction of the plastic or its components, or its degradation products with textiles. A common example is the reaction of oxidizing and acidic nitrogen oxide gases from degrading cellulose nitrate, such as Celluloid, with textiles. The acid completely destroys the fabric, resulting in loss of material, and leaving a hole. This commonly occurs in collar stays and stiffeners. This is an extreme case of acid catalyzed depolymerization of the textile polymer. Acidic degradation products from plastics commonly weaken textiles, making them prone to tearing. Acid attack by acidic degradation products from plastics is the most common form of remote (noncontact) damage caused to textiles by plastics.

Other damaging reactions occur. Decomposition products from polyurethane foam used for padding are often coloured products and cause irreversible yellow and brown stains which cannot be washed away. Peroxides produced by the oxidations of some plastics attack textile polymers, causing them to be oxidized and weakened, or faded.

Prevention and Reversal
of Damage to Textiles Caused by Plastics

Plastics that may cause damage can be either a component part of the object or an auxiliary exhibit and packing material. Although we can select plastics for exhibit and transport applications from a small number of safe plastics, we cannot do this with the plastics that are part of the textile objects. We must treat these plastics as objects.

Plastic components that are part of a textile object should be evaluated with regard to whether or not they will cause damage to the rest of the textile. We can predict certain kinds of problems for various plastics (see Table 1), and with this knowledge develop preventive treatment and handling procedures to minimize damage to the plastic component itself, and to other parts of the textile by the plastic component.

Handling of objects with brittle plastics should be kept to a minimum. Buttons, clasps, sequins, and other fittings and decorations in early 20th century textiles were often made of cellulose nitrate or cellulose acetate. These plastics are prone to breakage as they age because of embrittlement due to plasticizer loss and chemical degradation. Breakage is exacerbated by handling stresses when mounting and dismounting costumes during travelling exhibitions where garments might have to be repeatedly buttoned and unbuttoned. Procedures should be designed to account for this fragility and to avoid these actions. For example, an exhibit mount can be designed to serve as a support for transport. Then the object and mount can be handled as a unit and there is no need to remove the garment from the mount.

If possible, remove hazardous plastics from the objects, and if necessary, replace with nonhazardous substitutes. For example, cellulose nitrate collar stays should be removed from shirts to prevent acid decomposition of the adjacent textiles. These could be replaced with stable Mylar substitutes like those used in modern garments. Vinyl belts, most likely made from highly plasticized poly(vinyl chloride), should not be left on garments where they might cause plasticizer stains, but rather removed and stored out of contact with any textile.

Hazardous plastics that cannot be removed should be isolated from the rest of the textile by placing a barrier sheet between the offending plastic and the textile. For example, a sheet of Mylar or polyethylene could be slipped behind a plastic button, or between a vinyl belt and the dress on display, to isolate the plastic from the fabric. Polyethylene is softer and may be better to use than Mylar because its cut edges will be less likely to cut the threads holding the button.

Plastics that are fragile or become so as they age should be supported and protected from mishandling to prevent their being damaged. Plastics prone to damage by inappropriate environmental conditions should not be exposed to those conditions. (See Table 1.)

Embrittlement causes foam pads in garments to lose their resilience. When compressed, instead of bouncing back to their uncompressed shape, they remain deformed, either because the brittle and no longer rubbery foam has been bent into a new shape or because the cell walls of the foam actually shatter as the foam is deformed, destroying the foam structure. Care must be taken to ensure that old polyurethane foam padding is not deformed by compression or bending, such as when garments are folded during packing or when mounting on a mannequin. Consideration should be given to removing and replacing old hard and brittle polyurethane foam pads with new flexible ones of polyethylene that can stand the stresses that they might experience in a travelling exhibition.

Modern stretchy garments have lots of spandex, a polyurethane elastomer fibre. Raingear is often a laminated composite made of a fabric that has been coated with a polyurethane elastomer. These elastomers tend to become brittle as they age. Attempting to stretch a formerly stretchable spandex garment over a mannequin will break the elastomer fibres in the spandex. The stretch characteristics are destroyed and the fabric becomes baggy, rather than tightly form fitting. Bending, folding, or stretching the raingear will break the brittle elastomer coating, perhaps causing it to delaminate from the fabric substrate so that it hangs off the fabric in tatters.

Emissive plastics should be avoided in airtight enclosures. Their use should be permitted only for short periods of time, such as that required for transport, and only if there is an overriding reason for their use, such as the need for vibration dampening polyurethane foams in airtight crates that are to be transported through zones of widely varying relative humidity. The enclosure must be opened as soon as possible to allow dissipation of the volatile products.

If longer periods of airtight enclosure are anticipated, scavengers to absorb the reactive emitted volatile products should be sealed into the enclosure with the objects. Scavengers can be various products containing broad spectrum absorbers like activated charcoal, molecular sieves or zeolites, or specialty products containing specific compounds selected to target specific pollutants, such as silver tarnish protectants that absorb hydrogen sulfide. Some way of monitoring the buildup of noxious gaseous degradation products is most beneficial. For example, Fenn (1995) described indicators that detect nitrogen oxides emitted by degrading cellulose nitrate. An effective procedure is to combine the use of scavengers to control the emitted volatile compounds with indicators to monitor their build up, perhaps due to rapid increase in degradation rate or to exhaustion of scavenger.

When folding textiles, the parts of the garment should be arranged in such a way that there is maximum airflow past the emissive plastic components to sweep away the degradation gases. For example, do not bury cellulose nitrate buttons inside layers of folded material, but rather keep them exposed on top. Place scavengers as close as possible to the emissive plastic.

Where physical damage has occurred, such as staining by transferred material, it may be possible to remove the stain by washing or dry cleaning procedures. Stains and discolouration due to chemical reaction of the textile with substances from the plastic will need more aggressive chemical treatments and may not respond to any treatment. Similarly, physical and chemical damage will need interventive repair, and where there is loss of material, such as from acid catalyzed decomposition, replacement of material will be necessary.

Safe Plastics

The first step in determining whether a plastic is safe is to determine its chemical composition. For new plastic products, this information can be obtained from the supplier or manufacturer. If they will not supply the information, then avoid using the product. With knowledge of chemical composition in hand, selection decisions can be made. For older products and for plastics in objects, chemical analysis will probably be required. There are services available that can provide on-site nondestructive infrared spectroscopic analysis of plastics (Nilsen and Williams, 1997).

There are a number of resources that describe the relative merits of various plastics and products made for them.

General discussions of polymers and their properties are given by Horie (1987) and Baker (1995). Horie's book is especially valuable for its extensive discussion of polymers and gives many examples of their appropriate and inappropriate use in conservation applications. Problems with additives in plastics are discussed by Williams (1993).

The Department of Conservation at the British Museum has been active for decades in the evaluation of materials for storage and display of museum objects. Lee and Thickett (1996) recently published a compendium of methods used to test materials for their potential to emit harmful volatiles and their properties of importance for materials in direct contact with objects (mainly pH). This paper contains appendices with lists of materials that have passed their tests and are considered to be safe, including fabrics, paints, foams, plastic films and adhesives.

It would be nice to produce a list of plastics that are chemically stable then try to find products made from these plastics, with the appropriate form to do the job required. Current practice is much more along the lines of looking for, or serendipitously finding, products of appropriate form then requesting information about the chemical composition to determine whether they are appropriate for conservation applications. Different types of objects and different applications impose different requirements on the exhibit and transport materials. Comprehensive lists cannot

Table 2
Safe and Unsafe Plastics for Museum Use

Plastics regarded as generally safe for museum use

polyethylene and other polyolefins such as polypropylene
polycarbonate
polystyrene
acrylics
polytetrafluoroethylene (Teflon)
polyester, poly(ethylene terephthalate)

Plastics known to cause problems

nitrocellulose	Problems with early manufacturing processes resulted in a variable, often highly unstable product. Though the modern product is more consistent, it still cannot be recommended for use in conservation.
cellulose acetate	Some examples may be stable, but others have been known to release acetic acid. Test before use.
poly(vinyl chloride) (PVC)	This and other chlorinated hydrocarbons can release hydrochloric acid, and often contain volatile additives.
poly(vinyl acetate)	Some samples may be stable, but others, especially some emulsions, release acetic acid. Test before use.
poly(vinyl alcohol)	Prepared from poly(vinyl acetate), and subject to the same provisions.
polyurethanes	These are inherently thermally and photolytically unstable, and always contain additives.

be produced. However, plastics at each end (good and bad) of the suitability spectrum have been identified and listed.

A relatively short list of safe and unsafe materials was published by Padfield et al. (1982). This list in slightly modified form was republished by Erhardt (1991) for construction of packing crates for transport of paintings, and by Von Endt et al. (1995) for constructing storage cases. These articles have good discussions of how products are evaluated for safety. Their list of plastics and comments are reproduced in Table 2.

Whenever possible, choose plastics that are in the safe list and avoid those that cause problems.

Conclusions

Plastics can damage textiles, whether the plastic is a component of the textile or is an auxiliary exhibit and transport product. Damage depends on whether or not the plastic is in direct contact with the textile, and whether the plastic and the textile are in an airtight, or well ventilated, enclosure. It is imperative to determine which condition exists for each plastic-textile combination, because the selection of plastic products or preventive actions that are required to protect the textiles are affected by whichever situation prevails. Typical forms of deterioration that plastics suffer are listed, examples of the type of damage caused to textiles by plastics are given, and safe and unsafe plastics to use when making exhibit and storage appliances are listed. From these lists and examples, the risks that plastics in textile collections are exposed to, and the damage that these plastics may cause to the textiles, can be predicted and evaluated, and appropriate preventive conservation measures taken.

References

Baker, Mary T. "Synthetic Polymers," *Storage of Natural History Collections: A Preventive Conservation Approach*, Carolyn L. Rose, Catharine A. Hawks, and Hugh H. Genoways, eds. Society for the Preservation of Natural History Collections, 1995, pp. 305-323.

Erhardt, David. "Art in Transit: Material Considerations," *Art in Transit: Studies in the Transport of Paintings*, Marion F. Mecklenburg, ed. Washington: National Gallery of Art, 1991, pp. 25-34.

Fenn, Julia. "The Cellulose Nitrate Time Bomb: Using Sulphonephthalein Indicators to Evaluate Storage Strategies," *From Marble to Chocolate. The Conservation of Modern Sculpture*, Jackie Heuman, ed. Tate Gallery Conference, 18-20 September 1995, pp. 87-92.

Horie, C.V. *Materials for Conservation: Organic Consolidants, Adhesives and Coatings*. Butterworths Series in Conservation and Museology. London: Butterworths & Co. (Publishers) Ltd., 1987.

Lee, L.R. and D. Thickett. *Selection of Materials for the Storage or Display of Museum Objects*. British Museum Occasional Paper 111. London: The British Museum, 1996, 54 pages.

Nilsen, Lisa and R. Williams Scott. "Identification of Plastics In-Situ with a Portable Infrared Spectrometer," *CCI Newsletter*, no. 19 (March 1997), pp. 8-10.

Padfield, Tim, David Erhardt, and Walter Hopwood. "Trouble in Store," *Science and Technology in the Service of Conservation. Preprints of the IIC Congress 1982 in Washington*, N.S. Brommelle and G. Thomson, eds. London: IIC, 1982, pp. 24-27.

Von Endt, David W., W. David Erhardt, and Walter R. Hopwood. "Evaluating Materials Used for Constructing Storage Cases," *Storage of Natural History Collections: A Preventive Conservation Approach*, Carolyn L. Rose, Catharine A. Hawks, and Hugh H. Genoways, eds. Society for the Preservation of Natural History Collections, 1995, pp. 269-282.

Williams, R. Scott. "Composition Implications of Plastic Artifacts: A Survey of Additives and Their Effects on the Longevity of Plastics," *Saving the Twentieth Century: The Conservation of Modern Materials*, David W. Grattan, ed. Ottawa: Canadian Conservation Institute, 1993, pp. 135-152.

Résumé

Préoccupations au sujet des matières plastiques durant l'exposition et le transport des textiles

De nombreux textiles (y compris les textiles plats, costumes et accessoires) fabriqués au XXe siècle contiennent des éléments en plastique. Les plastiques peuvent réagir avec les composantes textiles et autres de l'œuvre. L'article traite des réactions qui peuvent se produire durant l'exposition et le transport relativement aux propriétés inhérentes initiales des plastiques et celles qu'ils acquièrent avec l'âge. Les produits en plastique modernes sont couramment utilisés dans la fabrication des dispositifs d'exposition et de transport des expositions itinérantes. Les plastiques non appropriés sont susceptibles de réagir avec les objets textiles et de provoquer des dommages d'ordre physique (p.ex. taches, abrasion), chimique (p. ex. désintégration par hydrolyse acide) et mécanique (p. ex. ruptures et déchirures). Les propriétés physico-chimiques et les caractéristiques de vieillissement de certains produits plastiques font l'objet d'un exposé général, accompagné de lignes directrices de sélection des produits plastiques convenant aux textiles.

The Lighting Decision

Stefan Michalski

Canadian Conservation Institute
1030 Innes Road
Ottawa, ON K1A 0M5 Canada
Tel.: (613) 998-3721
E-mail: stefan_michalski@pch.gc.ca

Abstract

Recent guidelines from the Canadian Conservation Institute (CCI) on the lighting of artifacts suggest an explicit balance between visibility and vulnerability. Visibility requirements reduce to one benchmark, 50 lux, and three possible reasons for increments in this benchmark: for low contrast details (up to x3), for dark objects (up to x3), and for old age (up to x3). The source of these simplified factors is reviewed, and their application to viewing textiles is explored. Vulnerability in textiles ranges from the very high to the very low. This range, and how one can know what one has, is reviewed. The CCI microspot fibre optics fading test offers a solution for textiles.

1. Is There Anything New Under the Sun?

The fundamental lighting dilemma, visibility versus vulnerability, is the same today as it has been for centuries. It was never unique to museums, housekeepers have always known it. Can anything new be said?

Conservators can decide on intelligent negotiation rather than their 50 lux mantra. Although 50 lux can and will be justified as the fundamental benchmark, we must recover the flexibility Thomson intended, a flexibility that can bend towards more exposure, and bend towards less exposure, as circumstances demand.

Vulnerability data is not so much new as unused by our profession. It is not an exact or easy science, but it is the best answer to the most important question: how much damage will occur how soon for what lighting. A direct microscopic test for important artifacts is suggested for definitive predictions.

Visibility, which has often been taken for granted by our profession, can draw on a new model from lighting research. It will explain the legitimate complaints aimed at museum lighting, and it will explain why bright lighting by scholars and conservators is not always, just sometimes, professional hypocrisy.

A summary table of this "new" lighting decision has been developed at CCI, shown as Table 1. Note that there are no longer broad generalizations across artifact categories such as "50 lux for paper and textiles" and "200 lux for oil paintings."

2. Lighting and Visibility of Artifacts

2.1 Visibility and Colour Arguments

As shown in Figure 1, the transition from monochromatic night vision to colour vision is completely finished by about 2 lux (Figure 1). The exact nature of this transition has only recently been clarified.[1] In the 1961 article that established 50 lux as a museum benchmark, Thomson argued on the basis of common experience, and noted similar minimums in French and Japanese recommendations from thirty years earlier.[2] Thus conservation argued that at 50 lux we see well enough, particularly colours. Together with the widely invoked 1956 study by Kruithof that showed viewers preferred warm (2800°K) sources at low intensities,[3] the die was cast for museum lighting.

In 1973, Crawford showed that the boundary at which our eye lost its ability to see small colour differences did indeed occur near 2 lux[4] (Figure 2). By the 1987 Bristol Lighting conference, Boyce[5] could cite more colour discrimination data[6] that showed maximum performance by about 10 lux (Figure 2). Loe[7] described data on viewer

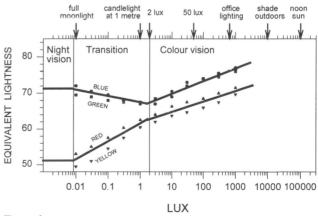

Figure 1.

Table 1

	Basic Rules for Lighting	To Adjust for Visibility	To Adjust for Vulnerability
If total control of lighting is possible For rooms with total control of display lighting, where object lifetimes must be maximized.	**For all organic materials, and those inorganic materials that are light or UV sensitive:** Light: 50 lux, only when viewers present UV: less than 10 µW/lm Note: only those under 30 years of age will be content, and only when they are viewing low contrast coloured surfaces without low contrast detail. **For all inorganic materials not sensitive to light or UV:** Light level unlimited, but lighting must not raise the surface temperature of the artifact more than 5°C above ambient air temperature. As a simple guide, the lightbeam should not noticeably warm your hands.	For low contrast details............ up to x3 For dark surfaces............ up to x3 For older viewers............ up to x3 Limited time, complex search............ up to x3 For combinations of the above, multiply by each of the factors in turn. For example, if low contrast details in a dark surface are to be seen quickly and well by a 65 year old, then the calculation is: (50 lux) x 3 x 3 x 3 x 3 = 4050 lux, i.e., about 4,000 lux. In general, an older conservator, curator, scholar, or connoisseur, making a careful inspection of a dark artifact, but given ample time for the task, needs (50 lux) x 3 x 3 x 3 = 1350 lux. It makes sense to limit such activities by senior experts to brief periods of time, and to provide task lighting that can be adjusted to various angles. Only indirect daylight, fluorescent lights, and special cool incandescent lights can achieve such intensities without risk of overheating the object.	Determine the light sensitivities of the colorants in the artifacts. Given that determination, the following actions will reduce the rate of colour loss to a maximum of about one perceptible step per ten years, which will give almost complete colour loss in 300-500 years. To extend lifetimes beyond this will require proportionally greater reductions than those given below. **Fugitive colorants: (ISO 1,2,3)** Reduce all long-term adjustments for visibility to a total of x3, i.e., 150 lux maximum, and display for only 10% of the time. (Brief periods of inspection should not exceed 1500 lux for 1% of the time or equivalent). **Intermediate colorants: (ISO 4,5,6)** Reduce all long-term adjustments for visibility to a total of x3, i.e., 150 lux maximum for permanent display. Any display at higher visibility levels will have to be proportionally reduced in time. (Brief periods of inspection should not exceed 1500 lux for 10% of the time, or equivalent). **Durable colorants: (ISO 7,8,+)** Reduce all long-term adjustments for visibility to a total of x30, i.e., 1500 lux maximum. (Brief periods of inspection should not exceed 4500 lux). **Permanent or absent colorants:** Given slow yellowing and disintegration of organic materials due to trace UV and unavoidable violet and blue light, follow guidelines for durable colorants above.
If partial control of lighting is possible For rooms with limited control of lighting (historic houses, offices, homes), where object lifetimes must be maximized.	**For all organic materials, and those inorganic materials that are light or UV sensitive:** Light: Avoid the range 1,000-100,000 lux, i.e., bright electric lights and daylight near windows UV: less than 75 µW/lm **For all inorganic materials not sensitive to light or UV:** Avoid direct sun on the artifact, especially if it has brittle components, such as aged enamel .	Move artifacts, especially those with significant details, into locations that give acceptable lighting for whomever is meant to see the artifact.	Determine the light sensitivities of the colorants in the artifacts. Given that determination, the following actions will reduce the rate of colour loss to a maximum of about one perceptible step per ten years, which will give almost complete colour loss in 300-500 years. To extend lifetimes beyond this will require proportionally greater reductions than those given below. **Fugitive colorants: (ISO 1,2,3)** Place these away from any locations that exceed 150 lux average over a ten hour day, and display only 10% of the time. If average intensity exceeds 150 lux, exhibit proportionally less than 10% of the time. **Intermediate colorants: (ISO 4,5,6)** Place these artifacts away from any locations that exceed 150 lux average over a ten hour day. If average intensity exceeds 150 lux, then exhibit proportionally less. **Durable colorants: (ISO 7,8,+)** Place these artifacts away from any locations that exceed 1500 lux average over a ten hour day. If average intensity exceeds 1500 lux, then exhibit proportionally less. **Permanent or absent colorants:** Given slow yellowing and disintegration of organic materials due to trace UV and unavoidable violet and blue light, follow guidelines for durable colorants above.

Artifacts and Lighting: *Visibility* vs. *Vulnerability*

Version 3.1, Stefan Michalski, Canadian Conservation Institute, Ottawa, May, 1997

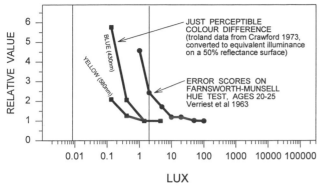

Figure 2.

satisfaction with lighting in a gallery. He fitted a soft curve with a knee near 200 lux, but one can also fit a sharp transition curve, and conclude that most of the satisfaction is reached by 50 lux. Thus 50 lux was proven to be well in excess of what was needed for colour perception, but it was a bare minimum for viewer comfort.

Scholarly dissatisfaction with 50 lux in museums has usually focussed on the "quality" of colours, or invoked the quagmires of historic or artistic "intent." Such dissatisfaction can often be traced simply to poor colour rendering sources, or competing colour temperatures across a single space, or poor gallery design for adaptation of the eye. On the other hand, there has been clarification of at least one real intensity effect: coloured materials are perceived as "brighter" in brighter light.[1] That is, their ranking relative to a noncoloured (grey) scale increases (equivalent lightness, in Figure 1). This effect may explain what some artists mean when they state that the colours in their works need lots of light, or conversely, when others state that their colours should not be "washed out" by too much light.[8]

Overlooked in the colour perception arguments, however, was the fact that the data concerned large patches of colour, viewed invariably by young students. Common experience tells us that seeing the details in our face is not just a little different with bright light but radically clearer, especially as we age.

2.2 Visibility, the Lighting Engineer, and the CIE
Unlike conservators, lighting engineers have always considered details as the primary criterion for visibility, not colours. By the 1970s, enough was known about the perception of detail for the Illuminating Engineering Society of North America (IESNA) to consider 50-100 lux as suitable only for "simple orientation for short temporary visits." "Visual tasks of medium contrast or small size" needed 500-1,000 lux while "tasks of extremely low contrast and small size" needed 10,000-20,000 lux.[9] In the 1996 IESNA *Museum and Art Gallery Lighting: A Recommended Practice*,[10] however, the traditional conservation rule of 50 lux for textiles, paper, etc.

appears without explanation. The sole discussion of visibility states "there must be sufficient light on objects to make them visible to all visitors."

The rigorous basis for any discussion of visibility has its most recent version in the 1981 CIE publication *An Analytic Model for Describing the Influence of Lighting Parameters upon Visual Performance*.[11] The key concept, "visual performance," measures exactly what we mean by artifact visibility - the accuracy with which we see the artifact in all its details, as we stroll through an exhibition. CCI has considered the CIE model, and extracted the simplified rules shown under Adjustments for Visibility in Table 1. Explanations will be given in sections 2.3 to 2.7, all of which derive from the CIE publication.[11]

2.3 Contrast, the RCS Curve, and Visual Performance
As light intensity increases, we can see details of lower contrast. The "relative contrast sensitivity" (RCS) curve plots this threshold for a simple dot, unambiguously presented in our line of sight. The curve was known by Thomson, but it did not offer optimistic transitions at low intensities, instead it climbed to full sunshine. (Contrast C and the RCS curves are actually in terms of luminance, but for our purposes reflectance (R) will do. Thus $C=|Rd-Rb|/Rb$, where d is detail and b is background.)

The CIE model begins with the RCS curve, but incorporates further studies on its deterioration with viewer age. The model then considers studies on dynamic viewing of clusters of details, where the difficulty of the viewer's task (D) can be increased by reducing the object exposure time, increasing the spread of the cluster, or asking for more information about the cluster. Visual performance is then the accuracy with which a detail of a certain size is seen (noted) as compared to the maximum accuracy possible for that detail when viewed by a young viewer, at maximum contrast, with maximum light (essentially full sunlight) and no task difficulty.

2.4 Visibility at the Traditional 50 Lux
In Figure 3, all curves are for moderately fine detail: 4 minutes arc, or 1.2 mm viewed at 1 metre. This is equivalent to the weave detail in a textile of 8 threads per cm (20 threads per inch) viewed at 1 m, or the period at the end of this sentence (0.6 mm) held at arms length (50 cm).

In Figure 3, the heavy black line is visual performance for a viewer of age 25 (A25), on a low difficulty task (D30), and details of moderate contrast 0.5 (C0.5). For the textile example, it means the viewer is given ample time, and the interstices reflect 0.5 as much as the fabric. The CIE suggests a lighting design target of 80% of maximum performance (at full daylight) for a particular visual task. This is the diamond on the knee of the curve. If the artifact is of intermediate reflectance (R=50%) then the lower lux axis applies. Reading the lower lux axis, the diamond is near

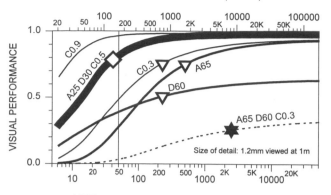

LUX IF DARK OBJECT (R=15%)

LUX IF MIDDLE BRIGHTNESS OBJECT (R=50%)

Figure 3.

50 lux. Thus we can confirm that the traditional benchmark of 50 lux gives good visibility for moderately fine details of moderate contrast for a young viewer given ample time.

2.5 Visibility Rule for Low Contrast Details

In Figure 3, the two thin solid curves differ from the benchmark conditions (A25, D30, C0.5) only in terms of contrast. The C0.9 line is for high contrast, such as the ink dot at the end of this sentence (ink about R=10%, paper about R=90%). The C0.3 line is for low contrast, such as the textile weave example if the interstices reflect 0.7 as much as the fabric. Its knee at 80% of maximum, marked by a triangle, reads 250 lux on the lower axis, so five times 50 lux.

Lower contrast (or finer) details are possible, but for this size detail, C0.3 is the lowest contrast that gives a maximum visual performance near 1.0 for full daylight. It seems unreasonable to ask for a higher standard than those soft details that we see perfectly in sunlight in our youth. CCI has opted for only part of the x5 factor needed to reach 80% performance on such details: a cautious "up to x3" for low contrast details.

2.6 Visibility Rule for Darkness of the Object

In Figure 3, the lower lux axis applies to intermediate brightness objects. The upper lux axis applies to dark objects, specifically R=15%. Thus this axis reads just over three times the light compared to the lower axis, and gives rise to a rule of "up to x3" for dark objects. Dark browns, dark blues, blacks, may fall as low as R=5%, and would argue for x10 lighting, but purposefully dark colours, such as textiles, are not meant to be seen in detail. Fortunately, inadvertently dark artifacts such as tarnished coins are not vulnerable to light, so plenty of light makes sense.

2.7 Visibility Rule for Age of the Viewer

In Figure 3, the dotted line gives performance for the same conditions as the thick benchmark curve, except that the viewer is age 65, rather than 25. The maximum plateau

still reaches close to 1.0, but the triangle at 80% maximum performance requires almost 500 lux on the lower axis, ten times that for the 25 year old.

This is not due to poor focus, which is assumed corrected. Part of the reason is that the fluid in our eye yellows, so that by age 65 we need four times the light to get the same light to our retina as in our youth. This is the ageing of the eye as camera. The eye as processor, as a dynamic searching system, also ages, hence the total lighting adjustment of ten times to maintain equal visual performance on clusters of details.

As noted in the CIE manual, it is unclear to what extent older viewers can compensate for their ageing visual performance. The simplest strategy is to spend longer looking. Much more difficult to assess are compensations due to experience. Thus a textile connoisseur may fill in details that a neophyte does not recognize, but does not need to!

For a cautious rule "up to x3" is assigned to viewer age, but it must be recognized as only a partial answer to "equal visual access." Museums may need to consider "bright light tours" for seniors only, or for openings with ageing critics and executives.

2.8 Visibility Rule for Limited Time, Complex Search

In Figure 3, the dashed line marked D60 is performance for the same conditions as the thick benchmark curve, except for increased task difficulty. Note that the maximum performance plateau has dropped to 0.6. The 80% knee at maximum performance, marked by a triangle, reads 250 lux on the bottom axis, five times 50 lux.

As noted under the rule for age, visual performance involves not just the eye as camera, but as a scanning processor too. In viewing artifacts with arrays of many details, irregularities, repairs, or defects, we need much more light to see them as readily as if they were pointed out to us.

A cautious lighting rule of "up to x3" has been assigned for complex search in a limited time.

2.9 Visibility and the Ethics of Maximum Adjustment

In Figure 3, the effect of age, difficulty and low contrast together is shown by the lowest curve. Note the low maximum. By reading the upper lux axis, we obtain the additional factor due to dark objects. To reach 80% of maximum shown by the star requires about 8,000 lux, so 160 times 50 lux. By using the simplified CCI rules, all four together yield 3x3x3x3=81, which is a cautious half of the 160 factor.

Senior scholars and conservators are older, and their visual tasks on artifacts are usually complex search of subtle details, but they can take their time, move closer, and use magnifiers. If we consider just the adjustments for low contrast, dark surfaces, and aged viewer, then 3x3x3=27, so about 1350 lux gives excellent inspection for all ages. It is no surprise, therefore, that careful inspection has traditionally meant moving to a window to use daylight, or that the IESNA recommends 1,000-2,000 lux for "tasks of low contrast or very small size."

In the adjustments for vulnerability in the CCI guidelines, Table 1, it is suggested that study exposure never exceed display exposure. If display of an artifact with a fugitive colorant is controlled to an exposure of 10% of the time at 150 lux, then inspection at 1500 lux should not exceed 1% of the time. If a conservation lab examining or treating this important artifact once every hundred years takes a year from start to finish, and the artifact languishes in labs at 750 lux, they will be responsible for as much light damage as half a century of controlled display. If they want to avoid hypocritical use of the artifact as lab decor, they must use opaque covers whenever possible.

2.10 Visibility and the Problem of Large Artifacts

With large objects, such as tapestries, the viewer stands back to see the whole thing. On the other hand, to see the authentic solid thing means to see its details. To see both together requires lighting similar to daylight. This phenomenon underlies the undeniable feel of daylight, the simultaneous experience of vast panorama and overwhelming detail. Museums must abandon such experience for light-sensitive materials, of course, but they must also recognize it as a desirable option for artifacts such as large metal and stone sculpture. There will, of course, be light adaptation problems to solve.

2.11 Visibility and Raking Lighting

It is an old lighting trick to enhance surface detail by raking the lighting from one direction, not at extreme disfiguring angles, but at 30°- 45°. This can be understood now in terms of increasing contrast (C) of the detail. Part of the increased contrast is simply the creation of shadows, part is decreased reflectance to our eye for surfaces tilted away from the light. In textiles the interstices gain in darkness and apparent width, so weave becomes more visible. Contrast enhancement is stronger for point light sources than area sources. Raking light does nothing, however, for design details such as different coloured yarns.

2.12 Visibility and Movement

For banners and costumes, movement of the fabric was intrinsic to the original visual experience. Movement not only gave rise to changes in conformation of the textile, but all the raking light phenomena outlined earlier also became dynamic for both weave and drape. For textiles with sheen, highlights become dynamic. And what worked well for sheen worked spectacularly for glitter. (Sheen and glitter elevate contrast to values many times above 1.0). One could argue that such fabrics were developed expressly

for the purpose of intensifying dynamic visibility in low intensity candlelight.

Overall, solid artifacts at low light levels will be seen in more detail if there is movement, such as slow rotation of a mannikin under directional lighting, or rotation of the lighting itself. Such movement also reduces the uneven fading of draped textiles due to static lighting, and reduces exposure per unit area by about one half.

3. Vulnerability of Textiles to Lighting

3.1 Wavelength Dependence and Ultraviolet (UV)

Light sources emit light (visible radiation) and UV (ultraviolet radiation). In practical summary, UV yellows, weakens, embrittles, or disintegrates organic materials such as textiles. Light is incapable of most such damage. Light and UV fade colorants, but light is 10 to 50 times more plentiful than UV in light sources. Thus if light is capable of fading the colorant at all, as it is for most fugitive colorants, then it dominates fading. If light is not capable of fading the colorant, as it is not for durable colorants, then UV dominates the fading by default.

In a more precise argument, Figures 4 and 5 compile the relevant damage spectra. The border between UV and light lies between 380 nm and 400 nm. Our young eye sees out to about 380 nm, hence the glass industry prefers this boundary for calculating %UV transmittance. The museum world prefers 400 nm as a border, since UV type damage is still strong in the 380-400 nm band. Except for the curious yellowing blip at 520 nm, the wool data in Figure 4 is typical for paper, wood and oil media too: UV makes yellow colorant, and blue light bleaches it. The essential difference between the spectra in Figures 4 and 5 is obvious: disintegration and yellowing (Figure 4) follow steep, ascending lines in the UV/violet region, fading of colorants (Figure 5) follow flat or wavy lines across most wavelengths of light.

Researchers, starting with lighting engineer Harrison in 1953,[12] and continuing with others such as Krochman,[13]

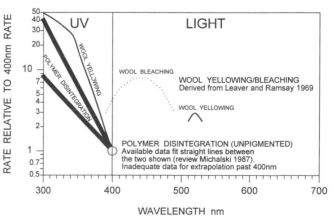

Figure 4.

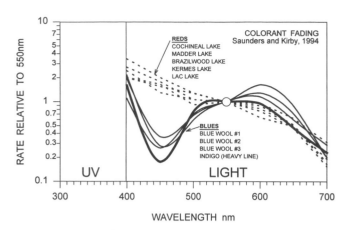

Figure 5.

have calculated weighting functions using straight lines such as these in Figure 5. (The equation form: Damage rate at Xnm = Damage rate at 400nm*10^(400nm-Xnm)/Cnm, where C is typically 100nm.) This function is then used to calculate a relative damage rating for the spectrum of a light source. These light source damage factors are valid only for the types of damage associated with UV, and most of this damage is controlled by UV filtration. These "lamp damage ratings" must not be applied to colour fading by light. Saunders and Kirby[14] have shown convincingly that while red and yellow dyes (in lake pigments) may be slightly more vulnerable to blue light than longer wavelengths, blue dyes reverse this rule (Figure 5).

3.2 Lightfastness Data
The most widely used international lightfastness scale is the ISO Blue Wools. Some of the rankings of historic textile colorants on this scale have been compiled in Table 2.[15-18] A few useful generalizations emerge from the literature. A given dye is more fugitive on silk and cotton than on wool, typically one or two steps worse on the scale. A pale tint (as new) is half or one step more fugitive than its standard depth shade, while a heavy dyeing may be one or two steps more durable. The mordant is very influential, one cannot estimate a dye's lightfastness without knowing it.

Unlike a new pale shade, a pale remnant of an already faded colour can be much more durable than the original colour. This small mercy comes about since a colourant forms a range of lightfastnesses so that the most fugitive components fade first, leaving the least fugitive components as the remnant. Kashiwagi and Yamasaki[18] have shown final fading of very fugitive dyes changes little from initial rates, but some dyes rated ISO#3 initially can jump three or more steps at final stages of fade. Table 2 measures this effect.

The practical problem for prediction of light damage in terms of exposure is the conversion of these lightfastness rankings to absolute sensitivities to light. This correlation has been the subject of much debate, and there is no

doubt it is inherently messy for many reasons, but the approximate correlation derived by Michalski in his review,[19] and as used in the UV+ scale on the CCI *Light Damage Slide Rule*, has been used for the scale in Table 2. This correlation is an idealized fit which spaces all eight standards evenly (dose in Mlx h to fade ISO blue wool number # to GS4 is: dose=0.22x2.43^(#-1). This correlation is for daylight through glass (or xenon arc or fluorescent lamps that approximate the same), since almost all lightfastness data has been collected with this UV-rich spectrum.

In a museum that cares about light damage, one can assume UV filtration, so an exposure equivalence to the Blue Wool ratings for UV filtered light is needed. This equivalence, as used in Table 2, and in the UV-scale on the CCI *Light Damage Slide Rule* is based on the data of MacLaren on 400 direct dyes and the ISO Blue Wools themselves,[20] as well as the confirming trend of other data on historic colourants. The data show that ISO#1 and equivalent colours are helped very little, but each subsequent ISO number is helped more and more. The result is a dose increase of about x3 between each ISO step, and a total span of 1000:1 between fugitive ISO#1, such as many greens, yellows and mauves on silk, and durable ISO#8, such as a heavy indigo on wool. This is the reason banners and ribbons fade early in military museums, while navy blue on wool seems to last longer than the wool itself.

3.3 Vulnerability Assessment by Analysis
Vulnerability analysis can be historical or chemical. History of textile technology will tell a knowledgeable curator or conservator whether a colour is likely to be one of the well known natural dyes, such as indigo or madder, or one of a group of known fugitive dyes, such as the anilines. For some colours, such as yellow, mauve, and green, the major historic dyes are all fugitive (Table 2), so analysis is only needed if one is hoping to find a more durable synthetic colourant. It is important for all chemical analyses to be shared, so that the pool of historic knowledge increases.

3.4 Vulnerability Assessment by Direct Testing
For important artifacts, one may be looking for unequivocal predictions that analysis cannot provide. Besides, one may also be looking for more powerful evidence with which to influence disbelievers. A direct fading test of a tiny spot on the artifact will satisfy both. Textile artifacts in particular lend themselves to this approach, since colours can always be found in unobtrusive areas, such as the back of the textile, inside a hem or seam, even the back of a yarn. CCI has developed a simple technique using a standard fibre optic lamp that delivers about 200,000 lux.[21] A metal mask with a 2 mm hole is used to reduce the spot to even less than the fibre optic bundle diameter.

Table 2 — Lightfastness Ratings of the Natural Dyes on Wool, Cotton, and Silk

The center of each dye phrase is aligned with its published rating on the ISO blue wool standards, either 1 to 8, or midpoints, e.g. 1-2. Sources of data:

(PL): Padfield and Landhi, 1966, ref. 17. Daylight through glass. Their data table II has been abridged: Their rating "1-2" has been set as 2 , their "4-5" as 4, since this agrees with their exposures for those columns, i.e., double the GS4 exposure of this table.

(D): Duff, Sinclair and Stirling 1977, or Grierson, Duff, and Sinclair,1985, ref. 18,19. Microscal lamp, simulation of daylight through glass.

(KY): Kashiwagi and Yamasaki, 1982, ref 20. Daylight through glass. Abbreviations: COT= Cotton. INIT= Initial fade rate, FINAL= Fade rate after significant fading has already taken place.

Only single dyes under "daylight" reported here, see original papers for some mixtures of these dyes, some studies with fluorescent lamps.

Mordants: [AL: Alum] [ALCL: aluminum chloride] [ALA: aluminum acetate] [SN: tin] [FE: iron] [CU: Copper]

Color Index Natural Dye number given, if known, e.g. R8. (BR:Brown, R:Red, O:Orange, Y:Yellow, G:Green, B:Blue, BK:Black, PB:Pigment Blue). If not, then dominant constituents from authors (KY), or H. Schweppe, 1993 *Handbuche der Naturfarbstoffe*. A: Atranorin, C:Chrysanthemin, F:Fraxin, L:Luteolin, M:Myrecetin, Q:Quercetin (major but not sole component of Y10), S:Shikonin see Colour Index 75535, SC: Sambucyanin, T:Tannins

TIME FOR NOTICEABLE FADE AT 50 LUX: (1 Year=3000 hours=150 klx h. Noticeable=GS4. Full fade takes about 30 such steps.)

Daylight through window glass:

1	2	3	4	5	6	7	8
1.5y	4y	10y	25y	60y	140y	340y	800y

Light with all UV removed: (Average behaviour. Some dyes benefit less from UV removal, so the scale above can be used as worst case.)

| 2y | 6y | 20y | 60y | 200y | 600y | 1500y | 4000y |

BROWNS

WOOL (PL): LIMAWOOD.R24[CU] SANDERSWOOD[CU,FE] VENTILAGO.O1[CU,FE] CAMWOOD.R22[CU,FE] BARWOOD.R22[CU,FE]
{COCHINEAL.R4[CU,FE]; MORINDA.R18[CU,FE]; MANG KUDU.R19[CU,FE]}
{CHAY ROOT.R6[CU,FE]; MUNJEET.R16[CU,FE]; MADDER.R8[CU,FE]}
{LAC DYE.R25[CU,FE]}
{Dyes in categories 5-7 are not distinguished in the PL study}

WOOL (D): CROTTLE LICHEN.A

REDS

WOOL (PL): LIMAWOOD.R24[AL,SN] COCHINEAL.R4[AL] LAC DYE.R25[AL]
ORCHIL.R28 BARWOOD.R22[SN] KERMES.R3[AL] MUNJEET.R16[AL]
BARWOOD.R22[AL] SANDERSWOOD.R22[SN]
SANDERSWOOD.R22[AL] CAMWOOD.R22[AL,SN]
VENTILAGO.O1[AL,SN]
{COCHINEAL.R4[SN]; KERMES.R3[SN]; LAC DYE.R25[SN]}
{MADDER.R8[AL]; TURKEY RED.R8}
{Dyes in categories 5-7 are not distinguished in the PL study}

WOOL (D): COCHINEAL.R4[SN] ALIZARIN.R8[AL]
LAC DYE.R25[SN] ALIZARIN.R8[SN]
LADYS BEDSTRAW.R14[AL] LADYS BEDSTRAW.R14[SN]

COTTON AND SILK (KY): COCHINEAL[SN]R4COT.INIT. SILK.INIT COT,SILK FINAL
MADDER[AL]R8COT.INIT. SILK INIT COT. FINAL SILK FINAL
SAPPANWOOD.R24[AL]COT,SILK INIT. COTTON,SILK FINAL
SAPPANWOOD.R24[ALCL]COT.SILK INIT. COT.SILK FINAL
SAFFLOWER.R26/COT,SILK INIT. COT,SILK FINAL

ORANGES, YELLOWS

WOOL (PL): WELD.Y2[AL] WELD.Y2[SN]
ANNATO.O4 KAMALA.O2[AL] MORINDA.R18
SAFFRON.Y6 JAK WOOD.Y11[AL,SN]
TURMERIC.Y3 OLD FUSTIC.Y11[AL,SN]
TESU.Y28[AL] QUERCITRON.Y10[AL,SN]
GARDENIA.Y6 TESU.Y28[SN]
COSCINIUM.Y18 PERSIAN BERRIES.Y13[AL,SN]
EVODIA
YOUNG FUSTIC.BR1[AL] YOUNG FUSTIC.BR1[SN]
{MUNJEET.R16[SN]; MORINDA.R18[SN]; SOPHORA.Y10[SN]}
{MADDER.R8[SN]; CHAY ROOT R6[SN]}
{Dyes in categories 5-7 are not distinguished in the PL study}

WOOL (D): PERSIAN BERRIES.Y13[SN]
LING HEATHER TIPS.Q.M[AL]
OLD FUSTIC.Y11[SN]

SILK (PL): KAMALA

COTTON AND SILK (KY): OAK.F[FE]COT.SILK INIT SILK FINAL, COT>8
MYRICA.M[CU]COT.SILK INIT COT.SILK FINAL
MYRICA.M[FE]COT.SILK INIT COT.SILK FINAL
PAGODA TREE.Y10[ALA]SILK INIT COT.INIT COT.FINAL SILK FINAL
MARYGOLD.Y27?[SN]COT.SILK FINAL COT.SILK FINAL
AMUR CORK.Y18[ALA]COT.SILK INIT COT.SILK FINAL

BLUES, GREENS

WOOL (PL): LOGWOOD.BK1[AL] {INDIGO.B2; PRUSSIAN BLUE.PB27}
WOOL (D): SULPHONATED INDIGO.B2 INDIGO.B2
LING HEATHER TIPS.Q.M[AL] PRIVET BERRIES.BK5[AL/FE] SEAWEED[CU] LING HEATHER TIPS.Q.M[AL/FE/CU] FOXGLOVE.L[AL/FE]
COTTON (PL): LO KAV.G1
COTTON AND SILK (KY): INDIGO.B2 SILK INIT COT.INIT SILK FINAL, COT>8

PURPLES

WOOL (PL): LOGWOOD.BK1[SN]
WOOL (D): ELDER BERRIES.C.SC
CUDBEAR LICHEN.L
COTTON AND SILK (KY): SHIKONE.S[ALCL]COT.SILK INIT COT.SILK FINAL
SHIKONE.S[SN]COT.INIT SILK INIT COT.SILK FINAL

BLACKS

WOOL (PL): LIMAWOOD.R24[FE] LOGWOOD.BK1[FE]
WOOL (D): WATER LILY ROOTS.T[FE]

Endnotes

1. Ikeda, M., C.C. Huang, and S. Ashizawa. "Equivalent lightness of colored objects at illuminances from the scotopic to the photopic level," *Color Research and Application* (1989), pp. 198-206.

2. Thomson, G. "A new look at colour rendering, level of illumination, and protection from ultraviolet radiation in museum lighting," *Studies in Conservation*, vol. 6 (1961), pp. 49-70.

3. Kruithof, A.A., and J.L. Ouweltjes. "Colour and colour rendering of tubular fluorescent lamps," *Philips Technical Review*, vol. 18 (1956), pp. 249-261.

4. Crawford, B.H. "Just perceptible colour differences in relation to level of illumination," *Studies in Conservation*, vol. 18 (1973), pp. 159-166.

5. Boyce, P. "Visual acuity, colour discrimination, and light level," *Lighting in Museums, Galleries and Historic Houses*, London: UK Institute for Conservation and the Museums Association, 1987, pp. 50-57.

6. Verriest, G., A. Buyssens, and R. Vanderdonck. "Étude quantitative de l'effet qu'exerce sur les résultats de quelques tests de la discrimination chromatique une diminution non sélective du niveau d'un éclairage C," *Revue Optique,* vol. 428 (1963), pp. 105-119.

7. Loe, D. "Preferred lighting for the display of paintings with conservation in mind," *Lighting in Museums, Galleries and Historic Houses*, London: UK Institute for Conservation and the Museums Association, 1987, pp. 36-49.

8. Rothko, Mark. Letter to Bryan Robertson on how to hang an exhibition at Whitechapel Gallery, cited in the catalogue: Compton, M. *Mark Rothko.* London: The Tate Gallery, 1987, p. 59.

9. Kaufmann, J.E., and H. Haynes. *IES Lighting Handbook. 1981 Application Volume.* New York: Illuminating Engineering Society of North America, 1981, pp. 2-5.

10. IESNA Committee on Museum and Art Gallery Lighting. *Museum and Art Gallery Lighting: A Recommended Practice*, RP-30-96. New York: Illuminating Engineering Society of North America, 1996.

11. CIE. *An Analytic Model for Describing the Influence of Lighting Parameters Upon Visual Performance*, CIE No.19/2 (volumes 1 and 2). Paris: Commission Internationale De L'Éclairage, 1981.

12. Harrison, L.S. *Report on the Deteriorating Effects of Modern Light Sources.* New York: Metropolitan Museum of Art, 1953.

13. Krochmann, J. "Über die bestimmung der relativen spektralen lichtempfindlichkeit von Museumsgut," *Deutscher Restauratoren Verbard*, 1985/86, pp. 20-28.

14. Saunders, D., and J. Kirby. "Wavelength-dependent fading of artists' pigments," *Preventive Conservation Practice, Theory and Research*, A. Roy and P. Smith, eds. London: IIC, 1994, pp. 190-194.

15. Padfield, T., and S. Landhi. "The light-fastness of the natural dyes," *Studies in Conservation*, vol. 11 (1966), pp. 181-196.

16. Duff, D., R.S. Sinclair, and D.S. Stirling. "Light-induced colour changes of natural dyes," *Studies in Conservation*, vol. 22 (1977), pp. 161-169.

17. Grierson, S., D.G. Duff, and R.S. Sinclair. "The colour and fastness of natural dyes of the Scottish Highlands," *Journal of the Society of Dyers and Colorists*, vol. 101 (1985), pp. 220-228.

18. Kashiwagi, M., and S. Yamasaki. "The lightfastness properties of traditional vegetable dyes," *Scientific Papers on Japanese Antiques and Art Crafts*, no. 27 (1982), pp. 54-65. (English translation by Library of the Canadian Conservation Institute, Ottawa, 1984.)

19. Michalski, S. "Damage to museum objects by visible radiation (light) and ultraviolet radiation (UV)," *Lighting, A conference on lighting in museums, galleries, and historic houses*, London: The Museums Association, and the United Kingdom Institute for Conservation, 1987, pp. 3-16.

20. McLaren, K. "The spectral regions of daylight that cause fading of dyes," *Journal of the Society of Dyers and Colorists*, vol. 72 (1956), pp. 86-99.

21. Costain, C. Canadian Conservation Institute, personal communication, 1996.

Résumé

Décider de l'éclairage

Des lignes directrices élaborées dernièrement par l'Institut canadien de conservation (ICC) au sujet de l'éclairage des objets recommandent de chercher un compromis entre la visibilité et la vulnérabilité. Les exigences de visibilité se réduisent à une seule valeur de référence, 50 lux, et à trois cas qui pourraient justifier le dépassement de ce niveau d'éclairement : détails à faible contraste (jusqu'à 3x), objets sombres (jusqu'à 3x) et personnes âgées (jusqu'à 3x). On examine le raisonnement à l'origine de ces facteurs simplifiés et la façon dont ceux-ci s'appliquent à l'éclairage des textiles. Le degré de vulnérabilité des textiles va de très fort à très faible. On explique la plage de vulnérabilité et les moyens qui permettent de déterminer le degré de vulnérabilité d'un textile donné. Le test ponctuel de décoloration par fibres optiques, mis au point par l'ICC, constitue une solution intéressante.

Lighting for Preservation — Fiber Optics in Museum Exhibits

Larry V. Bowers

National Park Service
Division of Conservation
P. O. Box 50
Harpers Ferry, WV 25425 USA
Tel.: (304) 535-6052
E-mail: larry_bowers@nps.gov

Abstract

Fiber optics, a relative newcomer to the field of museum lighting, was once considered merely an interesting, though not particularly practical, lighting tool. It has arrived at a point of significant development. Fiber optics are certainly not suitable for all lighting applications and are not a replacement for conventional museum lighting. They do, however, represent a viable alternative for lighting our most sensitive artifacts. If used properly, they can provide efficient, focused lighting — virtually free of harmful infrared and ultraviolet radiation — in an exhibit environment. Increased concern for rising energy costs, coupled with advances in optical fiber, lenses, and illuminator design give every expectation that this developing technology will have a greater impact on the future of museum lighting. The pros and cons of fiber optic lighting for museums will be addressed, and various fiber optic applications, both in North America and abroad, will be reviewed.

As more is learned about the nature of material degradation, conservators press for greater control over object environments and insist on stricter exhibit guidelines. As advocates for the artifact, it is incumbent upon us to keep abreast of the technological developments which can impact exhibit decisions. In recent years advances in case design, environmental monitoring, relative humidity (RH) control, and exhibit lighting have changed greatly the way objects are exhibited.

Textile artifacts, owing to their structure and/or their component materials, are often placed in the "most sensitive" category, requiring exhibit circumstances which greatly limit footcandle levels and total light exposure. Light, which shapes, defines, and ultimately gives life to our exhibits, simultaneously holds the power to destroy those artifacts enclosed.

Conventional lighting manufacturers now produce a wide variety of lamps and luminaires that fulfill many museum lighting requirements. However, traditional museum lighting is not always capable of easily meeting today's most stringent standards. Developing technologies such as fiber optics and light pipes, and recent advances in LED and solid state technology, which may have future application, offer greater possibilities to satisfy conservation needs.

Fiber optics have been in use for approximately fifteen years now. A number of museums have already tried and rejected them, either because they performed badly or were cumbersome, time consuming to install, or inefficient in application. In addition, many early attempts have sacrificed aesthetic presentation at the altar of object preservation. Advances in fiber optic technology now offers the promise of good lighting design wedded to good conservation.

The National Park Service has been using and testing fiber optic systems for exhibit lighting for almost seven years. We began our interest in 1990 when we were faced with a complex exhibit of sensitive textile and paper artifacts that were particularly difficult to light. The plan had called for the objects to be displayed in small boxes attached to a series of vertical panels stretched diagonally across a room. As conventional lighting would have produced too much radiant heating and been difficult to control, we decided on fiber optics as the only possible alternative.

Subsequent to that first crude but successful exhibit, we have installed a small laboratory in the Division of Conservation to test a variety of lighting components. It has allowed us the opportunity to test some of the leading fiber optic systems currently available and given us a set of standards for fiber optic application.

The lighting decision, and whether or not you choose fiber optics, should reflect a balance of the conservation and aesthetic needs of the objects and contain some of the following criteria:
1. The nature of the exhibit and object sensitivity.
2. The length of the exhibit in relation to the system choice.
3. The relative costs, measured in terms of hardware expense, installation, and overall maintenance costs (both labor and lamp replacement).

As with any technology though, fiber optics embraces both the positive and the negative. It is by no means perfect and should be approached from a thoughtful, educated perspective.

Figure 1. Fiber optic lighting of Lord Nelson's Uniform.
Courtesy of Schott Glass, Fiber Optics Division.

The Positive:

1. First and foremost, and of primary concern to the conservator, the use of fiber optics can completely eliminate ultraviolet and infrared radiation, thereby removing from the exhibit environment two of the most egregious agents of artifact deterioration.

2. Objects in close proximity to one another can be lit at quite different footcandle levels, allowing greater freedom of exhibit design, at no cost to artifact safety.

3. Fiber optics, if properly employed, can be a source of significant energy reduction, especially in instances where one illuminator is used to light multiple cases. A caveat here is that efficiency of operation, and therefore reduced energy costs, is directly related to exhibit design and system selection.

4. Due to the relatively small size of the output devices, fiber optics can literally disappear into the exhibit environment or case, providing unobtrusive, often unseen, directional lighting.

The Negative:

1. Despite the claims of some manufacturers, fiber optics cannot take the place of all conventional exhibit lighting, at least at this stage of development. Our own testing has unfortunately shown that manufacturers' data (photometrics, lamp life, etc.) are sometimes greatly exaggerated. Performance does not always meet expectations.

2. Most exhibit and lighting designers are not skilled enough in the application of fiber optics, often resulting in an inappropriate use or overuse of the technology. Insecure designers will sometimes hand over all the fiber optic aspects of an exhibit to the lighting manufacturer, which can prove quite costly.

3. Fiber optics are not always the most economical option. You may be able to solve your lighting problems with conventional hardware and a little creativity. As Stefan Michalski has often shown in demonstration, a lamp, a couple of mirrors, and some UV filtering glazing may be all that is required.

4. You cannot expect that installation of fiber optics will automatically solve all your exhibit and conservation problems. An inappropriate system choice may have associated difficulties that vastly outweigh the expected benefits and may prove quite expensive.

Alexander Pope's admonition, "A little learning is a dangerous thing," seems entirely appropriate here.

How Fiber Optics Work

Fiber optics work through a process known as total internal reflection, by which a reflective surface is created within the fiber, allowing light to be transmitted over substantial distances. This optical fiber is composed of two different types of material. The core material of glass, silica, or plastic, having a known index of refraction, is surrounded by a second material, known as the cladding. The cladding has a slightly lower index of refraction, the difference between the two indices creating this reflective interface, resulting in transmission of the light down the length of the fiber rather than out the side. The efficiency of light transmission will depend on the constituent materials, the quality of the bond between the core and cladding, hardware connectors, and end polishing.

The decrease in intensity of light transmission as it travels along a fiber is known as attenuation. It will be a factor determining the effective length of application. Depending on the type of fiber employed, a loss of between 2-4% per 30 cm (1 ft.) of travel is considered normal. Individual cable manufacturers have made quite different claims

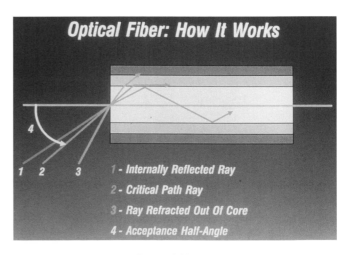

Figure 2. Cross section of optical fiber.
Courtesy of General Electric Lighting.

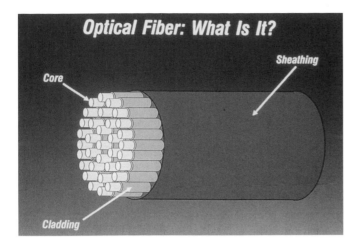

Optical Fiber: What Is It?

Core

Sheathing

Cladding

Figure 3. Typical glass fiber bundle with sheathing.
Courtesy of General Electric Lighting.

regarding transmission characteristics, and applications should be tested fully before committing to a system. For practical and transmission considerations, cable runs are normally kept to within 6 - 7.5 m (20-25 ft.). Fiber lengths in exhibit cases are often not longer than 3 - 3.6 m (10-12 ft.) as the illuminator is usually located in or directly adjacent to the case.

The Fiber

For lighting purposes the core material is usually glass or acrylic (polymethyl methacrylate). Each type of fiber has advantages and disadvantages, and the fiber choice will depend on case design, exhibit complexity, performance demands, and system compatibility.

Glass

Glass fiber comes in a number of different qualities, with quite different light transmission characteristics. High quality optical fiber made of crown and flint glass[1] excels in light transmission and is superior to all others in light quality. Lower quality glass fibers are available, although there is often a color shift (usually to green) after transmission lengths of only 2.1 - 2.4 m (7-8 ft.), owing to absorption of certain wavelengths of the visible light spectrum. This makes it unacceptable for most museum applications.

A single glass fiber of between 0.025 - 0.075 mm (.001-.003 in.) in diameter produces very little light. Consequently, fibers are bundled together to produce light guides[2] of varying sizes. The individual bundles are sheathed in an outer coating of Teflon, polyethylene, PVC, metal, etc., then capped in a ferrule at the output end and (usually) epoxied into a common end for insertion into the light source. Glass fiber must be cut to length and prepared by the manufacturer.

Glass has excellent flexibility relative to solid core plastic fiber and the bend radius is smaller, an important

consideration in applications where space for installation and any subsequent repair may be limited. It can also withstand much higher illuminator temperatures, increasing its applicability to a greater variety of light sources, with a concomitant reduction in concerns for deterioration and safety.

High quality glass fiber will transmit infrared wavelengths and a small amount of high end ultraviolet. Infrared is dealt with by filtration at the light source and ultraviolet radiation will virtually be eliminated by absorption if the cable is more than a few feet long. Our tests of Schott cable, as used by Absolute Action, an English manufacturer specializing in museum exhibits, showed zero μW/lumen of UV and a negligible increase in temperature in the exhibit environment over a protracted period.

Acrylic

Mitsubishi Rayon, Inc. began marketing their Eska (polymethyl methacrylate) fiber approximately fifteen years ago, opening the way to relatively simple and inexpensive fiber optic applications. This fiber comes in a variety of styles, has excellent light quality, low attenuation, and transmits zero infrared or ultraviolet radiation.

The most commonly used form of this cable in North America is the 3 mm solid core fiber. It is designed to be cut and polished in the field, offering greater design flexibility and latitude for modifications during installation. NoUVIR Research, an American firm, offers a wide variety of sophisticated lenses using this fiber.

One significant drawback of the 3 mm PMMA fiber is its lack of flexibility, resulting in a larger bend radius relative to glass fiber. Resistance to heat is also relatively low compared to glass. Above 70°C, the fiber will begin to deteriorate and transmission will fall off; at sustained temperatures above 100°C, PMMA fiber will begin to melt. Those wishing to design their own system should therefore use special care in planning the illuminator/cable interface.

Philips (Europe) makes fiber optic systems utilizing the more flexible, smaller diameter PMMA cable, bundled and sheathed like glass fiber, for which they now offer a wide variety of lenses and accessories. However, Philips has decided to delay introducing them to the North American market due to technical problems and lamp difficulties.

Thermoset Resin

A number of manufacturers have developed plastic optical fiber constructed of a variety of thermoset resins. A number of museum installations using this fiber have experienced problems of fiber embrittlement and physical deterioration, resulting in a loss of light quality, light quantity, and shifts in color balance. Manufacturers are working hard to solve these problems and this fiber may eventually prove to be a valuable addition to exhibit lighting. For now though, plastic resin cables should be considered still in the developmental stage and useful only for very short term exhibits.

Light Sources (Illuminators)

Effective transmission of light requires a focused light source properly matched to the acceptance angle of the fiber. For that reason, the best results usually come from a systems approach where the manufacturer has thoughtfully designed all the component elements. You *can* design the system yourself and marry hardware from various manufacturers, but, as mentioned previously, be aware of the potential hazards, and be sure to allow sufficient time for testing.

Illuminators fall into two basic types: halogen and metal halide, both available in a variety of configurations.

Halogen illuminators are usually considered best for museum installations. The light source is usually an MR-16 type projection lamp rated between 3000°-3400° Kelvin[3], and having excellent color rendition. Depending on the manufacturer, they are offered in standard line voltage or low voltage systems, with bulb life expectancy ranging from 50-5000 hours. Halogen bulbs are also instant-on and lend themselves well to use with occupancy sensors.

Various methods are used at the illuminator to control output. Some illuminators come with rheostats to adjust light levels. Lowering the rheostat *does* reduce the amount of light, but a significant color shift toward yellow will begin to occur as a 25% reduction is approached. Methods of reducing footcandle levels without affecting color temperature include the use of mechanical diaphragms, light reducing screens installed in the illuminator, or neutral density filters mounted in or attached to the lenses.

Metal halide and the new Xenon metal halide illuminators are capable of producing a great deal more light than those using halogen bulbs, and are especially well suited to general merchandise display, industrial, outdoor, and architectural applications. Their use in museums is limited and depends directly on the exhibit requirements and the particular manufacturer.

The color rendering index[4] of metal halide lamps ranges from 60 CRI, which is considered poor, to 85 CRI, the minimum acceptable standard for museum service. By comparison, tungsten halogen light sources are rated at nearly 100 CRI. Life expectancy of metal halide bulbs is excellent, with some approaching 20,000 hours, but replacement cost can also be high, often between $100-$300 per lamp.

Most metal halide lamps also require a substantial warm-up period and are not instant-on, eliminating their use with an occupancy sensor. Infrared radiation is handled by reflectorized coatings and/or filtration, depending on the manufacturer. Ultraviolet radiation is eliminated by filtration or by cable absorption.

We can expect developments to continue in this area. European and American manufacturers are using thin film technology to produce intense, focused metal halide light sources, while reducing size and increasing performance characteristics.

Output Devices - Lenses, Light Bars, Etc.

Most manufacturers offer some kind of hardware for directing light output. They vary enormously, from very simple, one-element acrylic lenses to complex lenses, with multiple elements, capable of directing relatively powerful, focused beams across a room.

Some manufacturers also offer light bars having aimable, multiple points of light. Other than making your own lenses or using open fibers, light bars offer the easiest, and often least expensive, method of directing fiber optic light. These come in various configurations, the best of which offer the opportunity to create a wash of light as well as focused, individual spots.

Exhibit complexity may affect whether or not you choose to deal with fiber optics in-house. Some exhibits may require the skills of a lighting designer familiar with fiber optics. When choosing a designer or system manufacturer always ask for a list of previous *museum* installations. Find out if those museums were satisfied. Did it meet their conservation and aesthetic expectations? Is the system performing well? Are there any maintenance problems? A few minutes inquiry at this juncture can forestall a lot of future headaches.

Most of the research and development in fiber optics since their inception has been directed toward data communication, sensing, and other scientific and industrial applications. Spurred by mandated energy reductions and technological improvements, industry now is committing more research dollars to fiber optic lighting.

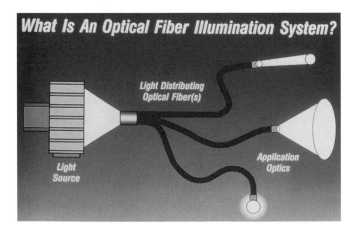

Figure 4. Components of a fiber optic system. Courtesy of General Electric Lighting.

Firms such as Absolute Action in England and NoUVIR and Lighting Services, Inc. in the United States specialize in exhibit lighting. Companies as large as General Electric and Philips see fiber optics as a growing market and are developing a range of fiber optic products. As they and smaller, specialized companies enter the marketplace we can expect fiber optics to have a greater and greater impact on the future of museum lighting. The technology will become more accessible and future uses may include fiber optics connected to passive solar collectors, providing UV and IR free sunlight to museum galleries and visitor areas.

As previously stated, fiber optics are not the answer to all your lighting problems. However, they do offer your museum the possibility of beautiful, technologically advanced object lighting which at the same time can maximize preservation.

Endnotes

1 Crown (lime) glass and flint (lead) glass: extremely high quality optical glasses meeting requirements for high refractive index, light dispersion, and surface brilliance.

2 Light Guide: A non-coherent fiber bundle used for illumination or detection.

3 Kelvin (K): The standard unit of measuring the color temperature of a light source. Ordinary incandescent lamps arc rated 2500°- 2800° K, producing a light yellow in coloration and considered "warm." Tungsten halogen lamps are rated 2900°- 3400° K. Neutral range is 3400°-3800° K.

Figure 5. Exhibit case (during installation) showing Zouave jacket lit at 6-8 fc, label copy at 15-20 fc, and canteen at 12 fc. Courtesy of US National Park Service.

Figure 6. Imperial War Museum; ribbons. Courtesy of Absolute Action Fiber Optics.

4 Color Rendering Index (CRI): The degree to which a tested light source accurately renders color compared to a Black Body at the same Kelvin color temperature. Rated on a scale of 0-100.

Bibliography

Albana, C., P.E. Gurlino. "Creative Light," *Museum*, (UNESCO, Paris), vol. XLIII, no. 172 (Nov. 4), 1991.

Burch, St. J., et al. "Fiber Optic Lighting in Museums, Galleries, and Historic Houses," *A Conference on Lighting in Museums, Galleries, and Historic Houses*, The Museums Association, UK Institute for Conservation.

Cuttle, C. "Lighting Works of Art for Exhibition and Conservation," *Lighting Research and Technology*, vol. 20, no. 2 (1988).

Feller, R.L. "Control of Deteriorating Effects of Light on Museum Objects: Heating Effects of Illumination by Incandescent Lamps," *Museum News* (1964).

Huber, J.C. "Getting Down to the Basics of Fiber-Optic Transmission," *R & D Magazine* (Feb. 1994).

Mathiesen, P. "Color, Cut, and Clarity," *LD & A* (October 1994).

McGiffin, R. "Museum Lighting: The Next Generation," *Spur*, Gene Autry Western Heritage Museum, vol. 6, no. 1 (January/February 1993).

Miller, J.V. *Evaluating Fading Characteristics of Light Sources*. NoUVIR Research Co., 1993.

Mueller, R.H., et al. "Sorting out the Roles of High and Low Loss Fiber," *The Photonics Design and Applications Handbook*, 1990, pp. 35-41.

Muehlmann, M. "Optical Fibers for Illumination," *The Photonics Design and Applications Handbook*, 1991, p. 31- 33.

Rea, M. S., ed. *I.E.S. Lighting Handbook*. Reference and Applications Vol. 8th Edition. Illuminating Engineering Society of North America, 1993.

Roveri, A. M. D. "Let There Be Light, "*Museum* (UNESCO, Paris), vol. XLIII, no. 172, no. 4. (1991).

Sikkens, M., Ansems, J.P.M. "Remote Source Lighting, Part One - Fiber Optic Light Guides," *International Lighting Review*, Issue 3 (1993).

Walker, A. "Optic Nerve," *Design* (April 1994).

Selected List of Fiber Optic Manufacturers

Absolute Action, Ltd.
Mantle House
Broomhill Road
London SW18 4JQ United Kingdom
011-44-181-871-5005

Calsak Corporation
P.O. Box 9036
Compton, CA 90224 USA – (310) 637-2000
Distributor of Mitsubishi Eska polymethyl methacrylate (PMMA) fiber.

Dolan Jenner Industries, Inc.
678 Andover Street
Lawrence, MA 01843 USA – (800) 833-4237
Manufacturer and supplier of illuminators, fiber optic light guides, specialty fibers; custom applications.

Fiberoptics Technology, Inc.
1 Fiber Road
Pomfret, CT 06258 USA – (203) 928-0443
Manufacturer and supplier of illuminators, fiber optic light guides, specialty fibers; custom applications.

FOSTEC, Inc.
272 Genesee Street
Auburn, NY 13021 USA – (315) 255-2791
Manufacturer and supplier of illuminators, fiber optic light guides, specialty fibers; custom applications.

General Fiber Optics, Inc.
1 Washington Avenue
Fairfield, NJ 07004 USA – (201) 239-3400
Suppliers of fiber optic light guides, illuminators

Lighting Services, Inc.
Industrial Park Route 9W
Stony Point, NY 10980-1996 USA – (914) 942-2800

Manufacturer and supplier of illuminators, fiber optic light guides, lenses, light bars; custom applications.

Lumitex, Inc.
8443 Dow Circle
Strongsville, OH 44136 USA – (800) 969-5483
Manufacturer and supplier of woven Eska PMMA fiber; custom applications.

Mitsubishi International Corporation
520 Madison Ave.
New York, NY 10022-4223 USA – (212) 605-2392
Manufacturer and supplier of Eska PMMA fiber.

NoUVIR Research
RR Box 748
Highway 13 & Loop 532
Seaford, DE 19973 USA – (302) 628-9933
Manufacturer and supplier of illuminators, fiber optic luminaires, fiber optic track lighting; custom application.

Optical Display Lighting
P.O. Box 74
Ellenton, FL 34222 USA – (800) 833-3756
Manufacturers and suppliers of fiber optic display lighting; light bars.

Résumé

L'éclairage et la préservation — Les fibres optiques dans les expositions muséales

Nouvelles venues dans le domaine de l'éclairage dans les musées, les fibres optiques étaient encore considérées, il y a peu de temps, comme un moyen d'éclairage potentielle-ment intéressant, mais sans grande application pratique. Toutefois, la technologie de la fibre optique a fait d'énormes progrès depuis. Les fibres optiques ne conviennent certes pas à toutes les applications d'éclairage et ne peuvent rem-placer l'éclairage classique. Par contre, elles représentent une solution de rechange judicieuse pour les pièces les plus fragiles. Convenablement utilisées dans une exposition, elles constituent un moyen d'éclairage efficace et ponctuel, pratiquement exempt de rayons infrarouges et ultraviolets dommageables. Les préoccupations quant au coût croissant de l'électricité et les progrès qui ont été réalisés dans le domaine des fibres optiques, des lentilles, des sources lumineuses donnent toutes les raisons de s'attendre à ce que cette technique en pleine évolution trouve de plus en plus d'applications au chapitre de l'éclairage dans les musées. L'article traite des avantages et des inconvénients de l'éclairage aux fibres optiques et examine diverses applications des fibres optiques en Amérique du Nord et à l'étranger.

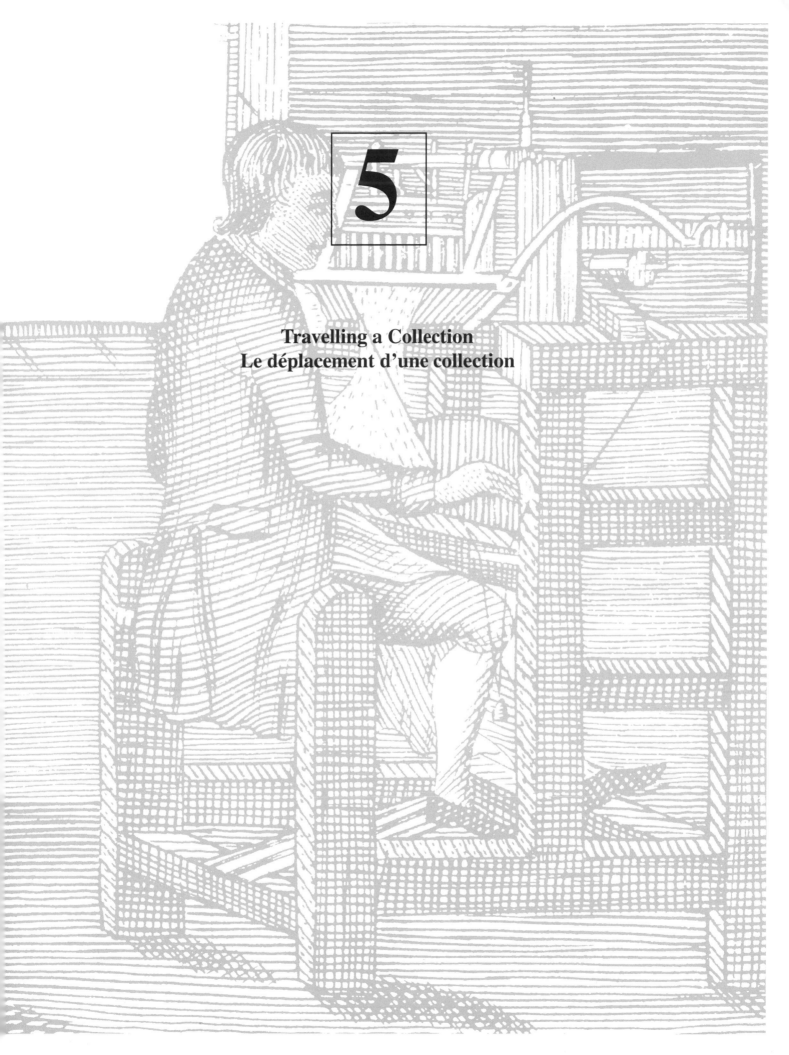

5

Travelling a Collection
Le déplacement d'une collection

Exhibiting Historical Costumes from a Living Tradition: Cantonese Opera in Canada

Elizabeth Lominska Johnson and Darrin Morrison

U.B.C. Museum of Anthropology
6393 Northwest Marine Drive
Vancouver, BC V6T 1Z2 Canada
Tel.: (604) 822-5087
E-mail: darrin@unixg.ubc.ca
E-mail: ljohnso@unixg.ubc.ca

Abstract

This paper discusses the human and pragmatic side of exhibiting a large collection of historic Cantonese opera costumes offered to the University of British Columbia Museum of Anthropology by a Vancouver-based Chinese musical association. In the first section, curator Elizabeth Johnson introduces the social context of working with the local Chinese community in an effort to involve, as much as possible, the people represented in the exhibit in determining the content. In the second section, Darrin Morrison addresses economical conservation solutions to the challenges of mounting and travelling over 200 fragile and elaborate costumes, accessories and props including a 10.8 m (36 ft.) long embroidered silk curtain.

I. The Social Context of the Exhibition

The human side of the exhibition process is rarely simple and straightforward, especially in situations where curators and conservators are committed to considering the interests and concerns of the people whose objects are being shown. Likewise, the technical side of an exhibition of textiles poses particular challenges because of the inherent complexity and fragility of the materials. In the second half of this presentation, Darrin Morrison will discuss conservation solutions to the challenges of exhibiting a large number of Cantonese opera costumes and accessories. As curator, I will introduce the collection in its human context. My particular concern is to analyze the complexities of producing such a large travelling exhibit in conformity to grant deadlines, while also trying to meet the expectations of the people from whom the costumes had come. The process exposed certain differences between dedicated performers and museum professionals in their attitudes towards the costumes, but also involved an ongoing dialogue between the performers and Museum staff throughout the exhibit planning and production process.

The Cantonese opera collection at the University of British Columbia Museum of Anthropology might be described as a curator's dream. In many ways it conforms to what museum curators value most. It is the largest collection of old Cantonese opera costumes in the world. Although they were made in China, they were used in Canada and so have local relevance. The costumes date from the 1910s-40s, and they are lavish, spectacular, and rich in handmade detail. Very few similar costumes survived in Hong Kong and south China because of climate, lack of storage space, war, revolution, and especially the Cultural Revolution in the 1960s. Several recent Chinese films have dramatically shown the willful destruction of such materials at that time. There are also other reasons, which I will explain, why performers in China may have chosen not to keep old costumes. As curators, though, we delight in old, rare, and endangered objects, and we do our best to preserve and exhibit them.

Figure 1. Photograph of the Kwok Fung Lin Troupe, taken in Vancouver, 1923. They are wearing costumes similar to those in the Museum of Anthropology collection. Courtesy of Wallace Chung.

In Vancouver, costumes were left in the care of the Jin Wah Sing Musical Association, an association established in 1934 to teach amateur performers, and to sponsor amateur and professional performances. The association used some of them until the 1960s, and then continued to store them, using effective traditional methods, in a basement in Vancouver's Chinatown. Because the costumes were no longer useful, and after having nearly sold them through a local shop to raise funds to buy new ones, the Association sold a large number of costumes to the Museum of Anthropology in 1973. They donated more in the early 1990s for our exhibit. Their senior teacher, Master Wong Toa, helped us in selecting those to be donated but then wondered at the care the Museum lavished on them, exclaiming at one point: "We considered them to be garbage!" Despite this, he worked with us enthusiastically throughout the project, identifying costumes, demonstrating their use, and advising us on proper ways of exhibiting them. Similarly, another advisor, also active in Cantonese opera, said that the Museum's treatment of the costumes, and research on them, made him realize their great historical value.

At the Museum of Anthropology, we accept the principle that people represented in an exhibit should be involved in determining its content as much as possible. The entire process — concept, curatorship, conservation — ideally becomes an ongoing dialogue between equal partners. In the case of this exhibition, however this process was not completely satisfactory. For one thing, the people active in Cantonese opera today do not feel links to the old costumes; they are very different from those used now and only the oldest Jin Wah Sing members have any memory of using them. Furthermore, the process of the exhibit was very much driven by the demands of the grants that made it possible. The decision to do an exhibit, and the basic concept, had to be articulated for grant applications before extensive community consultation, funded by the grants, could begin. After that point, schedules determined by grants and their requirement that the exhibit travel put us under considerable pressure and allowed little time for reflection or for changes to decisions taken earlier. The costumes to be exhibited had to be selected very early to allow time for conservation treatments, and were selected partly on the basis of their condition. The entire exhibition process could not be very flexible. The fact that the labels had to be produced in Chinese, English, and French did not encourage changes. People gave permission for us to use their words and images, but only our primary advisor had the chance to assess the overall concept. Complex politics within the local community meant that consensus would have been unlikely anyway.

We tried to build in as much consultation as possible. We were advised throughout our work by Master Wong Toa and Prof. Huang Jinpei, a senior musician from China knowledgeable about Cantonese opera. Following Prof. Huang's advice, we formed a committee of local advisors who met with us for discussions (in Chinese) in which they gave their views on our plans. Within Chinese culture, it is generally impolite to express direct criticism or opposition, however, so we may not have fully elicited the feedback for which we had hoped. When we did, practical concerns sometimes prevented us from meeting their expectations.

Some advisors expressed their desire that the costumes should be mounted and arranged to show a scene from an opera. If this could not be done with costumes, then they hoped a model scene could be made, but we were unable to find anyone here or in China who could make one. With great regret, we had to explain to them why we could not create a scene with the costumes. First of all, the costumes are incomplete; in the whole collection there is probably not one full costume, complete from headdress to boots. They are, after all, fragments, objects left behind. They are also not balanced in terms of gender or role types. Aside from the problem of costumes, we could not use mannequins because of prohibitive production and shipping costs, conservation concerns, and our lack of information on styles of theatre makeup and hairdressing from the time period.

As a result, we had to display the costumes like textile art: decontextualized, suspended flat, without heads, limbs, or the gestures so important in Cantonese opera. We tried instead to animate the exhibit and to show costumes in use by commissioning a video of a local performance, sensitively filmed by Mary Wong, Wong Toa's daughter, a contemporary artist. We also tried to create the context of a stage by hanging a very large, fragile, sequined silk curtain as backdrop to the exhibit, although conservation concerns forbade the brilliant lighting typical of a Cantonese opera stage.

In general, non-Chinese visitors to the exhibit responded to the costumes as art, exclaiming in our comment books about their beauty, their colour, and their remarkable techniques. They also said that the exhibit informed them about a part of Chinese-Canadian cultural history previously unknown to them. The comments of visitors of Chinese origin, in contrast, tended to express their appreciation for the exhibit's depiction of their long cultural history in Canada, and the personal memories it evoked.

We are grateful for the help of the members of the various local opera associations, who welcomed us to their performances and gave us their full cooperation in producing the exhibit, providing us with information and advice. They supported us throughout the exhibit process despite the fact that their primary interest is in performance, not exhibits, and in theatre, not museums. Although our extraordinary commitment to showing old, discarded costumes may have puzzled them, they respected our interest and worked with us. We only regret that the process could not have been more fully cooperative, and that practical and professional concerns prevented our meeting all their expectations.

II. The Pragmatics of Display

The preparation of over 200 costumes, accessories and opera stage props for exhibition and travel to six venues seemed like a daunting task and occupied much of conservation's time and resources for nearly two years. In the initial planning stage, hundreds of objects from the Museum's collection were assessed for their overall condition and suitability for display and travel. Under the basement conditions in which these costumes had been stored, it was easy to assume that they would be in relatively poor condition. However, the vast majority were remarkably well preserved and credit must be given to the

Jin Wah Sing Musical Association's forethought in carefully maintaining the collection. In fact, costumes with loose threads, dirt and wear was a result of their frequent use in performance and not because of poor storage conditions. Other costumes were pristine as if they never had been used.

The 35 robes, dresses and suits chosen for "A Rare Flower: A Century of Cantonese Opera in Canada" are primarily made from silk, cotton and bast fibres. Although incomplete, each of these complicated costumes is testament to the toil and skill of the craftspeople involved in their creation. Many of the costumes consist of multiple components including vests, belts, hoods and pants. Many are heavily ornamented with metal discs, mirrors, sequins, beads and fur; most are decorated with metal wrapped threads hand couched into elaborate designs.

Much of the conservation treatment work conducted for the exhibition was done to stabilize the costumes and accessories so that they could be mounted and then travelled. This included attaching clasps and snaps in order to alleviate stress on the costumes and the original frogs (closures) and ties. Portions of loose metallic thread on some of the costumes were carefully recouched down using contrasting silk threads so that the loose threads would not be pulled and damaged further when handled. Overall cleaning, mostly to remove dust and loose dirt, was conducted using a gentle vacuum and screen. Some badly creased portions were successfully relaxed with humidification, using a layer of Gore-Tex to create a water vapour permeable barrier between damp blotters (the source of humidity) and the costume. Original perspiration marks from the actors that once wore the costumes were left as it was decided that these reflected the history of these pieces. Tears, deteriorated closures and weak seams were reinforced; holes were patched and loose sequins secured.

As discussed in the first section of this paper, the mounting of the costumes for the exhibition partially depended on the context of display. Advisors had hoped that each costume would be displayed on a fully attired mannequin in the context of a scene from an opera. For reasons mentioned previously, this idea was abandoned with regret early in the exhibit's preparation. Instead, the garments were displayed on invisible and inexpensive mounts made in-house with sleeves extended from the sides either at 90- or 45-degree angles. In order to achieve this goal, various materials and methods were investigated and eliminated; for example, wooden doweling and copper pipe proved cumbersome, expensive or unsafe for use with the costumes. Finally, through a process of trial and error and the ingenuity of Susan Sirovyak, a member of the exhibit team, an easily constructed system using standard commonly available ABS (acrylonitrile-butadiene-styrene) plumbing pipe and polyethylene foam pipe insulation was developed at a cost of approximately $35 CDN per mount.

Each ABS plumbing pipe mount was constructed in two parts; the first consisted of an H-shaped frame that fitted onto doweling in the base of the display case and second, an easily detachable upper section supported the costume's weight and arms. All mount joints were made from standard ABS plumbing elbows and connectors. In order to protect the costumes from the hard ABS pipe, the upper section of the support was padded with polyethylene pipe insulation wrapped in polyester batting and covered in cotton and/or a polyester or acetate lining fabric. Costumes with separate leg panels and pants were mounted onto the H-shaped frame fitted to a Coroplast (fluted polypropylene sheet) and Ethafoam (expanded polyethylene foam sheet) waist support. Velcro attachments stitched to the waistband of the leg panels and pants were used to secure these pieces to the mount.

The upper padded section of the mount was carefully inserted into the sleeves of the costume. Once this was done the costume could be lifted onto the H-frame and any clasps or ties secured. A significant amount of time was required to place the costumes on the upper portion of the mount and, because of this, the costumes would remain mounted on the upper section throughout handling.

The accessories, comprising the remaining 150 pieces in the exhibition, proved even more elaborate and diverse than the costumes and included weapons, hats, headdresses, shoes, boots, fans, flags, curtains, papier-mâché decapitated heads, large wooden trucks, wigs and beards, etc. Like the costumes, the accessories were made for the spectacle of the stage and are encrusted with mirrors, sequins, beads, pom poms and any number of movable bobbles. Unlike the costumes, there was no standard way to mount each piece and a variety of methods were developed.

All hats, headdresses, shoes and boots were mounted on polyethylene foam forms covered in polyester batting and cotton knit and/or lining material. A Plexiglas dowel anchored into the base of the hat and headdress mounts was used to attach them to the display furniture, while other objects simply rested on the furniture or the base of the display case. Several large opera trunks from the museum's collection had false tops constructed so that they could be adapted as exhibit furniture, and reflect the collection's origins and the traditional methods used to store and transport opera paraphernalia. Many of the accessories presented particular problems related to their complexity and much time was spent cleaning and securing loose and damaged components, much like the work done with the costumes.

The 10.8 m (36 ft.) long silk curtain, embellished with beads, embroidery and sequins was included in the exhibit and was a particular challenge to mount and display. Due to its large size and fragility, this was probably the only time the curtain would be displayed before returning to permanent storage. Conservation volunteers carefully hand

Figure 2. Photograph of Chan Kwok-yuen, a well-known designer of Cantonese opera, advising Elizabeth Johnson on the identification of a 75-year-old costume in the Museum's collection.

sewed a long cotton strip, with the loop side of Velcro attached, along the entire length of the curtain. As with the costumes, loose sequins were secured with contrasting silk thread, and holes and tears were repaired and reinforced with swatches of yellow silk. The curtain required two or more people to install and while one person stood on a ladder to attach the curtain to the opposite hook side of the Velcro already secured to the wall, the other slowly unfurled the curtain like a giant silk scroll. Although we minimized the risk of damage that this amount of handling could do, it was anticipated that already damaged sequins would fall off. Over the entire travel and exhibition schedule to six different venues, however, only a few sequins were dislodged.

The final project was to develop a packing system for the costumes and accessories so that the exhibition could travel to a variety of museums, including smaller venues unable to accommodate large crates. Because the exhibition was travelling by a dedicated shipment in an environmentally controlled truck it was possible to pack the costumes in soft boxes rather than in unwieldy plywood crates. Consequently, a lightweight packing system for all the costumes and accessories using Coroplast boxes and trays with external frames of plywood was developed. In selecting smaller boxes (each box measured 1 meter by 2 meters by 25 cm deep), a conscious decision to fold the costumes was made.

Each box interior was carefully planned so that folding would be minimized and creasing and other damage, such as that resulting from abrasion, would not occur. This was accomplished by padding a base of Coroplast (cut to the inside dimensions of the box) with polyester batting and covering this with a white cotton sheet (purchased second hand and inexpensively from a hotel). Before this cotton sheet was secured lengths of polyethylene pipe insulation were laid out underneath in the profile of each costume. This was done to prevent the costumes from shifting on the padded base.

The upper portion of each costume mount, with costume attached was carefully lifted off of its corresponding H-frame support and placed onto this base. All folds were padded with lengths of cotton-covered padded pipe insulation and secured in place with ties through the base. The dowels, protruding out of the mount, were padded with cotton and polyester pillows to prevent the insides of the costumes from being abraded. Another cotton sheet, attached to the base of the box, acted as a dust cover for the packed costumes held securely using wide cotton straps with Velcro fasteners. Two people easily carried the packed boxes once the lids were fastened. Many of the accessories were also packaged in this manner. In addition, premade boxes available from the manufacturer were used for the smaller pieces. The larger headdresses were packed in custom-made boxes with loose and mobile pieces secured to minimize movement during shipping. Although we made the mounting and packing of each object as straightforward as possible and a staff member travelled to assist in the installation layout, extensive packing and mounting instructions were necessary for the installation to be a success.

When the exhibition opened at the Museum of Anthropology, it included a consecrated shrine dedicated to the patron gods of opera performers. The shrine was purchased to inform museum visitors about the religious basis of Cantonese opera and to allow actors to worship before public performances held during the exhibition. On the day of the consecration, Wong Toa brought offerings of food and burned paper offerings and incense. Although we expected the burning of incense and had prepared for it, we did not know that the consecration ceremonies would involve food, fire and smoke; this proved yet another example of how objects relate to living cultures and not just museum displays. Out of respect for community wishes, and for the gods to whom the shrine was dedicated, incense was burned at each venue during the entire exhibition schedule.

As Elizabeth Johnson outlines in the first part of this paper, not all expectations for this exhibition could be met. Perhaps the compromises that were made were reasonable considering the complexities of fostering an open dialogue among the parties represented. The successful efforts of the over 20 people who worked and volunteered to produce and travel this exhibition was evidenced by the safe return of the costumes and accessories to the museum in 1996, marking the end of another long journey for this remarkable collection.

Acknowledgements

Associations:
Jin Wah Sing Musical Association, Ching Won Musical Society, Ngai Lum Musical Society, Elite Cantonese Opera Musical Society, You Sing Cantonese Opera and Folk Music Association, Mount Pleasant Music Society

Advisors:
Wong Toa, Huang Jinpei, Alex Hung, Winnie Poon, Terry Lee, Paul Li, Lawrence Law, Lucy Law

Video:
Mary Wong Sui-yee

Sources of information and lenders to exhibit:
Chan Fei-yin, Chan Kwok-yuen, Louis Chang, Walace Chung, Hung Zhigang, Monica Bai, Ruth Orr Huber, Sandra Lau, Rosa Lee, Raymond Li, Kevin Mah, Carrie Mak, Wayne Mak, Karrie Sebryk, Tan Dierong, Diana Tong, Wong Hok-sing, Victoria Yip, Yung Cheong-hoe

Financial support:
Museums Assistance Program of Communications Canada; Secretary of State, Multiculturalism Directorate; Cathay Pacific Airways Ltd.; Sandra Lau

Exhibition Team:
Advisor: Prof. Huang Jinpei
Curators: Elizabeth Johnson and Rosa Ho
Designers: David Cunningham, Ray Mah Design
Conservation: Darrin Morrison, Miriam Clavir, Susan Sirovyak, Conservation Committee of Volunteer Associates
Outside conservators: Jan Vuori, Joan Marshall, Gaby Kienitz
Registrar: Allison Cronin

Résumé

Exposition de costumes historiques témoins d'une coutume vivante : l'opéra cantonais au Canada

Cet article porte sur le côté humain et pragmatique de l'exposition d'une grande collection de costumes d'opéra cantonais offerts à l'University of British Columbia Museum of Anthropology par une association musicale chinoise de Vancouver. Dans la première partie, la conservatrice Elizabeth Johnson présente le contexte social du travail avec la communauté chinoise locale, qui représente un effort de faire participer, dans la mesure du possible, les personnes concernées à la détermination du contenu de l'exposition. Dans la deuxième partie, Darrin Morrison traite des solutions économiques de conservation au défi de monter et de déplacer plus de 200 articles fragiles et complexes comprenant des costumes et des accessoires, notamment un rideau de soie brodée de près de 11 mètres de long.

Conservation, Display and Transport of *Becoming American Women: Clothing and the Jewish Immigrant Experience, 1880-1920*

Nancy Buenger

Chicago Historical Society
Clark Street at North Avenue
Chicago, IL 60614-6099 USA
Tel.: (312) 642-5035, ext. 374
E-mail: buenger@chicagohs.org

Abstract

In 1994, the Chicago Historical Society (CHS) produced the traveling exhibition *Becoming American Women: Clothing and the Jewish Immigrant Experience, 1880-1920.* Curated by Barbara Schreier, the exhibition explored clothing's complex role in the American acculturation process. First-and second-generation Eastern European Jewish immigrants loaned treasured family clothing and textiles for the exhibition, and shared poignant stories of the struggle for assimilation. Conservation treatment choices for these keepsakes balanced the original appearance of the artifact, evidence of subsequent use, and the frequent handling associated with a traveling exhibition. Display mounts included mannequins personalized with plaster masks of women who participated in the project. Packing and transport of this large and complex exhibition required considerable planning to expedite the show's two-year journey across the United States. An overview of the conservation, display and transport of garments in this exhibition will be presented.

Introduction

Exhibition planning for *Becoming American Women* began with a national campaign for artifacts documenting the immigration of Eastern European Jewish women to America. Advertisements were placed in synagogue newsletters, on the radio, in the *Forward* and the *New York Times,* and extensive interviews were conducted with first- and second-generation immigrants. Over 450 artifacts were loaned for the exhibition, the majority from private individuals. All of these objects were irreplaceable family heirlooms that played an integral role in the passage to America. The unique and personal nature of these artifacts was an important factor in the conservation, display, and transport of this exhibition.

Clothing was an important symbol of assimilation for Jewish immigrants. Mastering a new language took months or years; a new hat or pair of shoes provided a ready means of displaying their new identity. The consequences of altering their appearances were profound for many women, who were torn between maintaining their Jewish identity, well-defined by long-standing clothing traditions in Eastern Europe, and adapting to their new lives as Americans. [1]

The belongings that the new immigrants brought to this country were precious and few. For many, an entire life had to be packed in a single trunk and bundle for the journey overseas. A goose-down feather bed brought from Poland by Lena Cooper Dick in 1916 was a prized possession in the old country. Women sometimes sold everything but their feather beds when they came to America. A pillow made from Lena's feather bed is a family keepsake of her journey. [2] A scrap of homespun linen is all that remains of a bedsheet brought from Poland by Sarah Rovner's mother. Sarah reminisced about life in the *shtetl,* the Yiddish term for small Jewish towns and villages in Eastern Europe, as she recalled harvesting and spinning the flax for the bedsheet: "Our hands used to be cut from pulling the plants up all day."

Figure 1. This postcard illustrates the dramatic changes immigrants underwent after their arrival in America.

In the winter, women and children gathered to spin the flax with drop spindles. "I used to do it myself. We used to get together and drink tea and have something to eat. We were all singing together. It was a lot of fun." [3]

The new immigrants frequently abandoned clothing from the old country on their arrival at Ellis Island, New York, to avoid being identified as greenhorns. Shoshona Hoffman's mother, a Russian immigrant to New York City in 1902, threw her carefully packed wicker trunk of clothes overboard when a fellow shipmate from New York told her that they wouldn't "do" in America. [4] Joe Braufman of Lehr, North Dakota, wrote to his mother-in-law, Riva Lazar, in Romania: "I want to inform you I sent money for tickets for second class passage. When you get this letter make sure you are ready to go. Don't take any clothing, because when you get here we will not let you wear those clothes. And please don't cry, because your eyes are supposed to be healthy." [5]

Expensive clothes and accessories were beyond the means of most new arrivals. Women scoured the neighborhood for bargains, buying from pushcart vendors and second-hand shops. [6] Some of this new American-style clothing has not

Figure 2. *More stylish than durable, Ruth Young Block's purple satin bathing suit and shoes bled profusely when she went swimming.*

survived because the cheap goods were used until they literally fell apart. Ruth Young Block bought a bathing suit for her first vacation in South Haven, Michigan in 1919. The purple satin suit and matching shoes were worn only once, as the dye bled profusely when she went swimming, leaving her streaked with purple. [7] Not all immigrants were of limited means; several of the dresses loaned for the exhibition were exquisitely hand-made by seamstresses or store-bought for special occasions.

Conservation

Conservation treatment decisions were complex for these irreplaceable family heirlooms. The original appearance of the garment, evidence of subsequent use, the extensive handling associated with traveling exhibitions, and owner preferences were all taken into consideration. Alterations and evidence of use were preserved whenever possible. Exceptions were made when damage, repairs, or alterations affected the structural integrity of the garments, or substantially modified the original appearance of fashionable dresses. All donors were consulted regarding treatment options.

Clothing was a scarce commodity in Europe, as well as in the new homeland. A child's cotton dress and pinafore, made by Sara Karp for a cousin in Indura, Russia, was worn only on the Sabbath or special holidays. Garments were frequently handed down from one family member to the next, and mended or altered several times over. Parallel fold lines from unstitched tucks in the dress show how it was let down as Sara's cousin grew. The dress was eventually returned to Sara so that her own daughter might wear it. Conservation treatment of the outfit was limited to cleaning of the pinafore, which was heavily soiled. The tucks in the dress were not restitched as they formed an important record of use.

A cotton dress with lace inlays and ornamental tucking received a more interventive treatment. The dress was originally worn by Fay Kanter, the daughter of a Russian immigrant, when she graduated from Oliver Goldsmith School in Chicago in 1907. Uneven finishing details on the dress suggest that it may have been a school assignment, typical for Chicago elementary schools at the turn-of-the-century. The dress had been heavily worn, substantially altered, and the cotton fabric was fragile. The bodice had been taken in to mask large tears near the sleeves and back closure, and was structurally unstable. The length of the skirt had been nearly halved by large horizontal tucks. A decision was made to remove alterations that affected the structural stability and basic proportions of the dress; all other repairs or original construction anomalies were preserved.

Alterations near the sleeves and back closure were removed. The excess skirt fabric was released to return the dress to its original length. The garment was wet-cleaned to reduce cellulose degradation products and creasing. Large loss areas in the bodice were supported with aged cotton fabric that was tucked to replace missing decorative elements. The bodice was given a full polyester organza support as there were numerous small loss areas and the fabric was too fragile to withstand repeated mannequin dressing and undressing. The transparent, dimensionally stable organza could be easily heat-cut to fit the complex bodice sections. Threads were drawn from the organza for invisible couched repairs of loss areas.

Originally, the graduation dress would have been starched and pressed to create a smooth fabric finish. Treatment to reduce creasing avoided the use of steamers that can generate temperatures near 103° C (215° F), accelerate fiber degradation, and distort lightweight fabrics. After wet-cleaning, the dress was allowed to dry flat until barely damp and then placed on a mannequin. The fabric was hand-manipulated and dried with a hair dryer set on "cool" to reduce creasing. Areas of the collar and lace trim were further smoothed with a low-temperature iron, which was monitored with a surface thermometer. The iron was kept below 37.7 ° C (100° F), the same temperature as a blow dryer at the "cool" setting. These techniques do not affect firmly set creases but can help to recreate the original smooth fabric finish of stable cotton garments that have been wet-cleaned.

Figure 3. A 1907 graduation dress from Oliver Goldsmith School in Chicago had been heavily worn and substantially altered.

Figure 4. Alterations that affected the structural stability and basic proportions of the graduation dress were removed; all other repairs or original construction anomalies were preserved.

Options for relaxing creases are more limited when garments cannot be wet-cleaned. A humidification technique was used to reduce extensive creasing in a wool flannel and lace dress made by Chicago seamstress "Madame Grossman" for a Russian immigrant around 1913. The gown was suspended on a polypropylene screen over standing water in a wet-cleaning table sealed in plastic. After two hours, the dress was placed on a mannequin and smoothed by hand to reduce distortions. Rows of deteriorated or missing silk-covered wooden buttons decorating the front and back of the dress were considered an integral aspect of the garment's design and were replaced with reproductions. Silk was dyed to match the original button covers and stitched over commercial plastic button forms lined with Mylar disks.

It is difficult to predict how much support an artifact will require for extended display. A pair of cotton bathing shoes with ankle ties was in excellent condition and did not receive treatment. The shoes were displayed on a seated mannequin and the ties, which were more decorative than functional, did not appear to be under stress. However, the ties were torn when the shoes were removed after the first nine month exhibition period. The ties were repaired and a pair of black cotton tapes was attached to the shoes. The tapes were wound around the mannequin's ankles beneath the original ties and no further damage occurred.

One of the most important traditional Jewish clothing customs is the covering of a married woman's head. The most observant women shave their heads and don a sheitel, or wig. For many American Jewish women, assimilation began with the shedding of a kerchief or sheitel. One woman received a letter from her husband cautioning her to grow her hair because "in America you don't wear no wigs." She contracted typhoid fever in Poland, lost her hair,

Figure 5. A Ukrainian woman wearing a sheitel.

and wore her sheitel on the boat to cover her bald head. When her husband spotted her, he angrily refused to take her off Ellis Island.[6] Two rare turn-of-the-century sheitels were donated for the exhibition. One of the sheitels was in excellent condition, but the second was problematic. The sheitel was made of human hair mounted on a cotton net with two tapes that tied behind the neck. An ivory silk ribbon inserted beneath a center part in the hair created an illusion of skin. The hair was in remarkably good condition but was no longer arranged in a bun, and in considerable disarray. There was a heavy accumulation of oily substances in the wig and the hair was matted into clumps. The silk ribbon beneath the center part was split. The unusual opportunity to study an intact sheitel as well as documentary

photographs made it possible to attempt a reconstruction. The clumps and tangles of hair were gently eased apart by hand. The hair was smoothed into a bun and held in place with hairpins. Only a small amount of hair was lost during restoration; perhaps hair oil is a potent preservative. The split in the center part was repaired by couching the silk ribbon to the underlying cotton net support.

Display

Mannequins for costume display were selected to reflect the personal tone of the exhibition, as well as the facial characteristics of Eastern European immigrants. Specialty mannequins available commercially were priced beyond the exhibition budget. Mannequins from previous CHS exhibitions were modified by an in-house design technician at a substantially lower cost. Mannequin fabrication also created a unique opportunity to encourage participation in the exhibition.

Chicago-area participants in the project were selected to pose for plaster face masks that were mounted on exhibition mannequins. Covering a donor's face in plaster is not without attendant risk, but all of our willing victims patiently withstood the procedure and emerged smiling. Our design technician, Donna Schudel, began by photographing each

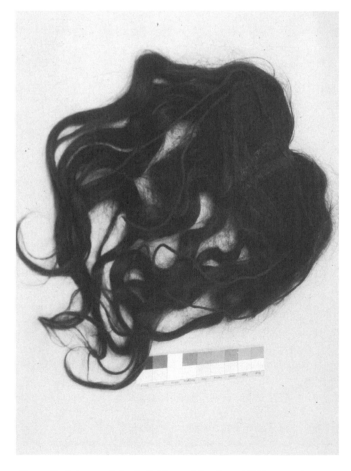

Figure 6. A human hair sheitel loaned for the exhibition was in considerable disarray but the hair was in remarkably good condition.

Figure 7. The original appearance of the wig was reconstructed by studying an intact sheitel.

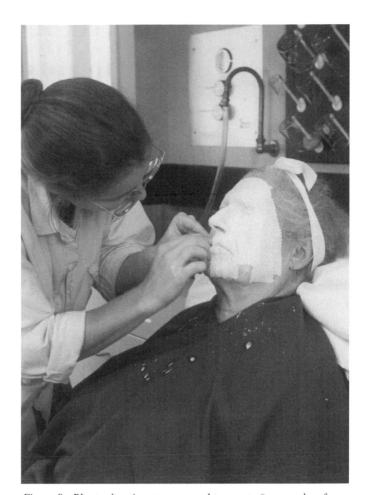

Figure 8. Plaster bandages were used to create face masks of women who participated in the project.

model for future reference. She coated the model's face, eyebrows and eyelashes with Nivea, a thick hand-cream. Plaster medical bandages were soaked in water and thinly coated on the model's face. Nostrils were left uncovered to avoid the need for straws. A hair dryer speeded drying; the entire procedure took an average of 20 minutes. When the mask was dry, it was carefully lifted at the edges and removed. Several models compared the process to receiving a facial and found the warm plaster calming.

The plaster masks were then mounted on previously used mannequins. A joint compound, which was primarily composed of plaster, was applied to the mannequins to adhere the masks and smooth the surface of the skin; the material passed an Oddy test prior to application. The faces and exposed limbs of the figures were finished with a tea-dyed Japanese paper that was pressed in place on the damp plaster. Hairstyles selected from period photographs were reproduced with additional Japanese paper.

Period undergarments and body pads were produced by volunteers to create appropriate body shapes and facilitate rapid dressing and undressing of the mannequins at the various venues. Undergarments fabricated for an 1897 wedding gown from Decatur, Illinois included a period corset and

petticoat, as well as bust and bustle pads. Corsets with underlayers of fiberfill can quickly change a mannequin's dimensions without sacrificing the correct period silhouette. A variety of body shapes were represented. Generous quantities of fiberfill stitched into cotton knit undergarments were useful for creating a more mature, well-endowed figure.

Representational mannequins were not required for all garments. Invisible mounts were created by cutting down the neck of mannequin torsos to follow the neckline of individual garments. The torsos were mounted on dress form bases. Kerchief and corset mounts were fabricated by covering mannequin heads and torsos with joint compound and Japanese paper.

Transport

Following display at the Chicago Historical Society, the exhibition made a two-year journey across the United States to the Ellis Island Immigration Museum in New York City, the National Museum of American Jewish History in Philadelphia, the Skirball Cultural Center in Los Angeles, and the Detroit Historical Museum. The exhibition was kept intact for travel to these venues. The lenders were enthusiastic to share their stories with a wider

Figure 9. Plaster masks were placed on mannequins from previous exhibits to create personalized facial characteristics appropriate for Eastern European Jewish women.

audience, and it would have been necessary to redesign the highly integrated exhibit to produce a smaller traveling display. Special considerations for transporting the show included the large quantity and variety of artifacts, including approximately 100 costumes and accessories; 340 photographs, books or documents; 20 household objects; 20 mannequins and garment mounts; and 35 exhibition cases. The Ellis Island Immigration Museum was undergoing restoration; access, installation and security arrangements were complex for this nationally listed historic building, which is visited by thousands on a daily basis.

CHS staff worked closely with Pickens-Kane Art, a Chicago fine arts storage, packing, and shipping firm, to plan the traveling exhibition and found them to be an invaluable asset for anticipating potential problems and designing creative solutions. The art-handling firm sent a representative to the Ellis Island Immigration Museum to measure the doors, hallways, and elevators in this historic structure that were frequently narrower and lower than modern-day standards. This precaution proved to be critical for planning crate sizes as the only available entrance during renovation was through a maze of narrow, underground tunnels with low overhead pipes, and tight corners. The shipping was subcontracted to independent truck owners and we negotiated to have the same drivers for each leg of the journey, an arrangement that saved time and frustration. The clothing and mannequins were packed separately. In addition to the high cost of fabricating crates for individual mannequins, the mounts were not suited to travel fully dressed. The close-fitting period garments could not be placed on the mannequins without detachable torsos, legs, and arms. The paper skin on exposed areas of the mannequins was fragile and rubbed off easily. Securing the multiple moving body parts without abrading the artifacts or the paper skin would have been a daunting proposition.

The costumes fit easily in standard archival costume boxes that were packed in wood crates. Clothing and undergarments for each mannequin were packed together in a single box with the exception of shoes, hats, and other large three-dimensional accessories. Packing forms were created from cotton stockinet, muslin, and fiberfill and labeled with artifact numbers to ensure that the garments were repacked with the same materials at each venue. Costume boxes were subdivided with corrugated board for three-dimensional accessories. Hat mounts were made from polystyrene wig stands mounted on foamboard and covered with cotton stockinet; cotton ties for the hats were stitched through the wig stands.

The mannequins were disassembled for travel. Each torso was immobilized at its base in a wooden skeleton crate. The skeleton crates were then placed in heavy-weight cardboard dish-packs. Arms were wrapped in bubble wrap, cushioned between foam, and layered in wood-reinforced cardboard crates. Legs and bases were placed in cardboard boxes, and cushioned with polystyrene packing peanuts sealed in plastic bags to ease repacking.

Photographs and non-textile objects were packed in foam cut-outs in wood crates. The packing firm convinced us

Figure 10. Mannequin torsos were mounted in wooden skeleton crates and then placed in heavy-weight cardboard dish-packs.

that it was safer and more cost-effective to pack these objects at their environmentally controlled storage facility rather than at the Historical Society. The non-textile objects were soft-packed in cardboard crates for transport to the facility, where the art handlers determined the most space-efficient packing arrangement and created customized foam cut-outs that precisely fit the objects. "Tea cozies" were stitched from moving blankets for the display cases; these covers were stored in the hollow bases beneath the vitrines during exhibition.

The exhibition took approximately one week to install or deinstall. Two full-time staff were needed to complete condition reports, dress or undress mannequins, and supervise artifact handling at each venue. CHS's registrar, Louise Brownell, accompanied the exhibition to each venue; a staff conservator or local costume preparator was responsible for the textile artifacts. Written mannequin dressing instructions were supplemented by photographs of each mannequin in its requisite undergarments as well as a view of the fully clothed figure. Every accessory, undergarment, or body pad was labeled with an exhibition number to prevent confusion and misplacement. Packing instructions included a step-by-step guide to padding each textile

Figure 12. Written dressing instructions were supplemented by photographs of each mannequin in its requisite undergarments, as well as a view of the fully clothed figure.

Figure 11. Period undergarments and body pads were produced by volunteers to create appropriate body shapes and facilitate dressing of the mannequins at each venue.

artifact and fitting it in the box, as well as a photograph of the fully-packed box.

Detailed case layout drawings were also sent to each venue. A CHS design staff person assisted with installation at Ellis Island as the facility posed an unusual challenge. The exhibition gallery was a former dormitory for immigrants detained overnight. Nothing could be attached directly to the walls, ceiling, or floors of this historic structure. Labels and frames were secured on temporary walls or with specialized picture hanging devices. Band cases that had been screwed to the floor at CHS were attached to larger display cases. The tiled floor of the room had several drain holes and the floor sloped near the drains; display cases had to be individually leveled with shims. Initially, open display had been planned for the representational mannequins. However, all of the exhibition artifacts had to be secured in closed cases as thousands of visitors pass through Ellis Island every day and security personnel cannot supervise individual galleries on a full-time basis. Despite these complications, it was particularly appropriate to install the exhibition at Ellis Island, where many of the artifacts and their lenders had passed on their arrival in America.

Conclusions

The prospect of preparing a traveling costume exhibition, which inevitably necessitates extended display and extensive handling, is enough to make any conservator weak in the knees. The demand for making museum collections more accessible to the public is increasing and museums are under pressure to respond in new ways: airports and shopping malls are establishing museum display cases and the National Endowment for the Humanities in the United States has created new grant priorities stipulating that exhibitions must travel for a museum to receive funding. Early and detailed planning is critical for the safety and success of a traveling exhibition, and conservators must be flexible members of the planning team.

The long-term display and extensive handling associated with traveling exhibitions will take a greater toll on costume artifacts than in-house exhibitions. Conservation treatments for traveling exhibitions may need to incorporate support fabrics for fragile textiles on a preventive basis rather than for existing damage. If this is not possible, it may be necessary to consider using an alternate object or a reproduction.

A traveling exhibition provides a wonderful opportunity to meet colleagues, learn how other museums function, and explore new cities. However, the size and complexity of *Becoming American Women* posed difficulties for both local and CHS staff at the traveling venues. Exhibition-related travel necessitated more than two months of time away from home for CHS staff. Most of the contracting museums did not have sufficient space to store exhibition materials until immediately prior to opening, necessitating a brief and intense installation period. Detailed instructions eased the workload and made it possible for contract staff to take over when necessary. However, it can be difficult for local staff to digest large amounts of written information within the condensed time frame that is usually available. If the traveling exhibition were planned today, it would probably be smaller and less complex.

Becoming American Women provided an opportunity to work with costumes and textiles that had powerful histories and to personally connect with people who had used or contributed the garments. The project elicited genuine excitement, generated by the enthusiastic lenders as well as the museum staff and large numbers of visitors who eagerly anticipated the exhibition at each venue. The exhibition represented a once-in-a-lifetime opportunity to display many of the artifacts and brought to life the poignant stories of these quintessential American women.

Endnotes

1. Schreier, Barbara A. *Becoming American Women: Clothing and the Jewish Immigrant Experience, 1880-1920*. Chicago: Chicago Historical Society, 1994, pp. 1-15

2. Interview with Rose Wandel, Chicago Historical Society, 1993.

3. Rovner, Sarah. Ellis Island Oral History Project, Ellis Island Immigration Museum.

4. Interview with Shoshana Hoffman, in *Becoming American Women*, Barbara Schreier, p. 4.

5. Joe Braufman correspondence, courtesy of Helen B. Lichterman, in *Becoming American Women*, Barbara Schreier, p. 4.

6. Schreier. *Becoming American Women*, pp. 93-96.

7. Block, Ruth Young, conversation with author, Chicago Historical Society, March 1994.

8. Interview with Ida Feldman, Chicago Historical Society, in *Becoming American Women*, Barbara Schreier, p. 50.

Illustration credits

1. Photograph courtesy of the John and Selma Appel Collection, Courtesy of Michigan State University Museum.
2. Photograph courtesy of Chicago Jewish Archives/ Spertus Institute.
3. Dress courtesy of Jackie Shapiro.
4. Dress courtesy of Jackie Shapiro.
5. Photograph courtesy of Muriel Golman.
6. Sheitel courtesy of Barbara Kramer.
7. Garments courtesy of Lois Cohen (apron), Julia Gershon (blouse), Edith Lebed (shawl), and Myrna Metz (sheitel).
12. Wedding Gown of Annie Oshinsky Berkson, Decatur, IL, January 24, 1897. Gift of Saretta Berkson Cohen and Willyne Bower. Gown courtesy of Skirball Cultural Center.

Résumé

Restauration, exposition et transport de l'exposition Becoming American Women: Clothing and the Jewish Immigrant Experience, 1880-1920

En 1994, la Chicago Historical Society (CHS) a créé l'exposition itinérante «Becoming American Women: Clothing and the Jewish Immigrant Experience, 1880-1920». Confiée à la conservatrice Barbara Schreier, l'exposition explore le rôle complexe de l'habillement dans le processus d'acculturation américain. Des immigrants juifs d'Europe de l'Est de première ou deuxième génération ont prêté des vêtements et autres textiles pour l'occasion, et partagé des histoires prenantes d'efforts d'intégration. Les traitements de restauration choisis pour ces articles visent à faire le juste poids entre l'apparence d'origine du vêtement, les signes d'utilisation et les manipulations fréquentes, caractéristiques des expositions itinérantes. Parmi les mesures spéciales de l'exposition, on notera la personnalisation des mannequins à l'aide de masques de plâtre des femmes qui ont participé au projet. L'emballage et le transport de cette exposition volumineuse et complexe a nécessité une planification considérable en vue d'un itinéraire de deux ans qui l'a portée aux quatre coins des États-Unis. On présente un aperçu de la restauration, de la présentation et du transport des vêtements qui ont constitué l'exposition.

Travelling with Panache: An Unconventional Packing Method for a Travelling Costume Exhibit

Carol Brynjolfson

Vancouver Museum
1100 Chestnut Street
Vancouver, BC V6J 3J9 Canada
Tel.: (604) 736-4431, local 371
Fax: (604) 736-5417
E-mail: carolb@vanmuseum.bc.ca

Abstract

A new conservator and history curator were challenged to prepare a previously displayed clothing exhibit for travel. The major complication was the use of very difficult-to-dress mannequins that had been commissioned for the exhibit. Dresses were travelled on the mannequins using a system of internal support and quilted garment covers. Most accessories were removed and packed separately. Mannequins were individually crated with a strut system inside the crates for support; crates travelled upright. The packing system was generally successful. The problems found and potential future solutions are discussed.

Introduction

In 1992, the new conservator and new history curator at the Vancouver Museum, Vancouver, British Columbia, were faced with the challenge of preparing a previously displayed exhibit for travel. The previous history curator had used Museum Assistance Plan (MAP) funding from the then Department of Communications (DOC) to plan and install a large textile exhibit at the Vancouver Museum. One of the conditions of MAP funding was that the exhibit must travel to at least three venues in other provinces.

Panache: 200 Years of the Fashionable Woman was a very popular exhibit. One of the perceived reasons was the specially commissioned mannequins. These were based on the *Lady Grace* full-sized doll and made by a specialist dollmaker. While these dolls added to the visual impact of the exhibit, they presented many problems for a travelling exhibit. Due to their very high cost, and the curator's feeling that they were an integral part of the exhibit, they had to be used. Twelve dresses were displayed on these mannequins, the remaining 14 were on commercial dress forms and Ethafoam disc body forms.[1]

The mannequins have porcelain heads, chests and lower arms; the lower torso and upper arms are stuffed and covered with cotton muslin. While the neck, upper and lower arms are all articulating, they were not dismountable. The wrists are not articulating and the hands have slightly splayed fingers. The lower arms are joined to the upper arms by a braided cord through the elbow, attached to

a washer inside the opening of the upper arm. This cord is covered with urethane foam. Due to the weight of the lower arms, the cords have either stretched or slipped down inside the upper arms, elongating the arm at the elbow. The mannequins are about three-quarters life size of the average modern female. The waist is very narrow (58 cm) and the hips wide (91 cm). There are also two stuffed cotton muslin legs which can be attached to the underside of the torso with Velcro strips; these were not used in the exhibit.

Packing Method — Dresses on Mannequins

All of the above characteristics of the mannequin caused a lot of conservation problems. Dressing the mannequins was very difficult, especially if a bodice had sleeves with

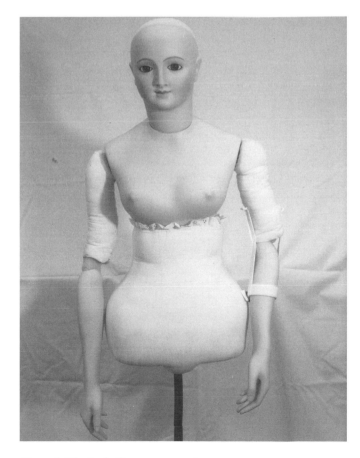

Figure 1. The Lady Grace mannequin.

narrow cuffs, or if the dress was one piece. It was therefore decided to investigate other methods of packing which involved leaving the dresses on the mannequins for travel. In 1992, there was very little in the conservation literature about travelling clothing exhibits. An article about a travelling ethnographic exhibit used a padded cover over a coat which was left on its mannequin.[2] It was decided to use a similar method and to support the dresses both internally and externally. To simplify packing and unpacking, the same method was used for the dresses displayed on the dress forms and Ethafoam disc body forms.

Figure 2. A custom hoop-skirt type petticoat used for a "triangular skirt" from the 1860s.

We used the body of the mannequin, as well as petticoats for internal support. The body shape of the mannequin was adjusted to fit the garment by padding with polyethylene batting under cotton jersey; this was wrapped over the porcelain parts of the mannequin torso and sewn to the soft parts. For the slimmer dresses, some of the stuffing was removed from the mannequins' hips. Hoop-skirt type petticoats were custom made for garments (see Figure 2). Cotton muslin petticoats were held in the appropriate shape with 2.5 cm (1 in.) polyethylene (HDPE) piping which was run through tabs sewn to the underside of the garment. The ends of the pipe were fastened so that they would not accidentally pop open. This gave a shape which would not flatten down during exhibit and travel. Suitable bustle pads and panniers were made of muslin, supported with plastic boning.

The arms of the mannequins had two particular problems caused by their manufacturing methods. First, the lower arms are heavy and tend to slip down at the elbow (see Figure 3a). Secondly, a slot in the upper end of the lower arm was slipped over a washer through which the connecting cord was knotted: there is a potential for the arm to slip off the washer. These two problems could result in the garment supporting the mannequin arms and causing a lot of stress on the shoulder area. The solution for most of the mannequins was to make an arm garter using 3 mm (1/8 in.) Evazote, a high friction foam, secured below the widest

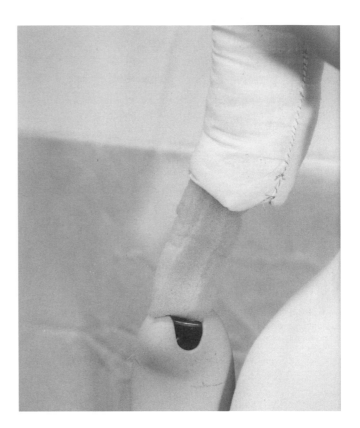

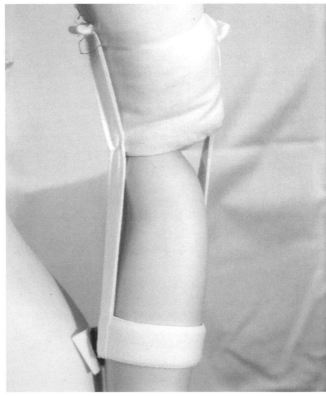

Figure 3a and 3b. a) The elongation of the elbow joint. b) The arm garter constructed to fix this problem.

part of the lower arm with twill tape and Velcro; twill-tape straps were sewn to the garters and the cotton of the upper arm (see Figure 3b). One dress had extremely short sleeves and the arm garters would have been unsightly, even under long kid leather gloves. For this mannequin, a long pair of cloth gloves were fitted over the arms and sewn to the upper end of the upper arms; the kid gloves were slid over the cloth ones.

Exterior support was provided by custom-made quilted covers. Commercially available quilting was used for most covers. Cotton jersey was on one side and polyester jersey on the reverse, with thin polyester fibrefill between. If extra padding seemed advisable, covers were made of two layers of cotton muslin padded with thick polyester fibrefill. Most garments had separate bodice and skirt covers. The covers were fastened by a series of cotton twill-tape ties down the front and/or back. Each piece was labelled with the number and description of the garment for which it was created. Packing instructions detailed the methods used to put each cover on the garment.

For wide skirts, covers were made with several gores to fit the shape. A bottom was sewn to the perimeter of each skirt cover; bottoms were either gathered by a drawstring around the mannequin support post or a slit was left to facilitate the support post.

Dresses with trains caused particular problems. These were dealt with in one of two ways. The first method involved rolling the train over a padded cotton muslin tube, avoiding wrinkles as one rolled. Long twill tapes sewn to each end of the tube were used to tie the ends of the roll to the mannequin's support post; the skirt cover supported the roll externally. One very complex train with fringes and tassels could not be dealt with in the same manner (see Figure 4). This train had a vertical central seam with its own tape sewn to the lining; the tape and lining were strong and stable. We fastened a long twill tape to the existing tape; the twill tape was then pulled so the train was held out to the back of the skirt in a horizontal position. The train folded naturally over the tape on its central seam. It was then swung around the right side of the skirt, over the skirt cover and the twill tape was tied to the front of the skirt cover. A flap on the skirt cover then covered over the train, keeping it from sliding back along the tape.

Bodice covers varied from simple to complex. Each was custom made, taking into account sleeve/shoulder styles, necklines and collars, bodice shape and decorations. Some were simple vest styles, others had flaps that went around the sides and tied in front or back. Where there was a possibility of mixing up which twill tapes to tie together, the ends of the twill tapes were colour coded with thread.

Unusual decorative items were accommodated. For example, a bow made of silk ribbons was on the shoulder of one dress. To avoid crushing the bow, a raised ring of quilted fabric was sewn to the inside of the garment cover; this rested on the dress and lifted the cover over the bow.

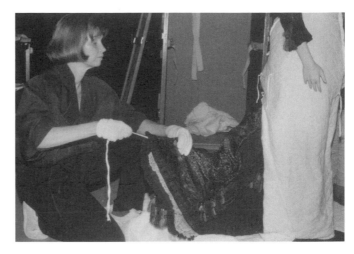

Figure 4. The complex train was folded over the twill tape, before being wrapped to one side over the garment cover.

Sleeve covers were usually made separately and tied to the shoulder area with twill tapes. Dresses with short, puff sleeves on dress-form mannequins were supported by creating a pouch at the shoulder of the bodice cover. Sleeves were gently eased into the pouch.

Some of the later (1916 to 1939) dresses were quite simple and straight in style. They were only given lightweight petticoat or slips internally, and covered with a simple, one-piece cover which had a drawstring bottom.

A few accessories travelled on the mannequins. Gloves and engageantes (removable undersleeves) were left on arms. On one mannequin, hair ornaments were sewn to the wig. One hat was quite stable on the mannequin head, and was secured for travel by covering it and the forehead with a hair net tied in place with twill tape. A cotton cap was also left on the head of another mannequin.

Each mannequin required its own packing crate. These were made in three sizes, the most common one being the smallest. The interior of the crate was fitted with wooden 5 x 10 cm (2 x 4 in.) struts to support the mannequin. The base plate of the mannequin stand was held securely on the base of the crate between two side struts, a back strut and a removable front strut. The back and front struts had channels cut on the underside which fit over the edge of the base plate.

The position of the base was carefully determined so that the mannequin's upper back just rested against a horizontal back cross-strut. A front cross-strut was then screwed in place. The height of the cross-struts was determined for each mannequin, so that they rested against an area of the chest where there was the least probability of damaging the dress. Left and right side supports were attached to the back and front cross-struts. The cross-bars and side supports were padded with rolled bubble-pack inside an Ethafoam layer.

The neck and head were secured by using two strips of 5 cm (2 in.) wide loop Velcro. The first strip went from the back of the back strut behind the right shoulder, crossed behind the back, went around the left side then the front of the neck, around the right side then crossed behind the back, to stick to the hook Velcro behind the left shoulder on the back strut. The second Velcro strip went from the front of the front strut, over one shoulder, crossed behind

the neck and above the previous Velcro back over the other shoulder and to the front strut. Before the second Velcro was fastened down, it was tightened slightly, which also tightened the first Velcro since it crossed above and pulled down on it. Most of the dresses on these mannequins did not have high collars, so there was little problem with the Velcro damaging the dress.

Arms were supported with Velcro straps across the hand to the sides of the crates. In the case of the very wide crates, struts were built to support the arms (see Figure 5).

Other Garments and Accessories

A beaded silk georgette evening sheath from the early 1920s could not travel on the mannequin: it was too heavy. It was relatively easy to put on a dress form. Its style allowed it to lie flat and be rolled, interleaved with acid-free tissue. It was then stored in a Coroplast box inside a small wooden crate. The large wooden crate which would have held this dress was partitioned to hold this small crate and the mannequin on the lower level. The upper level was used to hold cartons with accessories, extra tissue, the condition report/packing instruction book and the labels.

A very heavy silk velvet evening coat from 1939 was also folded and packed with tissue in a Coroplast box. Hats were supported on layers of Coroplast which had a padded mount; a cover of quilted batting was tied over each hat to keep it from lifting up or moving around. The hats and hat supports were put inside boxes. Pelerines and scarves were folded with tissue and packed in boxes.

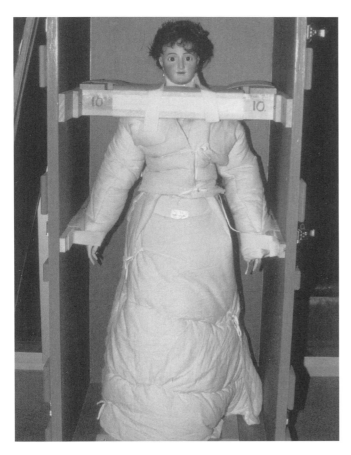

Figure 5. A dressed mannequin in its crate.

Most of the accessories (brooches, necklaces, bracelets, purses) were packed in custom carved holes in layers of Ethafoam on a Coroplast tray. The holes were lined with cotton jersey or, for the silver artifacts, Pacific Silver Cloth. The tray was covered with another layer of Ethafoam which was secured with twill tape. The covered trays were stacked in boxes.

The signature feathers (*Panache*) were gently wrapped in acid-free tissue and floated inside a thin 3 mm (1/8 in.) Ethafoam envelope which was attached to the upper side of a long box. A parasol was packed in a similar manner in the same box and a long bouquet was placed in the bottom of the box.

The crates were provided with lifting bars along two sides, and could also be tilted enough to load them onto a dolly. The crates were travelled upright, in the air-ride suspension truck from the Exhibit Transport Services of the Department of Communications. Loading and unloading was done by staff at the local museums. The Vancouver Museum conservator went to each venue to do condition reports and to help set up the exhibit. Since the budget did

Figure 6. Detail of upper support struts.

not permit the curator to travel, the conservator was given detailed display instructions for each garment.

Discussion

The decision to use the type of packing described above had an impact on which dresses were chosen for the exhibit. Also many of the dresses used in the original exhibit were on loan from a private collection and were not available for the travelling exhibit. Some of the Vancouver Museum's collection dresses used in the original exhibit were too fragile for this form of travel: a wedding dress had many rents in the silk taffeta underskirt, a black beaded evening gown had fragile, deteriorating beads which were also extremely heavy. Dresses were chosen for robustness and a need for only minimal conservation, as well as curatorial requirements.

Because the Vancouver Museum does not employ a textile conservator, advice was sought from a local private conservator who has done occasional work for the museum, as well as from the textile conservators at the Royal British Columbia Museum, the Canadian Conservation Institute, and the Canadian Museum of Civilization. Their advice enabled the Vancouver Museum staff to do the work necessary to prepare the dresses for exhibit. Due to the care with which the petticoats, garment covers and crates were made, little damage was sustained by the dresses.

One of the more fragile dresses was a greenish-grey and blue silk taffeta day dress from the early 1870s. Before travelling, the grey silk above the corded points on the overskirt showed some abrasion. During travel, the stress caused the abraded areas to deteriorate with broken warp thread and some loss of warp threads (see Figure 7). Shear forces also caused a horizontal adhesive repair at the rear of the overskirt to open 0.2 cm.

One wool poplin maternity dress showed some raising of nap on the surface, especially around the lower skirt. This

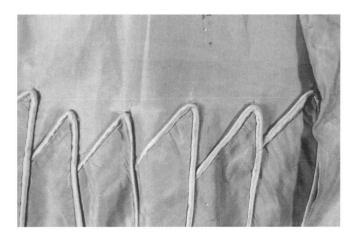

Figure 7. Overskirt of grey and blue taffeta dress: damage can be seen just above the points.

has tentatively been attributed to abrasion by the garment cover on the dress caused by the vibration of travel. This garment cover had the polyester side of the quilted material towards the garment, rather than the cotton side.

A yellow silk evening gown with cream damask panels, which was on a custom-made Ethafoam disc mannequin, showed enlargement of an area of deteriorating silk damask. The area had been repaired by couching prior to the exhibit, but on return, damage had gone beyond the area of repair. On review, the mannequin may have been a little too tight at the level of the armholes, causing stress on the garment.

The bustle pads and panniers tended to droop during travel. The plastic boning deformed under the weight of the garments over extended periods of time and the stress of travel.

Conclusions and Suggestions for Improvement

Many of the problems encountered can be solved if future uses of this travelling method are required. Some of the garment covers just barely met at the openings, especially on the bodice covers. This allowed some access for dust and also allowed any short fibres from the fibre fill to migrate to the garment. Cotton muslin flaps sewn to one edge of the cover and tucked behind the other edge would have covered the gaps.

An apron-style support for the heavy points of the overskirt of the grey and blue taffeta day dress would probably minimise stress and damage. Such a support could have a component which remained under the overskirt during the exhibit, but had an attachment which covered the front and tied around the waist during travel.

The raised surface nap on the wool poplin could be eliminated by choosing the cotton side of the quilt batting or by sewing another fabric (probably a slick silk of satin weave polyester) over the quilt batting.

Slightly undersizing the Ethafoam disc mannequin, used for the yellow silk and cream damask dress, would have been a better alternative, given that the vibrations and shock of transit could have caused the dress to shift on the mannequin.

Improvements could be made to the internal supports. The hoop-skirt petticoats did not all have as many hoops as they could have. One or two more hoops per petticoat would have given more even support without significantly adding to the weight of the mannequin. The bustle pads and panniers should have been stuffed internally so that they did not deform. The stuffing would have to be lightweight but not compressible; Ethafoam or Styrofoam may have worked.

This packing method is not one to be used for most travelling exhibits. It was designed to solve a particular problem with difficult-to-dress mannequins, which were considered to be integral to the exhibit. It was expensive to build one crate per garment as well as to ship the large number of crates. This method is certainly not advisable for fragile garments or heavily beaded ones. Overall, the method of packing dresses on internal supports with quilted covers worked well, except for the few problems described above.

Endnotes

1 Department of Clothing and Textiles, University of Alberta. Papers from "Disc Mannequin Workshop," November 8-10, 1985.

2 Gail Sundstrom Niinimaa. "Mounting Systems for Ethnographic Textiles and Objects," *Journal of the American Institute for Conservation*, vol. 26, no. 2 (Fall 1987), pp. 75-84.

Acknowledgements

Joan Seidl was the newly appointed history curator who worked closely with me on this project. A contract consultant (who has asked to remain anonymous) selected the costumes, contributed to the text of the exhibit and made the petticoats, bustle pads and panniers. A contract conservation assistant, Linda Tanaka, did much of the conservation work and designed and made all the garment covers. Crating was done by Ken Stephens of Denbigh Design in consultation with myself. I wish to thank them all for their contributions to this effort.

Résumé

Voyager avec panache : une méthode d'emballage originale pour une exposition itinérante de costumes

Un nouveau restaurateur et un conservateur des matériaux historiques relèvent le défi de préparer des vêtements déjà exposés en vue d'une exposition itinérante. La principale complication réside dans l'utilisation d'un type de mannequin spécial conçu pour l'exposition. Les costumes sont disposés sur les mannequins, pour le voyage, avec un système de supports internes et des couvre-vêtements matelassés. La plupart des accessoires sont retirés et emballés séparément. Chaque mannequin est placé dans une caisse individuelle dotée d'un système interne de soutien à vérins. Les caisses sont transportées verticalement. Le système d'emballage s'est révélé réussi dans l'ensemble. On traite des problèmes qui se sont manifestés et de leurs solutions potentielles.

6

Support and Presentation
Support et présentation

Dressed for the Occasion: Creative and Practical Ideas for Mounting Costume Exhibitions

Eva Burnham

McCord Museum of Canadian History
690 Sherbrooke West
Montreal, QC H3A 1E9 Canada
Tel.: (514) 398-7100
Fax: (514) 398-5045

Daniel Lalande

3721 Laval Avenue
Montreal, QC
H2X 2E1

Abstract

Costumes always provide interest and animation to museum exhibits. Whether as exhibits in themselves or as accessory figures within the context of other exhibits, costumes immediately provide a human element that attracts the viewer on a very personal level. When a single element of an exhibition can stimulate such an immediate and instinctive viewer reaction, it is unfortunate that all too frequently museums are put off from mounting costume exhibitions because of the difficulties involved in creating appropriate mannequins. In fact, the benefits of a successfully mounted show should far outweigh any problems in producing its various elements. This presentation will identify frequently encountered problems in mounting costume shows, and provide practical and innovative solutions. The everyday reality of budget constraints will not be forgotten, and a number of alternate options and their relative costs will be discussed for each aspect of mounting. The importance of giving an exhibition "style," whether it be traditional, historic or abstract, will also be discussed. The importance of preparation and of clear, timely communication between curators, designers and technicians, in order that an exhibition's objectives and concepts are clearly understood, will be emphasized. The various type of mannequins available will be discussed. The talk will be illustrated with slides taken during various stages of mounting an exhibition.

Due to unforseen circumstances, this paper was not available for publication.

Résumé

Vêtu pour l'occasion : idées créatives et pratiques pour le montage des expositions de costumes

Les costumes donnent toujours de la vie aux expositions. Qu'ils soient eux-mêmes l'objet de l'événement ou qu'ils servent d'accessoires dans d'autres expositions, les costumes apportent instantanément un élément humain qui attire le visiteur de façon très personnelle. Lorsque l'on songe au fait qu'un seul élément d'une exposition puisse susciter une réaction aussi immédiate et instinctive chez le visiteur, il est regrettable que, trop souvent, les musées renoncent à monter des expositions de vêtements en raison des difficultés qui entourent la création de mannequins appropriés. En réalité, les avantages d'une exposition convenablement montée dépassent largement les difficultés de réalisation de ses divers éléments. Dans la présentation, on décrit les problèmes courants qui touchent le montage d'une exposition de costumes et on propose des solutions pratiques et innovatrices. La réalité quotidienne des budgets qui doivent être respectés n'est pas oubliée; des solutions de rechange en matière de montage et leurs coûts seront discutés. L'importance de donner un «style» à l'exposition, qu'il soit traditionnel, historique ou abstrait, sera aussi traité. On souligne aussi l'importance de la préparation et d'une communication claire et opportune entre les conservateurs, les concepteurs et les techniciens afin que tous comprennent bien les concepts et les objectifs de l'exposition. On traite de divers types de mannequins. L'auteur agrémentera sa présentation avec des diapositives prises à diverses étapes du montage d'une exposition.

En raison de circonstances imprévues, seul le résumé de la communication a pu être publié.

Flying the Flag Down Under: A Discussion of the Significance of Flags, the Etiquette of Using Them and a Variety of Display Techniques

Catherine Challenor and Wendy Dodd

Australian War Memorial
P. O. Box 345
Campbell ACT 2601 Australia
Tel.: 06 2434531
E-mail: cathy.challenor@awm.gov.au
E-mail: wendy.dodd@awm.gov.au

Abstract

Throughout history, flags have been powerful symbols of purpose and identity. People express their loyalty and a sense of patriotic duty by showing respect to their flag. Consequently, flags can become important cultural and historic artefacts. This respect must also be reflected in museum handling and display methods. This paper briefly discusses the history of flags and military traditions and describes a variety of display and support methods.

Flag - a piece of cloth, commonly bunting, of varying size, shape, colour, and device, usually attached by one edge to a staff or cord and used as an ensign, standard, symbol, signal, decoration, display. Macquarie Concise Dictionary

Introduction

The study of flags, or vexillology, is a specialist field. We are not vexillologists, but a certain level of understanding of the importance and traditional etiquette associated with flags is important to enable conservators to describe, preserve and display flags appropriately. Because Australia was originally a British colony, our flag etiquette is derived from British traditions.

History and Significance of Flags

Throughout history flags have had many uses and meanings. Today they are still powerful symbols of purpose and identity. There are house flags, city flags, company flags, trade union banners, religious flags, flags of international organisations, sporting flags, signal flags, military and naval flags. In other words, most sections of a community have a flag.

National flags are held in the highest esteem and have the greatest significance. They evoke great emotion and are often considered to be sacred. Other flags, such as those flown by merchant ships, air ensigns, official government flags and the flags of political or social groups, are all symbols of the people. Prior to the 19th century, the flag was the symbol of the authority of the church or state rather than being a symbol of the people. The raising of national consciousness during events such as the French Revolution encouraged the use of flags by dissident voices. Political movements such as unions of students or workers adopted flags to represent their aims and ideals. As were other flags, they were used as rallying points. The flags of some of these dissident voices have become national flags. The French Tricolour is an excellent example.

National flags today are regarded as symbols of, and the property of the people. In some countries, such as the United States of America, residents are encouraged to fly their flags whenever possible, whereas other countries restrict their use to specific days. Some countries have a government flag and another flag for use by the public. That is on land. At sea, flag conduct and etiquette is almost universal. For example, when in a foreign port, all ships pay the courtesy of flying a small version of that country's flag.

In some countries, the respect displayed towards the flag is similar to that previously accorded to royalty. The national anthem is sung in honour of the flag rather than a monarch. The desecration of a flag is considered to be a major insult and in some countries is an offence. There are regulations about the use of civic flags in some countries whereas the United Kingdom, from which much of Australia's flag etiquette is derived, has no written regulations about the Union flag. In fact, the British put their symbol to many uses — some of which are quite irreverent.

Flags have regularly been used as a means of communication — for signalling intent or distress. A red flag means danger, mutiny or revolution; white, truce, goodwill or surrender; yellow an infectious illness; a green flag is hoisted over a wreck; black means mourning and death; a skull and cross bones, pirates, and a red cross within a white ground signifies a hospital or ambulance. Use of flags to signal has been an important part of naval training. Flags are still used as a form of communication at sea.

The capture of a flag carries with it a sense of victory over one's foes, and the planting of one's own flag signals triumph over enemies or over nature.

Flags can, for a variety of reasons, become important cultural and historic artefacts. Some flags are purely decorative and are valued for the skill and workmanship used to make them. Others have a practical purpose. Depending on the history of the use of a practical flag it may become an icon or an item of immense historical significance to a society or culture. The majority of flags have links to a seat of power and, consequently, have great significance to the military and in military history.

Each country has its own flag customs and etiquette much of which is based on long-standing traditions. Sometimes the procedures have developed as a sensible or practical way of acting, other procedures have been incorporated in legislation or form part of international treaties. There is a current movement towards standardisation of customs throughout the world.

Flag designing was originally a branch of heraldry and within its laws and traditions. For example, the colour yellow represented the metal gold and white represented silver. In designing a flag, these two metal colours should not be placed next to each other and all other colours should be separated by one of the metal colours. Today public competitions are held to encourage the whole community to participate in designing a flag and very little attention is paid to traditions.

Colours and Banners

The respect shown by citizens to their flag must be reflected in museum display and handling methods. Because of our British heritage many Australian military traditions follow the British model. The Sovereign's Colours of the Army, Air Force and Navy have a special place and are used only for ceremonial purposes. These Colours are presented to the regiment, ship or establishment by a member of the British Royal family or the Monarch's representative and are consecrated by a chaplain in a prescribed ceremony. Old Colours, which go out of service when new Colours are presented, have usually been laid up in a church where traditionally they were left to rot. The laying up of Colours has been compared to burial, and the removal of these Colours to an exhumation. With Australia's development as an independent multicultural country with its own identity, there has been a growing interest in its history. This interest in history is promoting a move to preserve old Colours which is reflected in changes to the ceremonial regulations governing the use and laying up of the ceremonial Colours.

Many of the early Australian Colours were hand-stitched by women from the community represented by the regiment. The stories of these women and their families is the history of the community. A resistance is developing to allowing a community symbol to disintegrate relatively uncared for by hanging it unsupported in an environment that promotes its degradation. However there are some conservative elements within the Army who still feel that we can only pay respect to these Colours by laying them up in a church or memorial and allowing them to fade away.

Some flags that have been layed up in a church are now being "rescued" once the degradation becomes obvious, and are presented to the War Memorial to preserve. Many are beyond active conservation, cannot be handled and can only be stored flat in a stable environment. Some are given minimal treatment for stabilisation others have been researched and given complex treatments. We do our best to preserve the Colours and banners in our care.

As museum professionals, we regularly give advice on the care of Colours, and are careful to point out that no heroic and expensive conservation treatments should be carried out if the Colours are to be returned to hang in an unsuitable environment.

Display Methods

The Australian War Memorial, which serves as a memorial to Australians who have lost their lives for their country, is also a large museum of historical military material. The Memorial holds an impressive collection of flags, banners and colours. These flags are made from a variety of fibres using many different techniques for embellishment and construction.

Our exhibition galleries display artefacts and artworks made from a multitude of materials. We have had to develop a variety of display methods to satisfy conservation, design and curatorial concerns.

Rod and Drape

This method was used to display a large (3.5 m by over 1 m) closely woven cotton/polyester banner in a temporary exhibition concerned with peacekeeping operations. It was to be included with a variety of other relics on a platform in an open display. The height of the display area was less than the height of the banner. It would have been possible to roll the banner to fit the height of the platform, but it was decided that, if possible, the whole of the banner's screen-printed design would be shown.

The upper edge of the banner was raw, but a row of holes a few centimetres from the edge indicated that a hanging system of some kind had previously been used. The top edge of the banner was folded back to the original sewing line to form a heading and stitched using stab stitch in the original holes. A padded metal rod was then inserted through the heading and suspended from fittings in the ceiling. The lower end of the banner was left to drape on the lower platform over a polyester film barrier.

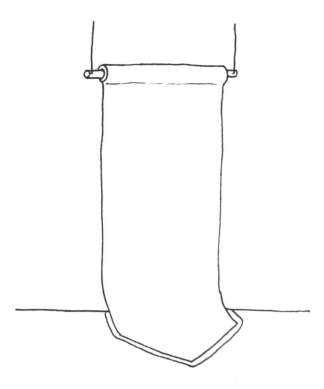

Figure 1. Long flag draped on a platform with barrier beneath.

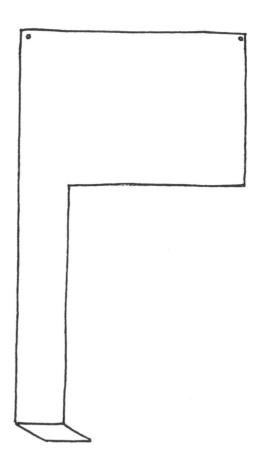

Figure 2b. Acrylic backing.

Fold or Roll and Drape

We have used this method when space is limited and a particular part of the flag is significant. The folds or roll are always well supported.

Small Flags on Sticks

This method was used for a collection of small patriotic flags used in a long-term display to commemorate seventy years since the end of World War I. The small flags, usually thickly printed on cotton, are attached to short sticks. They vary in shape and size. The designer wanted a lively display to illustrate the action of waving these flags in delight at the news of the armistice.

In this instance, the flags have been stitched or hinged on three sides to a fabric-covered Foamcor board which extended at least 1 cm beyond the edge of the flag.

Figure 2a. Fabric-covered board with channel for stick.

Figure 2c. Flags mounted onto boards and suspended using holes in acrylic support.

The stick extended beyond the board and a groove was cut in the Foamcor to take the stick where it was attached to the flag. The stick was held into the groove with a couple of stitches and the whole supported from behind and below by a piece of clear acrylic.

The flags were suspended using nylon thread attached to the acrylic. They were displayed in the showcase at various angles and depths to give a floating quality to the flags as though being waved in a crowd.

Semaphore Flags

A variation of the above technique was used to display two signal flags together. The vertical mounting technique in this instance gave the flags a rigid semaphore look, which was appropriate for the display as well as giving good support. These flags were attached to wooden sticks, 2 cm in width. The hoists were fitted very tightly over the sticks and attached with iron nails. The nails were rusted,

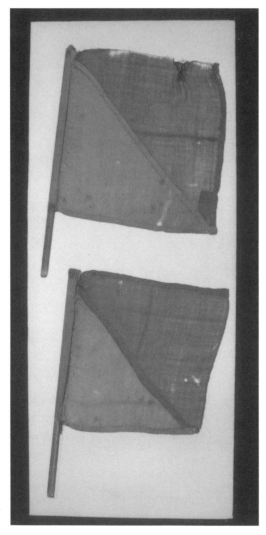

Figure 3. Semaphore flags supported in channelled grooves and stitched to fabric-covered board.

but not actively corroding. There was a possibility of damaging the flag if an attempt was made to separate the fabric from the sticks to treat the tears and rust stains in the hoist area. Adequate support for the sticks and fabric was the main concern.

To provide this support, channels were cut into a piece of Tycor and the channels reinforced with adhesive linen tape. The channelled board was covered with washed fabric and reinforced from beneath by adhering a sheet of 5 mm Foamcor. Once the tears and weak areas in the flag's fabric had been stabilised, the sticks were placed in the channels and the flag was stitched down on three sides. The fuller areas near the hoist were padded with Dacron to fully support the fabric.

Large Flags on Cloth-covered Boards

We have been able to successfully display quite large flags on fabric-covered boards. This woollen bunting flag, which measured almost 2 m in length, was particularly weakened in the hoist area by insect damage. On first inspection it was doubtful that it could withstand vertical display. The flag was to be displayed in the South African gallery, and to create an appropriate atmosphere needed to be displayed vertically.

After extensive stabilisation of the flag, which involved opening up the hoist to insert a suitable lining beneath the weakest areas near the hoist, Velcro was stitched to the back of the hoist and to the top of the fabric-covered mount board. The flag was also stitched about half way down each side to lessen the movement of the flag within the acrylic box frame which was made to fit snugly over the mount board and screw into the sides of the wooden frame attached to the back of the mount board.

This method was used on several other large flags in the same gallery. After seven years on display, the mount boards have not warped and there is no sign of stress or sagging in the flags.

Adhesive Strips to Attach Flag to Fabric Support

We have used this technique to mount embroideries and flags when the use of a needle would cause damage. A fabric-covered mount board is prepared but instead of stitching the embroidery down, strips of adhesive coated Stabiltex are used. These strips are made with the adhesive on half of each side of the Stabiltex. Half of each strip is adhered to the reverse edges of the embroidery and the other half to the backing fabric. The mount board can then be framed or covered with a acrylic box.

This method was used for some of the small patriotic flags where the thickness of printing ink makes the flags more like painted canvases. The inks fill the spaces between the threads of the fabric making sewing an unacceptable option.

Acrylic Rod Within an Acrylic Box

A King's banner presented to the Royal Australian Artillery in 1904 by Edward VII in recognition of service during the

Figure 4. Large flag supported with Velcro along hoist and partially stitched along the sides, protected in an acrylic box.

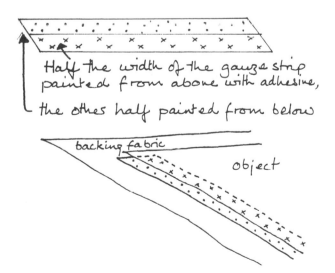

Figure 5. Gauze strip heat-set to object and backing fabric.

Boer War was required for display in the South African gallery. The banner was layed up at the Australian War Memorial in 1972 and is in quite good condition.

This display method involved no sewing or adhesion of the flag to a support and is suitable only for flags that are stable and strong enough to support their own weight. This banner was to be displayed with its ornate staff, although not hanging from it. This would have been impractical since the staff measured more than 2 m in length and the banner required a protective cover.

The banner was hung from its hoist on an acrylic rod which rests on acrylic brackets screwed into the top of a fabric-covered board. An acrylic box has been fitted around the board and the staff mounted vertically on the wall alongside.

The advantage of this method is that the natural draping quality of the flag can be seen rather than it being rigidly attached to a backing board. Unfortunately few old flags, particularly silk ones, can withstand this method and require some intervention and additional support.

Stitched to Loose Backing and Hung

This method is good for temporary displays where it is important to create a feeling of the flag floating or flying. A backing fabric just slightly larger than the flag is made with a heading which will accommodate a rod strong enough to support the flag. The flag is stitched or velcroed to the backing across the top and stitched two thirds down the sides so that the lower edge can hang free. The backing

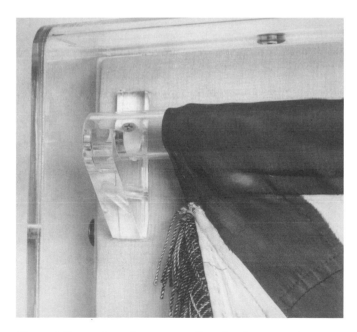

Figure 6. Banner hung from an acrylic rod and supported on acrylic brackets that screw through a fabric-covered board and wooden frame.

is suspended from the rod. We have successfully used this method to display flags and a group of souvenir scarves which were loaned for a short-term display.

Conclusion

Because the Australian War Memorial is a multifaceted organisation, there are a variety of stakeholders in any exhibition. Once the theme and concepts of an exhibition have been decided, there is much negotiation about which relics and artworks will be included in the display. There has to be mutual respect for collections so that there is a suitable balance between the messages conveyed and the integrity and preservation of the items displayed. The art and military heraldry curators do not want their paintings or flags (that have intrinsic artistic or historical value) simply used as wallpaper by a concept designer who wants to tell a particular story. Conservators have to find display methods to meet the requirements of the designer, the curators, the historians, and the object.

Figure 7. Naval ensign velcroed and stitched to a loose backing to create a feeling of movement.

It is important for people working in museums to consider the significance of flags and to follow the required etiquette when handling and displaying these objects which are of considerable significance to the culture of their origin.

Bibliography

Campbell, Gordon and I. O. Evans. *The Book of Flags.* London: Oxford University Press, 1957.

Ceremonial Manuals of the Australian Army, Navy and Airforce. January 1997.

Evans, Ivor. *Flags in General.* Melbourne: Evan Evans Pty. Ltd., (monograph).

Gordon, W. J. *Flags of the World Past and Present, Their Story and Associations.* London: Frederick Warne and Co., 1918.

Pedersen, Christian. *The International Flag Book in Colour.* English Edition. London: Blandford Press, 1971.

Smith, Whitney. *Flags Through the Ages.* United Kingdom: McGraw-Hill Book Company, 1975.

Résumé

La signification des drapeaux, les règles de conduite relatives à leur utilisation et diverses techniques de présentation

Tout au long de l'histoire, les drapeaux ont servi à symboliser de manière frappante les convictions et l'identité des peuples. Le respect du drapeau témoigne de la loyauté et du patriotisme du citoyen. Les drapeaux ont ainsi tendance à acquérir une importante charge culturelle et historique. La notion de respect qui les entoure doit se refléter dans les méthodes de manipulation et d'exposition dans les musées. L'article décrit brièvement l'histoire du drapeau, la place qu'il occupe dans les traditions militaires, ainsi que plusieurs méthodes d'exposition et de fabrication de supports.

Making the Most of Mounts: Expanding the Role of Display Mounts in the Preservation and Interpretation of Historic Textiles

Alison Lister

The Textile Conservation Centre
Apartment 22, Hampton Court Palace
East Molesey, Surrey KT8 9AU United Kingdom
Tel.: 0181 977 4943
Fax.: 0181 977 9081
E-mail: 106065.1467@compuserve.com

Abstract

This paper addresses some of the problems arising from the conflicting demands for artefacts to be made more accessible to visitors and for less interventive approaches in conservation. The concept of minimum intervention is outlined, and the benefits of extending the role of the conservator in the interpretation and presentation of objects are discussed. The difficulties, both physical and conceptual, in displaying objects that have received limited intervention are highlighted. One of the ways in which mounts can be used to overcome these difficulties is described and illustrated using two case studies.

Introduction

The mounting of an historic textile for display aims to provide it with a secure and attractive presentation device. It is frequently the case that objects are conserved specifically in order that they are in a sufficiently stable and "complete" condition to withstand being mounted for display. Mount design and production, therefore, often are considered important but essentially separate and additional processes to those concerned with actually conserving the object. As awareness increases concerning the benefits of taking a less interventive approach to the treatment of objects, it is clear that this view of mount making may become inappropriate. A different approach is required: one that combines the safe display of objects that have received limited treatment and ensures they continue to fulfil their role in the museum context.

Minimum Intervention

Minimum intervention can be defined as doing no more in the way of treatment to an object than is absolutely necessary (Lister 1995: 12). It is a principle that acknowledges that important information relating to the physical nature and context of an object can be irreversibly altered or removed by certain interventive treatments. In textile conservation it is an approach traditionally considered most appropriate for archaeological artefacts, but its use is being extended to other types of textiles. Although the concept of minimum intervention is receiving widespread support amongst conservators and curators, it is becoming clear that in the area of display it can create both physical and conceptual problems. There is a need for practical solutions to be found that address these problems. If these are not forthcoming, there is a real danger of minimum intervention being viewed only as an impediment to the use of historic objects as sources of information and enjoyment, and not as an approach that has tangible benefits for all.

It is the author's opinion that the problems created by minimum intervention fall into two categories. The first concerns the physical demands made of objects whilst on display. Objects that have received limited treatment may be unable to withstand the physical rigours of certain display systems without further damage, deterioration or loss occurring to the objects or the very features of evidential value that minimum intervention aims to preserve. In the display of textiles these problems are exacerbated by the nature of the objects and the contextual material often found in association with them. The materials and construction mechanisms used to create textiles make them highly vulnerable to unsuitable handling and display, and this susceptibility is greatly increased if the textiles retain features of evidential value, for example, soils, creases, repairs and alterations. The fragility and vulnerability to permanent change, reduction or loss of these features, as well as the objects themselves, must also be acknowledged (Brooks et al. 1996: 16).

The second problem concerns the way in which these objects may be perceived by the museum visitor. The display of objects that have received little interventive treatment could generate negative or confused responses from an audience used to seeing objects presented in a clean and "complete" state. If minimum intervention merely results in objects that are at best confusing and at worst totally incomprehensible to the average museum visitor, then the use of historic objects as primary sources of information is undermined. It is this aspect of display that is of the greatest interest in terms of the proposed use of mounts, and as such it requires further explanation. The concept of the "meaningfulness" of objects is one that features strongly in recent debates about the role of museums and collections in, for example, education. Loomis' discussion of learning in museums states that psychologists, such as himself, have "known for a long time that if something is meaningful to the individual it is easier to learn and more apt to be remembered" (Loomis 1996: 12). In his view, objects themselves can convey meaning but that museum visitors often require help in understanding this. Other commentators, although supportive of the idea that the meaning of objects must be communicated, dispute the assumption that objects can "speak for themselves". Weil (1992) considers this notion to be one that "carries genuine and potentially negative consequences", and argues that by relying on the objects to communicate for themselves, museums run the risk of excluding some visitors and inhibiting the development of a common understanding about objects between the public and the individuals responsible for their preservation. He cites another commentator on this issue who believes that meaning can only arise through the interaction of object and observer, and that rather than being inherent in the objects themselves meaning is contextual (Weil 1992: 6/7). Pearce (1994: 26) believes that the meaning of objects in a museum setting lies somewhere between the object and the viewer's response to it. This very brief account of the debate about the interpretation of objects serves to illustrate the importance of ensuring that objects are displayed in accessible and meaningful ways.

The Role of the Conservator in Display

As someone who is involved in the education of textile conservators[1], the issues discussed above are of interest for a number of reasons. It is essential that students do not perceive the concept of minimum intervention as "doing less" but rather as "doing differently". A conservator's involvement with an object is changed rather than lessened: the reduction in intervention in one area (the object) is offset by increased intervention in another (for example, interpretation). Developing students' understanding of what constitutes the "true nature" of an object (United Kingdom Institute for Conservation 1990: 8), and the impact conservation can have on this is therefore a key educational objective. Raising students' awareness and appreciation of contextual issues relevant to textiles forms an important element of their professional education. It is essential that conservators realise that in fulfilling their professional role they are also uniquely placed to extract and record information from objects. The conservation process automatically involves them in the methods identified as being of use in the investigation of material culture (Prown 1994: 134). Contrary to the view expressed by Cannon-Brookes that "evidence [provided by the physical condition of an object] is best read by the scholar-curator whose task it is to accumulate a much deeper, specific knowledge of related material than the technological familiarity based on representative examples which forms part of the training of conservators" (1994: 48), it is the author's opinion that conservators can and should contribute to the debate about the meaning of objects. Conservators must see

themselves, and be seen by others, as active participants in the processes that determine the presentation and interpretation of objects. Students are therefore encouraged to take a wider view of their responsibility to objects and to develop the necessary skills to enable them to use the knowledge and insights gained through the conservation process to "communicate meaningfully with colleagues specializing in the other disciplines" (Cannon-Brookes 1994: 48).

Perspectives on Mounts

Returning to the problems related to the display of objects that have received limited conservation treatment. One possible solution is to consider using mounts in more significant ways: not just as "coat hangers" on which to show an object, but as active contributors to their long-term support, stabilisation and interpretation. The benefits of creating supportive, physically stable and chemically inert mounts for artefact storage are well known, and a considerable amount of information and expertise already exists on this topic. The greater availability of "conservation grade" mounting materials has significantly increased the possibilities for conservators to create high quality, precision mounts that are safe, durable and attractive. Much of the knowledge and experience generated by preventive conservation research is being made use of by some conservators in the area of display, but there still remains a need for mount making to be more widely viewed as a proactive rather than a reactive measure. It is the author's belief that mount design and production should be seen as integral parts of the conservation strategy defined for an object, rather than processes that are additional to it. An appropriately designed and skilfully crafted mount can assume a substantial part of the supportive and stabilising role currently provided by more interventive treatments. It can enhance or even replace more conventional conservation support techniques, and can be designed to accommodate every feature of an object, regardless of whether it is stiffened by dirt, distorted through use or burial, or is fragmentary. In essence, a "bespoke" design can be created that directly responds to the unique needs of an object including the features of evidential value it contains. In the area of interpretation, mounts can be used to "animate" a static object, give it "body" and form, set it at an angle that suggests its original function, and reduce the visual disturbance of areas of loss so that it regains a "complete" and coherent appearance if this is required. Informed choices can be made concerning the style, form and even colour of the mount with the specific purpose of creating an image that is easily recognisable and meaningful even if the object itself is unfamiliar or in a soiled, distorted or incomplete state. None of the skills required to create such mounts should be beyond the capabilities of conservators experienced in dealing with the vagaries of many historic objects. What may be needed is more extensive research into the context of objects, and the identification of issues and problems relevant to their conservation *and* interpretation.

Case Studies

The following two case studies are presented as instances where the provision of a mount was an integral part of a conservation strategy, and one that had the specific purposes of providing the object with physical support and enhancing its understanding. The first illustrates the potential for using mounts as substitutes for certain interventive treatments, while the second demonstrates how the provision of a mount can extend the physical and interpretative consequences of intervention.

Case study 1 - Cap from a genizah

This case study concerns a cap retrieved from a genizah[2] in a synagogue in Southern Germany, a region that was inhabited by German Jewish communities until the 1930s. The cap represents a rare example of the costume worn by rural people of the "small, forgotten Jewish communities of whose artefacts almost nothing remains" (Friedlander 1992: 11). It is to be included in future travelling exhibitions featuring genizah material organised by The Hidden Legacy Foundation[3]. The purpose of these exhibitions is to "gain public recognition of the outstanding importance of these "concealed finds", and of their value to historical, bibliographical and theological research" (Friedlander 1992: 11).

The cap consists of a crown made of numerous shaped strips of wool fabric joined to create a complex spiral pattern, a headband made of the same fabric and stiffened with paper and leather, and a wide leather peak stitched to the headband. Prior to conservation, the cap was heavily soiled and stained with surface and ingrained dirt (from the genizah site and possibly from use), and was severely distorted and flattened. The back seam of the headband was torn and the peak was almost completely detached (Figure 1).

Following extensive research into the object, its condition, historical/cultural context and future role as part of a travelling exhibition, it was determined that intervention should be kept to the minimum necessary to preserve the object and evidence of its use, but enable its construction and original profile to be revealed (Javér 1996). Following detailed examination and documentation of the cap before treatment, the loose surface dirt was removed (and retained), and the distorted leather stiffening of the headband was humidified. A patch of nylon net was placed across the torn seam of the headband to reduce the stress on this area. A two-part mount was prepared. The upper part, designed to accommodate the fullness of the crown, consists of a flexible, fabric-covered ring of wadding that can be inserted without putting strain on the headband. The lower part of the mount, designed to support and align the heavy and still partially detached peak and protect the lower edges of the headband from stress and abrasion, is constructed from Ethafoam (expanded polyethylene foam) carved to the appropriate shape, padded and covered with fabric (Figure 2). A rigid baseboard with a mount-shaped recess was also prepared to protect the cap during transportation.

Figure 1. The upper face of the cap before conservation. The soiling, distortion and damage obscures the complex construction and original form of the cap.

Figure 2. The upper face of the cap after conservation. The mount (not visible from this viewpoint) fills out the crown, making the cap's construction visible, and holds the partially detached peak in its original alignment with the headband.

Case study 2 - Bead-net dress

This case study concerns a rare Fifth Dynasty (c. 2456-2323 BC) Egyptian bead-net dress. The dress, from the collection of the Petrie Museum of Egyptian Archaeology, University College London, is believed to be a garment that was worn (possibly without undergarments) by a young female dancer (Janssen 1995: 5). It is composed of a threaded network of faience beads, two faience "cups" (thought to be breast coverings), and a shell and bead fringe. The history of its excavation and partial rethreading in the 1950s, and an explanation of the conservation strategy devised and implemented for its subsequent partial reconstruction have been recorded elsewhere (Seth-Smith and Lister 1995), but the making of the form is outlined below.

The Petrie Museum defines itself as "a teaching, research and study collection, not an art museum" in which the aim is to "illustrate the development of Egyptian culture, technology and daily life" (Anon. 1977: 1). In accordance with this institutional aim, the curator who initiated the reassessment and retreatment of the artefact felt it was extremely important that the original use of the bead network as a dress be made explicit to the Museum's visitors. As the dress was believed to be a garment worn in life, as opposed to one used exclusively for burial, its presentation in a manner that specifically indicated this was considered essential. The objectives of the mounting element of the conservation strategy were to preserve the surviving components, assist the stabilising and supportive effect of the reconstruction process, and present the bead network in a such a way that its original function would be fully and clearly communicated. As the project progressed it became apparent that displaying the dress mounted in a flat (horizontal or vertical) orientation would not be appropriate because this mode of display would not clearly indicate its function nor enhance the remarkable physical and visual characteristics of the bead network. Although only the front half of the dress was reconstructed, it was decided that a fully three-dimensional form would be provided as this would give a more life-like effect than one limited to the dimensions of the reconstructed part.

The mount took the form of a upright, headless torso. It was created from Ethafoam supported by a stainless steel pole. Ethafoam was chosen for its rigidity, inertness and ease of shaping. Using the dimensions of the reconstructed dress front, measurements taken from a colleague's daughter, and a knowledge of anatomy and modelling from life (acquired by the author at art school), the form was sculpted into the required shape. Considerable attention was given to producing a shapely, even sensuous, human-like form, but one that was not overtly erotic. The anatomical features of the lower part of the human body therefore were not reproduced. Selecting a suitable colour for the outer fabric proved crucial to the success of the form. It was essential that the chosen colour, when viewed under

the lighting conditions of the museum, had a flesh-like appearance and complimented the colours of the beads and shells. Reproductions of ancient Egyptian wall paintings of women (men are usually shown as having skin of a darker shade) were viewed in the area of the museum where the dress was to be displayed. The selected colour was a pale pinkish orange. The resulting form provided the reconstructed dress with additional physical support to enable it to withstand permanent upright display, and gave it a visually pleasing and lifelike appearance (Figures 3 and 4).

Discussion

The advantages of using mounts in more active ways have been described and illustrated. In discussing any conservation approach, however, there is a need to consider the disadvantages that may arise from it. Possible drawbacks of using mounts in the ways described are therefore considered below.

The deterioration or removal of the mount will result in partial or complete loss or reduction of support to the object. There is a widely held and justifiable belief that the process of support should be separate from that of mounting. The underlying concern here is that unless independently supported the object will be put at risk should the mount fail

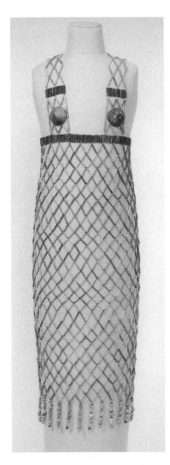 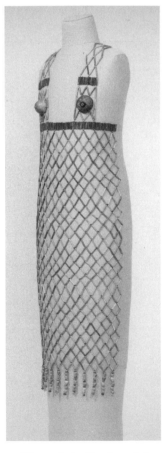

Figure 3. The reconstructed dress front mounted on the form.

Figure 4. A side view of the dress on the form.

or be removed. This is a very real possibility with objects that move frequently between storage and display. It could be argued, however, that this risk of failure could apply to some interventive support treatments, and that the implications for the object, should this occur, are likely to be more dramatic than those resulting from the loss of a mount. A deteriorated, damaged or missing mount is easier to spot by even an untrained eye than a similarly affected support treatment, and much easier and less hazardous to the object to replace. It seems more appropriate and efficient to guard against deterioration by ensuring that mounts are well made from durable materials, and prevent removal by creating effective operational systems, including labelling and documentation, than to resort to more interventive treatments.

The mount and the artefact become, in effect, "the object".
If an artefact is heavily dependant on its mount for physical support and interpretation, there is a danger that artefact and mount will become "fused" in the perception of the viewer. Although the potential for this problem must be acknowledged, again it is important to recognise that it is one that also can occur with certain interventive treatments. As with such treatments the conservator has a responsibility to ensure that the mount remains distinguishable from the artefact whilst at the same time unobtrusive, and it should be possible to achieve this through a judicial choice of style, shape, colour and texture of the mount, and through information given in labels and catalogue entries.

The mount creates an impression of the physical form and/or interpretation of the object that is later found to be inappropriate/incorrect.
This is a problem, but it is not exclusive to mounts. Labels, themed displays and other interpretative data are all subject to the effects of fashion, misinformation and misunderstanding. The interpretation of an object, in whatever form, can only reflect current knowledge and thinking, just as all conservation treatments must reflect the ethical frameworks in place at the time of their implementation. One of the main advantages of taking a less interventive approach is that the potential for reinterpretation is greater. It would seem preferable to simply change a mount in response to new information or an alternative interpretation than to reverse (if this is possible) a more interventive treatment.

The disadvantages discussed above illustrate that conservation is never able to achieve ideal results. For every successful action there are often actual or potential drawbacks. The advantages and disadvantages of any treatment approach should not be viewed in isolation from the alternatives or from the defined aims and objectives of treatment. The success of an approach should be determined by the degree to which it meets the defined aims and minimises the need for inappropriate compromise both now and in the future.

Conclusions

The safe display and effective interpretation of objects that have received little or no interventive treatment requires a radical rethink of the design and function of the systems used to exhibit them. If objects and the information they contain are to be protected and preserved greater emphasis must be given to devising display approaches and methods that specifically ensure the survival of both these aspects. If objects are to continue to have value and meaning to all those who desire to see them it is imperative that they are presented in accessible and understandable ways. In this paper, the use of mounts as one way of responding to these issues has been considered. There are others: for example, the use of replicas and computer generated images, and the potential of these techniques should be explored further. The benefits of extending the role of conservators in the area of display have also been highlighted, along with the need for better informed dialogue between conservators, curators, educators and exhibition designers. As illustrated by the theme of this conference the value of interdisciplinary exchange of information and ideas is increasingly being recognised. Such collaborative efforts suggest that the issues raised in this paper merit further debate.

Acknowledgements

The author would like to thank Nell Hoare, Director of the Textile Conservation Centre, for permission to publish and for her support in allowing access to the Centre's resources. I would also like to thank Dinah Eastop for her invaluable support, encouragement and constructive comments on earlier drafts of this paper, and Helen Colwell for photography

Endnotes

[1] Alison Lister is a Lecturer in Textile Conservation and the co-ordinator of the second year of the three year post-graduate Diploma course in textile conservation run by the Textile Conservation Centre, in affiliation with the Courtauld Institute of Art, University of London.

[2] In Talmudic literature a "genizah" is defined as a room "in which something is hidden or placed for safekeeping". Among rural German Jews, the attics of synagogues were used to store or ritually inter old or obsolete objects connected with the practice of religion (Wiesemann 1992: 16/17).

[3] The Hidden Legacy Foundation was established in 1988 to salvage and preserve the genizah material from the small village synagogues in Southern Germany, and make it available for scholarly research and display to the public (publicity leaflet, The Hidden Legacy Foundation).

References

Anon. *Guide to the Petrie Museum of Egyptian Archaeology.* London: University College London, 1977.

Brooks, M., A. Lister, D. Eastop, and T. Bennett. "Artifact or Information? Articulating the Conflicts in Conserving Archaeological Textiles," *Archaeological Conservation and Its Consequences*, (Preprints of the contributions to the International Institute for Conservation (IIC) Copenhagen Congress, 26-30 August 1996.) Roy, A., and P. Smith eds., London: IIC, 1996, pp. 16-21.

Cannon-Brookes, P. "The Role of the Scholar-Curator in Conservation," *Care of Collections*, Knell, P., ed. London: Routledge, 1994, pp. 47-50.

Janssen, R. "Newly Displayed Garments," *Friends of The Petrie Museum Newsletter*, no. 12 (Spring 1995), pp. 4-5.

Javér, A. *Treatment Report for a Genizah Cap: TCC 1846.2.* Unpublished conservation report, Textile Conservation Centre, 1996.

Friedlander, E. "Foreword," *Genizah - Hidden Legacies of the German Village Jews*, Exhibition catalogue, Wiesemann, F. Vienna: Wiener Verlag, 1992, pp. 11-14.

Lister, A. *Guidelines for the Conservation of Textiles.* London: English Heritage, 1995.

Loomis, R. "Learning in Museums: Motivation, Control and Meaningfulness," *International Council of Museums (ICOM) Committee for Education and Cultural Action (CECA)*, Study Series, October 1996.

Pearce, S. "Objects as Meanings; or Narrating the Past," *Interpreting Objects and Collections*, Pearce, S., ed. London: Routledge, 1994, pp. 19-29.

Prown, J. "Mind in Matter: An Introduction to Material Culture Theory and Method," *Interpreting Objects and Collections*, Pearce, S., ed. London: Routledge, 1994, pp. 133-138.

Seth-Smith, A. and A. Lister. "The Research and Reconstruction of a 5th Dynasty Egyptian Bead-Net Dress," *Conservation in Ancient Egyptian Collections*, Brown, C., F. Macalister, and M. Wright, eds. London: Archetype Publications, 1995, pp. 165-172.

United Kingdom Institute for Conservation. "Guidance for Conservation Practice," *UKIC Members Handbook*, London: UKIC, 1990, pp. 8-9.

Weil, S. "Speaking About Museums: A Meditation on Language," *Alberta Museums Review*, vol. 18, issue 1 (1992), pp. 3-9.

Wiesemann, F. "Hidden Testimonies of German Rural Jewry. An Introduction to the Exhibition," *Genizah - Hidden Legacies of the German Village Jews*, Exhibition Catalogue, Wiesemann, F. Vienna: Wiener Verlag, 1992, pp. 15- 31.

Résumé

Optimisation des supports : extension du rôle des supports dans la préservation et l'interprétation des textiles historiques

Dans cet article, on aborde certains problèmes qui découlent d'une contradiction entre deux exigences, soit augmenter l'accessibilité des objets aux visiteurs et adopter une approche moins interventionniste en conservation. Le concept de l'intervention minimale est décrit, ainsi que les avantages de l'extension du rôle du restaurateur à l'interprétation et la présentation des objets. On souligne les difficultés, à la fois physiques et conceptuelles, d'exposer des objets qui n'ont subi qu'une intervention limitée. L'une des manières dont les supports permettent de surmonter ces difficultés est décrite et illustrée par deux études de cas.

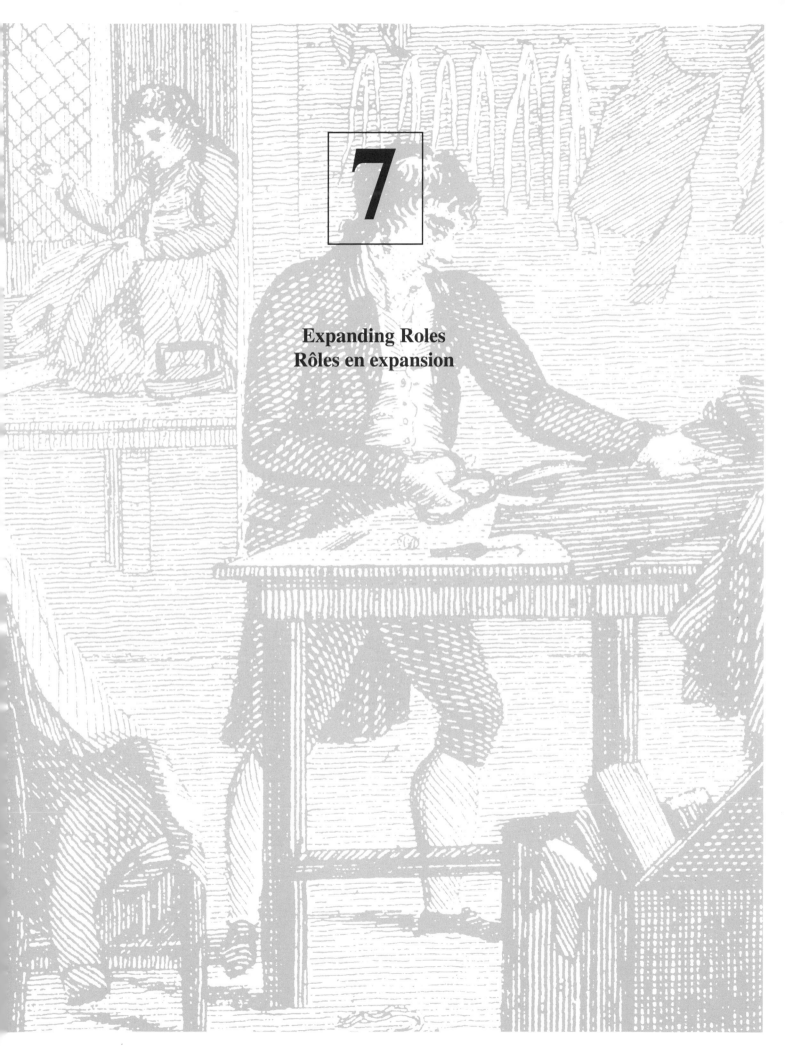

7

Expanding Roles
Rôles en expansion

The Real West: A Collaborative Exhibit at Three Venues

Jeanne Brako

Colorado Historical Society
1300 Broadway
Denver, CO 80203 USA
Tel.: (303) 866-4693
E-mail: chssysop@usa.net

Abstract

The Colorado Historical Society participated in a multi-venue exhibit, "The Real West" with the Denver Public Library and the Denver Art Museum. Exhibit planning was done in teams comprised of staff, consultants and advisory groups from the various institutions. Over 1,600 artifacts were prepared for exhibition. Managing a project this size was aided by developing a database from the exhibit list to track tasks and assignments, especially conservation. Conservation issues included mounting a toxic waste outfit, tee-shirts displayed on cyclone fencing, the use of lifelike mannequins versus abstract forms for American Indian costume display, loading a Conestoga wagon, and insect control for historic and modern materials. Interactive CD-ROM programs connecting storytelling, legends and artifacts produced for the exhibit provided new ways of exhibiting and interpreting artifacts, including textiles. This paper focuses on preparing and exhibiting textiles at all venues of "The Real West" exhibit.

A recent experiment in museum collaboration that offered unique challenges to the role of conservation in exhibit preparation was *The Real West*, the product of a partnership between the Colorado Historical Society, the Denver Art Museum, and the Denver Public Library. This innovative exhibit was presented in three parts, with each institution simultaneously hosting part of the installation. Each venue would have its own themes and character, but the three venues would form a coherent whole. The exhibit would be a physical manifestation of the exhibit's working title *Colorado: One Land, Many Visions*.

The idea for a joint exhibit came out of an earlier collaboration. In 1990, the three institutions formed the Civic Center Cultural Complex Committee to address urban planning issues that involved these adjacent institutions. A joint exhibit was proposed as a future public activity of this partnership.

The Real West exhibit opened in Denver, Colorado on March 30, 1996. This paper chronicles the management, preparation, and presentation of artifacts in this 6,000 m^2 (20,000 ft.^{2}) exhibit using the textiles as a focal point. Textiles important to this exhibit were not limited to historical artifacts, such as quilts and christening dresses, but also included non-collections items. Textiles were used to divide and articulate space, to control light levels, to serve as props, as references to other objects, and to deliver text-based messages. Textiles were also featured in action through the use of interactive videos. This comprehensive use of textile materials added a tactile and humanizing component to the exhibition experience.

Until work began on *The Real West*, most exhibits at the Denver Art Museum and Colorado Historical Society had been either prepared completely in-house, or they were set up as packaged, traveling exhibits. The plan for *The Real West* exhibit called for an outside design firm that would work with the exhibit teams to prepare installation drawings. The installation would then be executed by in-house staff and contractors.

Planning and fund raising for the exhibit began in 1991. In 1994, three curatorial teams were formed to work on the conceptual framework for the exhibit. In late 1995, the curatorial teams presented their artifact lists to the design and collections management teams.

It was recognized early on that although each venue was no more than a city block apart, this type of exhibit would require extensive planning and coordination. The project was additionally complicated by the fact that the Denver Public Library did not routinely create and install exhibits. Fortuitously, the library had recently expanded its facilities and one entire floor still remained vacant. This floor would be converted to a gallery for the duration of the exhibit.

Development of an Exhibition Database

In the early stages of exhibit planning, each curator had a good idea of what his or her individual sections of the exhibit would include. However, until concept drawings had been completed, no one would have an overview of the whole. It was recognized that an important organizational step was to develop an efficient way to track exhibit information. It was agreed that a custom-designed database would be useful. The database information, combined with drawings of each section of the exhibit, would provide an organizing framework and blueprint for the exhibit preparation and installation process.

Over 1,600 artifacts divided between three venues were used in *The Real West.* They included paintings, textiles, prints, photographs, sculpture, and objects and props ranging from prehistoric specimens to the latest technology for handling radioactive waste, including the actual radioactive isotopes. All 1,600-plus artifacts would pass from lender to curator to designer to conservator to preparator to installer. Given normal changes in the development of any exhibit, the object list would also be expected to change up to the date the exhibit opened.

Paradox was the program we chose for the exhibit database. Although both the Denver Art Museum and Colorado Historical Society use Argus, a museum management database for daily activities, we wanted to use a more flexible database for this project. Basic information from other systems were "dumped" into the Paradox framework.

The Real West database was designed to provide updated information in a number of categories to the many people involved in exhibit preparation. The database structure began with the information the curators had been asked to provide for label copy. This included object name, accession or loan number, owner, materials, and label copy. After curators and conservator met to decide what information would be useful in the database, the database fields were expanded.

We hired a project assistant to manage the database, enter changes and updates, and distribute reports. The Colorado Historical Society's one-person computer department was responsible for designing and printing out new and updated reports.

A number of activities would be tracked on the database. As exhibit textile conservator, I wanted to use the database to find out how many mannequins or mounts would be needed, which textiles needed what types of mounts, how much Velcro needed to be purchased, when certain items would be available for preparation work, and the location of the items concerned. The conservation technician would need to know whether individual items needed padding, which edge of a quilt Velcro would be sewn to, and what the installation date for each section was. If the designer could let us know via the database what colors were being used as background in different sections of the exhibit and how deep individual cases would be, we would be even better off. Fields in the final database included information on an artifact's permanent location, holding location, conservation needs (including surface cleaning and additional treatment), framing and mounting needs, special handling instructions, security requirements, and exhibition and preparation status.

The database proved especially effective for tracking preparation activities. In addition to the problem of artifacts going into three different venues, preparation of different types of artifacts would take place at various locations. Although designating central areas for various exhibit prep activities would increase efficiency in some ways, it would require significant choreography to get all artifacts to and from their temporary holding areas to their scheduled prep locations and then into their proper venue sections. This was efficiently done by planning and tracking intended activities on the database, and then printing lists or reports to help keep everyone on track. Artifact handling assistants were given lists of loan artifacts that were in holding at the Colorado History Museum that needed to be moved to the Denver Public Library for framing. They would later receive lists of items that had been framed and were now ready to be delivered to a certain exhibit section for installation. As project textile conservator, I received lists of clothing items the art museum was lending to the library, but required relocation to the history museum conservation lab to be mounted by my assistants.

One of the most useful categories in the database was labeled "format". Using the materials information given on the exhibit labels, we created a limited number of "format" categories. "Format" referred to whether an item was flat or three dimensional, and into what broad artifact category it would fit for exhibition preparation purposes. Categories I found useful to track were "textile flat", "textile 3D", and "other". For instance, if leather or hide garments were going to need mannequins or padding typical of textile preparations, they were coded as "textile 3D". This allowed participants to receive lists limited to the artifacts for which they were responsible. The "other" category was useful in calling up unusual items such as leather mail bags, which might need textile type treatments, such as soft padding.

The following shows two of the customized reports that were produced. The actual Paradox reports look slightly different than those shown here, as these were generated in a word-processing program.

This was the first time the Colorado Historical Society had managed an exhibit using database technology. The system had its growing pains, but it would have been extremely difficult to manage an exhibit of this scope in a short turnaround time without it.

Artifact Preparation and Mounting

In planning, each venue would have its own character, but some aspects of the mounts and exhibit prep process could be standardized. Every artifact, as appropriate, would at least be vacuumed or dusted before going on exhibit. Textiles in the same section of an exhibit would be mounted onto similar colored fabric. Textile mounts that were visible to the public would be covered with the same

DPL Venue Exhibit Section
Fort Textile Conservation Report March 5, 1996

Rec#	Acc#	Object	LocPerm	LocHold	Format	Surface Clean	Other Cons
124	H.726.D	Sombrero, Straw	3D1.E15	Lab	Tex-3	Vacuum	Humidify
129	H.5937.1	Cap, Miner's, Canvas	3D1.E27	3D1.E4	Tex-3	Done	N/A
599	DPL-108	Dress, Josephine Meeker	Loan	3D1.E6	Tex-3	Vacuum	N/A

DPL Venue Exhibit Section
Fort Registrar's Report March 1, 1996

Rec#	Lender	Loan#	Acc#	Status	Object	Arrival Date	Loan Forms	CondRpt	Photoed
68	DAM	DPL103	1972.71	OK	Embroidery	3/14/96	Yes	Yes	No
694	DAM	DPL118	1949.58	OK	Women's Boots	3/14/96	Yes	Yes	No
690	DAM	DPL127	1951.10	OK	Woman's Dress	3/14/96	Yes	Yes	No

neutral colored fabric. Necklines of mannequins and other clothing mounts would take a standard form, with some adjustments made to the style of the period. All mounts would be archival. Mounts had to be as simple as possible, given the fast turnaround for the exhibit and the number of objects to be prepared.

All 1,600 artifacts were prepared for exhibit under the supervision of three conservators, myself from the Colorado Historical Society, Carl Patterson, objects conservator from the Denver Art Museum, and contract paper conservator, Eileen Clancy. We were supported by a paper conservation assistant, several contract mount makers, the exhibit and design staff of the Denver Art Museum and the Colorado Historical Society and numerous volunteers. The Colorado Historical Society and the Denver Art Museum split responsibility for preparing artifacts for the Denver Public Library venue. Several painting treatments were contracted out.

The most time-consuming aspect of exhibit preparation was the production of custom-sized clothing mounts. To standardize, mounts were limited to three types: full sized (in the round), half sized (about 7.5 cm [3 in.] thick) and thin (approximately 2.5 cm [1 in.] thick). Full-sized and half-sized mounts were made out of an Ethafoam core padded with batting and finished with a padded cotton knit cover. To custom-size the mounts, items were placed

onto tissue and traced one time. The tissue pattern was first used to cut two or four cotton-knit panels. Generally, two panels were cut and machine stitched together at the sides and top. This formed a protective cover over the Ethafoam core and held any additional padding in place. When four panels were cut, each pair was sewn to the same size batting panel and then the two padded forms were joined at the shoulders and/or sides. We preferred this system as it created an easily removable cover that was finished on both sides, but it was more time-consuming to produce.

After the cover was traced, the tissue pattern was cut down a standard amount at the sides and shoulders and used to size the Ethafoam that would form the mannequin's core. The Ethafoam forms were cut and sanded to body contours by the exhibit preparators, who also drilled 2.5 cm (1 in.) diameter holes in the bottom of the core to hold the support poles. The cotton-knit covers were pulled over the cores, the cores placed on Plexiglas poles, the poles screwed into painted bases, and the forms were dressed. Minor size adjustments were made by adding batting underneath the padded covers.

One of the most notable items in the exhibit mounted in this way was Josephine Meeker's dress. Josephine was the wife of Nathan Meeker, an Indian agent killed by the Utes in 1879 in what is known as the Meeker Incident. The dress was made by Josephine from Indian blankets while she was held captive during this period. The dress and an 1879 photo of Josephine wearing the dress are in the collection of the Greeley Museum in Greeley, Colorado.

A Ute wearing blanket used in the exhibit required a modification of this type of mount. The curator wanted the blanket to be shown on an abstract form that suggested arms and the wearing position. This was achieved by piercing padded wire hanger arms into the Ethafoam and posing them as arms. Polarfleece was used as the cover on this mount since its napped surface helped support the textile.

Half-sized and thin mannequins were similarly made, but these mounts had 6.2 mm (1/4 in.) fleece as padding and the thin mount used 6 mm Coroplast as the core material. All of the tee-shirts in the exhibit were mounted on the thin forms.

Several items required specialized mounts. Three hide Indian outfits were placed in abstract versions of dioramas at the Denver Public Library venue. Two dresses were painted; one had heavy bead work. One was presented with a heavy leather and metal belt.

The mounts for these items began with a steel armature of a type the Denver Art Museum had previously used for mounting Chinese robes. The shoulder height of the armature adjusts with set screws.

To custom-size these mounts, two Coroplast panels were cut using the upper body contour from a tissue pattern of the item. The Coroplast panels were tied with twill tape to the metal armature to give form to the shoulders and upper body. The padded cover—in this case Polarfleece rather than cotton knit—was laid over the shoulders of the form and tied at the waist with twill tape to keep it from slipping. Polarfleece was chosen for the cover of these mounts because its napped surface and the beige color chosen blended well with the color and texture of the hide garments. The garment was then placed over the padded form. In the case of the dress with the belt, the belt was suspended from the armholes of the dress by narrow linen twill tape. This kept the weight of the belt off the soft hide and prevented compression.

Use of Textiles in "The Real West" Exhibition

The Cheyenne Indian diorama at the Denver Public Library venue had a painted fabric backdrop that served to hide large windows behind the diorama. At first, the designers were not convinced that the windows needed to be blacked out for light control reasons. No solution appealed to them until we began to discuss using canvas curtains as an inexpensive way to block the light; the designers realized that canvas would blend with the teepee, and if a painted motif were used, the canvas could become a design feature. Canvas was then used to block out all of the gallery windows.

The use of canvas in this venue was compatible with design treatments of other areas. While an early exhibit idea had been to let people enter a teepee as part of the exhibit, the use of the teepee as part of an installation with historic artifacts precluded this. Instead, canvas panels set up in another area of the exhibit suggested an enclosed teepee space centered around the exhibition of a pipe. This use of canvas to delineate and suggest interior space was again used in a recent Colorado Historical Society exhibit *Cheyenne Dog Soldiers*. In this exhibit about the Sand Creek Massacre, new bright canvas panels are used near the start of the exhibit and represent the day before the attack; further through the exhibit, canvas with burn marks delineates the space representing the aftermath of the battle. The canvas works in these areas not only as a dramatic element, but locally reduces light levels in areas that highlight key artifacts but require low light levels. Demand lighting is used as visitors enter the "teepee" area.

One of the most successful presentations of an artifact in the Colorado Historical Society venue of *The Real West* exhibit was the Conestoga wagon. The Conestoga wagon had been on exhibit at the museum for a number of years, and while it initially served to draw visitors because of its size, they quickly lost interest in its empty interior. For *The Real West* exhibit, curators "packed" the wagon. The interior now holds an assortment of items transported across Colorado during western expansion. A number of the items shown are textiles, commonly brought West because of their compact, durable utilitarian nature. A Plexiglas panel placed at an angle across the back of the wagon makes this display very accessible. The wagon, because of its renewed popularity, is now the focal point of the entrance to the Colorado Historical Society's reconfigured installation on the West. The canvas cover on this wagon is a reproduction.

The accompanying slide presentation to this paper shows a number of other examples of the way textiles were presented in *The Real West* exhibition. Presentations ranged from oversized photo panels of textiles in historic use to a life-sized cardboard image of John Wayne in cowboy regalia; coarse cotton utilitarian objects to paintings draped in silk, calling up the salon experience; and historic Indian blankets to modern rodeo costume. Overall, the exhibit was successful in telling its story and portraying the texture and fabric of western life.

I would like to thank all the participants in *The Real West* exhibition for their collaborative efforts and also the conference organizing committee of Symposium 97 for providing a forum for sharing this information.

Résumé

The Real West : *une exposition coopérative répartie dans trois sites*

La Colorado Historical Society a participé à une exposition intitulée «The Real West» (le vrai Far West) en collaboration avec la bibliothèque publique et le musée des beaux-arts de Denver. La planification de l'exposition est le fruit des efforts d'équipes composées de personnel, de consultants et de groupes de conseil des divers établissements participants. Les organisateurs ont ainsi préparé plus de 1 600 pièces. La gestion d'un projet de cette envergure a été facilitée par la création d'une base de données à partir de la liste de pièces et par le suivi des tâches et des attributions, surtout en ce qui a trait aux activités de conservation. Plusieurs éléments de l'exposition étaient plûtot particuliers : montage d'un uniforme de protection contre les déchets dangereux, exposition de t-shirts sur une clôture anticyclone, utilisation de mannequins réalistes au lieu de mannequins stylisés pour exposer les vêtements amérindiens, chargement d'un wagon de la Conestoga; il a en outre fallu prévoir des mesures de lutte contre les insectes nuisibles aux matériaux anciens et modernes. Des programmes interactifs sur CD-Rom faisant le lien entre les objets de l'exposition et les histoires et légendes constituent une solution nouvelle pour l'exposition et l'interprétation des objets, notamment des textiles. L'article se concentre sur la préparation et l'exposition des textiles dans tous les endroits où est répartie l'exposition «The Real West».

A Division of Skills: A Case History of Mounting an Exhibition on a Limited Budget

Ann French

Textile Conservation
Area Museum Council for the South West
4 Circus
Bath BA1 2EW United Kingdom
Tel.: 01225 477758
Fax: 01225 444793

Lesley Anne Kerr

Somerset County Museums Service
County Museum
Taunton Castle
Castle Green
Taunton TA1 4AA United Kingdom
Tel.: 01823 320200
Fax: 01823 320229

Susan Stanton

Department of Eastern Art
Ashmolean Museum
Beaumont Street
Oxford OX1 2PH United Kingdom
Tel.: 01865 278067
Fax: 01865 278078

Abstract

The paper will outline a case history of an approach to mounting a temporary exhibition of lace on a limited budget to conservation standards by adopting an approach of a careful division of skills. Textile conservators contributed their knowledge of techniques and materials with regard to both cost and suitability, the museum curator provided project management and supervision, and a team of trained volunteers mounted the lace for display. Key factors in making the project successful were the existence of an ongoing conservation survey of the textile and costume collection, the involvement of the Textile Conservation Service throughout, strong management from the professional curatorial and design staff, and the existence of a motivated team of volunteers.

Introduction

Needles and Pillows, an exhibition of lace and associated material, was planned and executed during 1996 by the Somerset County Museums Service and the Textile Conservation Service of the Area Museum Council for the South West, England. Somerset County Museums Service (SCMS) is a department of the local authority, Somerset County Council. The County Council is funded through the rate support grant controlled by central government and through taxes raised at local level. The departmental budget is approved by the County Council. The Area Museums Council for the South West (AMCSW) is one of 10 regional bodies funded by the Department of National Heritage to support and promote museums in their areas. The AMCSW employs eight conservators to provide advice, training and treatment for the region's 250 museums. Charges to the museums cover about one-third of the cost of conservation work carried out by the conservators, the rest being met by the AMCSW.

Somerset County Museums have a fine lace collection, much of which was collected during the early years of the 20th century, on behalf of the museum, by a Miss Babcock. There are approximately 2,000 items in the collection and the standard of the lace varies enormously, from simple handmade Torchon and European peasant laces to fine examples of Mechlin and Valenciennes. Many of the objects in the costume collection are also trimmed with lace. The exhibition was planned to perform several functions: to maintain the SCMS temporary exhibition programme, to provide easy public access to part of the reserve collections, to illustrate the strength and depth of those collections, as an opportunity to harness the expert knowledge of an individual volunteer, an opportunity for the Keeper to gain a deeper understanding of part of the collection under her care, and as a tribute to and public acknowledgement of the work carried out by a committed team of volunteers on the costume and textile collection.

The cataloguing, identification and re packing of the lace had been carried out by a single volunteer, Ethelwyn Osborne, over a four-year period, and it was in liaison with her that the exhibition was first planned. It was evident that the help of the AMCSW Textile Conservation would be essential, and they were approached before any further action was taken. An integrated approach was devised between AMCSW Textile Conservation and the Keeper - Social History, to enable the best use of resources, while still meeting conservation standards in the display and mounting of the lace.

This approach involved:

- Use of a continuing long-term condition survey of SCMS's entire textile collection by AMCSW Textile Conservation.

- The existence of a team of volunteers who could be trained in simple but safe display methods for mounting the lace.

- The provision of the necessary materials for display and mounting.

- A curator committed to providing management of the exhibition and supervision and support to the volunteer team.

- Limiting the conservation work of the regional textile conservation service to training a volunteer team leader, to carrying out any wet-cleaning and interventive treatment required, and to preparing the more complicated display mounts.

The Case History

Conservation Condition Survey

Since 1991, AMCSW Textile Conservation service has been working on a survey of SCMS's costume and textile collection. Each accessioned object in the collection is examined; condition, interventive conservation and preventive conservation needs, storage and display requirements and handling sensitivity are recorded. A scale of (1) to (4) is used to denote the degree of stability and treatment need, (1) being stable and non-urgent and (4) unstable and urgent. A rough estimate of conservation treatment hours required is also made. About ten visits a year have been made (at £93.00 a day per conservator for 1996), averaging 60 - 70 objects per visit. Fifty-five percent of the collection has been surveyed to date. Information from this survey has already been used to plan a new store, to move the collection, and to prioritise collection care projects. Regular survey visits by the conservators also had an initially unacknowledged benefit in allowing them to get to know both staff and volunteers at the museum.

When a lace exhibition was discussed, the existence of this documentation for the lace collection facilitated the initial selection of objects, anything with extensive treatment needs or complex display requirements could be excluded at an early stage.

Object Selection and Exhibition Planning

On 9th February 1996, Lesley Anne Kerr, Keeper - Social History and Ethelwyn Osborne, volunteer team leader, came to the AMCSW Textile Conservation Studio bringing the initial selection of lace with them. A day was spent reducing the amount of lace, and planning the work to follow. Factors which influenced this process were:

- The budget of £2,000 for the entire exhibition, excluding the cost of SCMS staff time.

- The plan and size of the temporary exhibition gallery.

- The number and size of the existing display cases and equipment.

- The time and human resources available, (for example volunteers do not work 37 hour weeks).

- The workload of the AMCSW Textile Conservation Studio, pre-existing commitments with deadlines for other museums had to be met.

The strategy adopted was that:

- SCMS would provide all curatorial, design and technical services.

- AMCSW Textile Conservation would provide training for the volunteer team in simple but safe display methods for mounting the lace, provide the necessary materials, carry out any wet-cleaning and interventive treatment required, and prepare the more complicated display mounts.

  The volunteer team would do as much display mounting as possible.

As a result of this visit, the number of pieces selected was considerably reduced, the constraint generally being case capacity. Object selection followed certain themes, i.e., early lace, production techniques, lace on costume, types of lace etc. Extensive interventive treatment and complex mounting could not be afforded within the budget, although some exceptions had to be made for pieces illustrating key aspects of the exhibition.

Display methods and materials were discussed and decided. Costumes would be displayed on mannequins or padded coat-hangers, flat pieces of lace and fans mounted onto fabric covered acid-free boards, with long pieces of lace partially rolled, parasols to be suspended from their handles and tips, and items such as bonnets put onto custom-made mounts. It was decided to use coloured silk to cover the mounts as the fine weave shows the construction of the lace to best advantage. Time constraints and the cost of sending silk samples to be tested meant that it was most economical for the silk to be bought wholesale by AMCSW Textile Conservation and then dyed to the shade required. The collection of dye recipe fabric samples in the studio proved invaluable to select colours. The colour chosen was a deep greenish blue which complemented both the undyed lace and the black lace. The same recipe was used throughout, but different percentage shades were used according to the colour of the lace, a 5 percent shade was used for the black lace and a 3 percent shade for the undyed lace. To prevent SCMS having to make time-consuming special orders of materials for small amounts, AMCSW Textile Conservation provided acid-free board cut to size, cotton bump and Melinex (Mylar) which are all stocked in the studio.

Curatorial Work

With the advice of the conservators, the final choice of lace was made taking each section of the display individually to produce a balanced selection which would illustrate the points made in the text. Once this had been done, each item was considered individually to assess the type of mounting it would require. If a piece was to be displayed flat, an approximate board size was noted. In the event, 39 boards were needed, and a number of standard sizes could be identified, the most common being 350 x 450 mm. By completing this process for every item, the requisite amount of each material was established.

This process also made the job of the volunteer considerably easier. With standard board sizes, organization of the work was less complicated and, working from a master list, everyone knew what size board was to be used for a particular piece - or pieces - of lace. Some of the lace, like lengths of Mechlin or Valenciennes, could be placed onto boards in groups. This not only removed the need to produce a large number of small finicky boards, but also allowed the visitor to make comparisons.

The other major decision that had to be made relatively early with the conservators concerned the piece of lace on which the poster and publicity material would be based. In the event a handkerchief with a border of Youghal lace was chosen. The textile conservation staff cleaned and mounted it immediately, enabling the design team to produce artwork for the poster. In addition, the mounted handkerchief acted as a standard for the volunteers in mounting techniques.

Conservation Work

i) Interventive Work

One hundred and one museum objects were selected for exhibition including small fragments, longer lengths of lace, and lace-decorated accessories such as fans, scarves, collars and a bonnet. These were left at the textile conservation studio where further details of each piece were recorded. These included: dimensions, mounting requirements, cleaning and interventive treatment required plus accurate estimates of the treatment time. This information was used to provide SCMS with a final quote for AMCSW time and materials. Wet cleaning, minor repairs, dying support fabrics and mounting fans and a cap was estimated at 43 hours work, plus one day of training for the volunteer team leader in making padded boards and mounting techniques. The total cost of conservator's time charged was £630.50 net, (full cost excluding grant-in-aid was £1728.63), and the cost of materials for all mounting was £170.68.

Sixty-four items were identified as requiring wet cleaning. Lace was divided into categories: white/cream cotton; dark/black cotton; white/cream silk; dark/black silk. The cotton lace was cleaned using a washing solution of Hostapon T (sodium methyl tauride) at 1g/litre water and sodium carboxymethyl cellulose at 0.5g/litre water. The silk objects were cleaned using a washing solution of Synperonic N (an aqueous solution of a condensate of nonyl phenol with ethylene oxide) at 1g/litre water and sodium carboxymethyl cellulose at 0.5g/litre water. The objects were washed flat on the washing table, a medium heat (30°C) was used to enhance the cleaning of the cotton lace. Washing solution was applied with a brush in a light rotating action and six rinses with deionised water were carried out. The lace was dried flat on the washing table.

Support treatment was given to a chemical lace collar, a sequined collar, and a lace bonnet by applying a backing support of 20 denier nylon net stitched in place with fine polyester thread. A mount was made for the bonnet from acid-free card padded with polyester wadding and covered with silk. A piece of "work in progress" on a bent and broken frame was mounted onto a board to hold it flat and to hold the broken ends in alignment.

ii) Display mounting

The fans were mounted on padded boards made from acid-free card, padded with polyester wadding and covered with the dyed silk. Additional raised padding of polyester wadding covered with silk was stitched to the board to support the exact shape and contours of each fan.

iii) Training of Volunteers

AMCSW Textile Conservation had carried out training for the volunteers at SCMS before, and knew what kind of projects they had been involved with and what they were capable of achieving. This previous experience was used to plan training for the team.

The volunteer team-leader spent a day at the AMCSW Textile Conservation Studio and was trained to make fabric-covered padded boards and in the techniques of mounting the lace on the boards. Some long pieces of lace needed to be rolled onto small silk covered Melinex (Mylar) tubes at each end so that they could fit onto the boards. The volunteer returned to the County Museum in Taunton and passed on these skills to the team of volunteers involved in preparing the exhibition.

Exhibition Installation

The actual covering of the boards and hangers and the mounting of the lace was carried out by a stalwart band of 10 volunteers. They worked at the County Museum for two days each week for a six week period and completed a total of 350 hours. Clearly, if the SCMS had not had this free and enthusiastic support, the exhibition would not have been feasible.

The text was completed by the Keeper - Social History and Mrs Osborne and passed to the SCMS design department with the graphics and object captions. They were also provided with the object lists and the board sizes or mounting information, i.e., two collars on hangers, to allow them to produce a draft layout for the display. Existing exhibition cases were utilised. These conformed to a system which had been developed by SCMS for travelling exhibitions and which provided cases in a variety of shapes and sizes while maintaining a coherent design. The cases and display panels were re-covered using two types of material in two different shades of grey, chosen to contrast with the colours of the silk. Display suede was used for case bases and plinths where objects, such as a dress train, would come into direct contact with the material and loop nylon was used for the text panels. The exhibition was installed by the design team and the Keeper without a conservator present. The two dresses in the display were mounted on dummies purchased from Stockmans, the lace boards were attached to the panels using adhesive Velcro and all items in the exhibition were behind glass with the light levels at 50 lux. The exhibition opened on the 15th June 1996.

Total Cost of Exhibition

The exhibition budget of £2,000 did not include SCMS staff time. The major costs incurred were the purchase of two mannequins from Stockmans (£893.00), the conservation and display material costs (£701.18), material for re-covering the cases (£120.00) and production of text panels and captions (£150.00). The latter costs were kept so low by keeping the work in-house and by providing low-cost solutions to problems, i.e., laser-printed text, the use of colour printers to produce graphics, etc. A grant of £150.00 was awarded by the Daphne Bullard Trust, administered by the Museums Association, towards the costs of conservation. The total expenditure was £1,864.18, but the mannequins, although needed, were more of a capital investment as they can be reused for other displays.

Evaluation

Positive Aspects of the Project

Everyone involved in the project has learnt a great deal and feels that this type of approach has great application for smaller museums without specialist conservation staff at a time of shrinking resources.

- AMCSW Textile Conservation was available to SCMS to advise and to work on the project, continuing their experience with volunteers which can now be applied to other museums.

- A limited budget does not mean that conservation has to be excluded, instead the role of conservation must adapt. The skills and knowledge of the conservator must be used cost-effectively which will mean that they may have to share tasks previously seen as theirs. Conservation knowledge must be applied to identifying

an appropriate division of skills: and conservators must learn to recognise relevant skills in others, such as volunteers, and to provide training and supervision.

- It is still possible to hold temporary exhibitions without compromising standards.

- Such a project can act as a powerful motivator and unifying force for volunteers. Two separate teams of volunteers were used, one the Friends of Taunton Castle and the other from the local branch of the National Fine and Decorative Arts Societies (NADFAS). The two groups have now merged and are both involved in further collection care projects such as the re-storage of the militaria collection.

- Involvement of the conservators at an early stage enabled the curatorial staff to make realistic decisions concerning selection of objects and exhibition design.

- The exercise produced a template which can be used as a guide to organising future exhibitions, looking at the skills available from both the professional staff and volunteers involved and how to make the most of limited resources of time and money.

Negative Aspects of the Project

A more accurate description of "negative aspects" is "what would be done differently". This includes:

- A conservator needs to be present during the actual exhibition installation to provide guidance and "tips". For example, Velcro was used to mount the lace boards and the adhesive variety used proved inadequate. A conservator present might well have anticipated this and recommended stitching the Velcro to the boards.

- The conservator must realise that a volunteer workforce will not have the experience to make the fine judgments of tension and weight when mounting. Account must be taken of this during training and planning. For example, the boards holding the larger and heavier pieces of lace should have been displayed at an angle to compensate for gravitational pull, as some slippage occurred with the boards displayed vertical.

- Costume mounting needs, such as underpinnings and mannequin adaptation, probably fall into the type of mounting that should be done by conservators.

- The problem of organising the reserve collection and storing the material after the exhibition was dismantled was not anticipated. SCMS wants to store the lace mounted on the boards, but as yet has no system of shallow boxes or drawers to do so.

Conclusion

The approach described in this paper is not a traditional one, nor is it necessarily appropriate for museums with full-time specialist conservation and curatorial staff. In the region covered by the AMCSW, 75 percent of museums are run by volunteers with no professional curatorial staff. Enabling and encouraging volunteers to carry out museum collections work has become a key part of the work of the AMCSW. In addition, in a period of diminishing resources for local authority museums with frozen or deleted posts, volunteers have become increasingly involved in museum work. Their contribution can enable otherwise unlikely projects to happen, for example exhibitions.

This contribution must be acknowledged with supervision, training and recognition of skills. Conservators and curators can provide this, and co-operate with volunteers to work on a large range of museum projects from collection care to exhibitions, without compromising standards.

Résumé

Répartition des tâches : cas concret de montage d'une exposition avec un budget réduit

Dans l'article, on décrit un cas concret où la répartition attentive des tâches en fonction des compétences a permis de respecter les normes de conservation lors de la mise sur pied d'une exposition temporaire de dentelle, malgré un budget réduit. Les restaurateurs de textiles ont mis à profit leurs connaissances des techniques et des matériaux pour équilibrer le coût et la qualité, le conservateur du musée a assuré la gestion du projet et la supervision, enfin, une équipe de bénévoles formés a monté les dentelles. Parmi les facteurs clés qui ont assuré la réussite du projet, on compte l'existence d'une vérification constante de l'état de la collection de textiles et de costumes, la participation du service de conservation des textiles du début à la fin du projet, la gestion rigoureuse exercée par le personnel de conservation et de conception et l'enthousiasme de l'équipe de bénévoles.

"Let Me Edu-tain You," Historic Artifacts and the World of Themed Entertainment

Cara Varnell

Conservation Department
Los Angeles County Museum of Art
5905 Wilshire Boulevard
Los Angeles, CA 90036 USA
Tel.: (213) 857-6169 − Fax: (213) 936-5755

Abstract

Themed entertainment, a broad umbrella term for business-es that provide entertainment and education in a themed setting, is a growing industry in North America. There is an increase in themed venues that incorporate historic artifacts into exhibition spaces, blurring the line between museums and entertainment. Enough high caliber objects are present-ly showcased to see a growing trend and to raise a concern about their preservation. This paper offers three points for the consulting conservator to consider. First, understand the organization before offering advice. Secondly, to be effective, the conservator must be both a teacher and a diplomat. Finally, the conservator must be fully prepared with answers and must be able to provide the client with concise, up-to-date technical and resource information to support all recommendations.

Once upon a time about 45 years ago a man named Walt Disney had this great idea. He decided to open an amusement park. His park would be like no other because it would be divided into different playgrounds each with its own identity based on an individual theme. The archi-tecture, the rides and all other activities in each of these sections would be related to that theme; Tomorrowland, Adventureland and Fantasyland would be some of the special places where visitors, young and old, could come to spend their day. He called his park Disneyland. And with that Themed Entertainment was born.

Themed Entertainment, an industry unique to the late 20th century, is a broad umbrella term covering many seemingly unrelated enterprises. There are the obvious themed amusement parks, such as Disneyland or Busch Gardens, but the Themed Entertainment industry actually covers a vast range of businesses. A "themed" venue can be as simple as a neighborhood Chinese restaurant where the dining room ambiance is created by the use of traditional Chinese art, music and design. It can be as complicated and temporary as the 1996 Summer Olympics in Atlanta, Georgia. It includes restaurants such as Planet Hollywood, or the Hard Rock Cafe, gaming resorts like Ceasar's Palace in Las Vegas, NV, and retail stores like Niketown on

57th St. in New York City. It is the new, popular cultural museums such as the Rock and Roll Hall of Fame and Museum in Cleveland, Ohio or the Experience Music Project scheduled to open in Seattle, Washington in 1999. It even can be an entire town such as Branson, Missouri. Whether a huge corporation or a small local establishment, these businesses provide the playgrounds for millions and millions of people every year. They give us entertainment, education, diversion and fun in a theatrical, themed setting whether it is the Golden Years of Hollywood, ancient Rome or a 1950s bebop cafe. In the realm of the arts, Themed Entertainment is the wave of the 21st century.

Why should this be of any more than a passing interest to conservators and curators? Because more and more themed venues, of the type cited, recognizing the provoca-tive nature of authentic artifacts, are incorporating pieces of historic and artistic value into galleries and exhibition spaces, blurring the line between museums and the world of entertainment. Original photographs, posters, costumes or other cultural materials are finding their way onto the walls and into the display cases of a variety of these venues. It has become apparent that the long-term survival of many of our cultural artifacts could be in question.

Certainly every object presently displayed at these sites cannot be considered historically valuable or unique, but enough high-caliber artifacts are presently showcased in themed settings to see the growing trend and to raise a con-cern. Currently, the most commonly exhibited objects are memorabilia from our modern society: movie, music and sports paraphernalia, for example. The future of this type of material is not a trivial concern for it must be remem-bered that what is considered ephemera today will become a part of history tomorrow.

The public display of art and artifacts outside a museum or gallery context is nothing new. Venues such as airports, lobbies of corporate buildings or public parks have been decorating their spaces with artworks and cultural artifacts for decades. The art brings a certain life to sometimes oth-erwise sterile environments; it can make a space feel more comfortable as well as enliven it. In these cases, the art is exhibited solely for decorative purposes as often as it is for its own sake. What is unique about a Themed

Entertainment site is that the incorporation of the artifacts is directly tied to the design and activity of the space; they help to define it. For example, when Planet Hollywood displays Marilyn Monroe's delicate costume from "Gentlemen Prefer Blondes," it cannot be rotated, for the sake of preservation, with just any other sturdier substitute from a stock of 1950s fashions. In this context, the inclusion of that particular dress in the site design becomes more important than its preservation.

As with other public spaces, Themed Entertainment exhibits offer many challenges not commonly found in the more traditional museum settings. It is not unusual for the public hours to be much longer than those of any museum and to include all 365 days a year. Many of these centers have more visitors in a year than most traditional museums could ever hope to have in the same time frame. The environmental problems associated with this type of exhibition, for example, security, humidity control, light exposure, infestation control, and exposure to pollutants, are similar whether the public space is an airport or an entertainment center. These unique issues create challenges which are more complex than many found in a traditional museum. Their scope is broader than what many in the museum community normally address; what are the ramifications of five million visitors a year moving in and out of the exhibition space, or the constant exposure to food fumes and cigarette smoke in restaurant venues, or the 5,475 hours of light exposure which come from continual display 15 hours per day over 365 days?

In addition to environmental issues, Themed Entertainment display requirements are often governed by criteria other than the needs of the artifact. It is not unusual to have artifacts prepared and mounted, in essence "boxed," by a dealer and sold to a venue ready to hang. The mounting materials used in these enclosed cases often are not archival, and have limited concern for the long-term effects. Also, the site designer may want a dynamic presentation of the artifacts and may not be particularly concerned about an object's ultimate safety; the design concept and the desired effects being more important.

Perhaps the most salient point, though, is that many of these venues are for-profit operations as opposed to most museums, themed or traditional, which are not-for-profit. For these for-profit companies, their business may be entertainment, but their bottom line is money. Their issues of cost-effective planning and exhibition design are very different from those of museums where the site exists to protect and display the artifacts; where the preservation of the artwork is paramount. In a Themed Entertainment context, the artifacts are there to enhance the venue. Once past the initial site opening, there may be no more money allocated for the continued care of the displays or for rotation of sensitive material. In the short view, permanent displays are seen as unquestionably the most cost-effective.

There are two categories of display objectives which have clearly emerged in these new situations. First is the inclusion of a gallery/museum space, specifically for the exhibition of related original material. For example, Warner Bros. Studios in Burbank, California has built a museum on their backlot to be visited by the public at the conclusion of their studio tour. The second includes venues such as Planet Hollywood and the Hard Rock Cafe where the artifacts become an essential feature of the decor, helping to create a mood.

Where does the art conservator fit into this picture at this point? If they are included at all, it usually seems to be after the plans are made, the cases designed and the lighting fixtures chosen. Though this tends to be a high-tech industry with an unlimited imagination, the subtleties of artifact preservation and safe display can be completely mysterious to those not familiar with the field of collections care. Too often the conservator is brought in at the end of the design process, when plans have been set in motion and compromises in standards have become unavoidable. Ideally, if historic artifacts are integral to the design concept, then a conservator would be a part of the initial planning team, prior to the implementation of irreversible decisions. In order to insure that conservators be included as critical cogs in the design wheel, we need to become more publicly active and outspoken about our concerns for the preservation of our cultural heritage. In other words, how can the Themed Entertainment community know that they need a conservator if they do not understand who we are and what we have to offer or even that we exist?

Regardless of when a conservator is brought into the project there are three points which should be kept in mind. First,[1] before offering any advice, listen carefully to the site designers and staff. Understand the general goals of the organization, know both the background and the ability of the staff, and be clear on the perception of their responsibility toward the artifacts. As earnest as they may be about the preservation of the material, often the personnel come from an entertainment background, not from museum training. This difference can translate into conflicts over the presentation and care of the objects. An astute sensitivity to the overall situation will be rewarded with a greater influence in the decision-making process.

Second, education is the most valuable commodity that a conservator has to offer. There is no point for a consultant to condemn design choices or predict the worst in artifact damage without first laying a foundation of information. What is evident to a museum professional can also be obvious to a non-professional once they have the facts. For example, simply and explicitly explaining why environmental conditions are a serious concern can clear the way for the discussions of a long-term collections care policy. Effectively playing this role of teacher and diplomat in the early stages of a project means more than a smooth working relationship. It is the most efficient way to maximize the conservator's input, resolve problems and find the best possible solutions for the objects involved.

Finally, come prepared with answers and information at hand. Well-documented data, from the effects of environmental conditions to the various case designs, can only help in building the argument for the development of museum quality standards within the exhibition space. Providing this information in an easy to understand format also can help the staff prepare their future presentations within the organization. In other words, if they must justify their budget requests, give them the tools with which to do that. Be prepared to provide sources for lights, UV filters, monitoring equipment, vacuum cleaners, or future conservation services. The conservator's goal should be to help the staff understand the need for a collections care, to develop collections policy and exhibition standards appropriate to their specific situation and to give them the tools to defend, implement and maintain them.

If the current trend continues, it is clear that in the United States, Canada and much of the western world the line between culture, entertainment and education will begin to fade in the next 50 years, and it is not inconceivable that a wide variety of historic artifacts will eventually be included in these venues. Conservators and other trained museum professionals dedicated to the long-term preservation of our cultural heritage need to become a part of this process now in order to help establish high standards for artifact care in Themed Entertainment venues today and in anticipation of those to come.

[1] These recommendations are the result of my experience with venues that display Hollywood memorabilia.

Résumé

L'éducation et le divertissement : les objets historiques dans le monde du spectacle thématique

L'industrie des spectacles thématiques, expression générique qui regroupe les entreprises œuvrant dans le domaine du spectacle et de l'éducation dans un cadre thématique, est en pleine croissance en Amérique du Nord. On note une augmentation du nombre d'endroits incorporant des objets historiques dans des salles d'exposition, qui estompent la différence entre musée et divertissement. Le nombre d'objets de grande valeur actuellement en montre est suffisant pour que l'on commence à se préoccuper sérieusement de leur préservation. Dans l'article, on porte trois éléments à la connaissance des restaurateurs consultants. Premièrement, comprendre l'organisation avant de fournir des conseils. Deuxièmement, pour remplir efficacement son rôle, le restaurateur doit faire preuve à la fois de pédagogie et de diplomatie. Enfin, il doit être parfaitement préparé à répondre à toutes les questions possibles et être apte à fournir des renseignements concis au client sur les questions techniques et sur les ressources pour appuyer ses recommandations.

8

Demonstrations
Démonstrations

Demonstration of Color Measurement Techniques for Historic Textiles

Deborah Bede

Minnesota Historical Society
345 Kellogg Boulevard West
St. Paul, MN 55102 USA
Tel.: (612) 297-5490

Several aspects of color measurement will be interpreted specifically for use on historic textiles. Topics covered will include a comparison of color measurement instruments and color spaces, the placement of the measuring head, and the standardization of measurement techniques. The demonstration will compare several measurement techniques and discuss various interpretation methods.

Démonstration des techniques de mesure de la couleur des textiles historiques

Deborah Bede

Minnesota Historical Society
345 Kellogg Boulevard West
St. Paul, MN 55102 USA
Tél. : (612) 297-5490

Plusieurs aspects de la mesure de la couleur sont interprétés relativement aux textiles historiques. Parmi les sujets traités, on compte la comparaison des instruments de mesure de la couleur et l'espace chromatique, le positionnement de la tête de mesure et la normalisation des techniques de mesure. À titre de démonstration, on compare plusieurs techniques de mesure et on expose diverses méthodes d'interprétation.

Intersecting Silhouette Mannequins

Denis Larouche

Canadian Museum of Civilization
100 Laurier Street
P.O. Box 3100, Station B
Hull, PQ J8X 4H2 Canada
Tel.: (819) 776-8320
Fax: (819) 776-8300

In spring 1995, the River Gallery of the Canadian Museum of Civilization opened its doors to a major exhibit of Native costume called: "Threads of The Land." Items of clothing from collections throughout North America and Europe, were gathered together to present a comprehensive cross section of traditional styles prevailing in the culture of three Native groups of the Canadian Northwest: the Dene people, the Copper and the Caribou Inuit and the Nlaka'pamux (Plateau people of the southern Interior of British Columbia).

A significant part of the collection was made up of artifacts such as mittens, gloves, boots and other accessories. However, the most challenging portion of the exhibit, as far as the display studios were concerned, was the more than 150 parkas, tunics, dresses and other body-covering garments for which mannequins were to be made.

A technique previously used for conservation type mounts, the "Ethafoam Disks" method, did not seem appropriate for such a large number of individually crafted mannequins. The number of individually measured disks makes it a rather slow process, as well, round disks make round

mannequins and the human body is simply not round. A different approach was needed, something quicker and more straightforward.

After tinkering with several ideas, a prototype was built where two intersecting silhouettes (front view and profile), were cut to a garment's specific dimensions and assembled to form the core of a mannequin. Four more pieces were added to fill in the "gaps" and produce a complete torso totalling only six pieces of foam to cut. This torso is then padded with a stable material such as polyester fibrefill and finished off with a layer of cotton jersey. Both fibrefill and cotton jersey can be tucked into grooves cut into the foam of the mannequin, making their installation very quick and easy, as is their removal, should modifications be needed. For example, the jersey and padding are simply peeled away and the foam core can be either trimmed or added to, depending on what is needed, and the covering layers tucked lightly back into their grooves.

Once acquainted with it, the intersecting silhouette technique should prove a quick and (I hope) easy way to produce natural-looking, customized mounts for costume displays.

Les mannequins à silhouettes entrecroisées

Denis Larouche

Musée canadien des civilisations
100, rue Laurier
Case postale 3100, Succ. B
Hull (Qc) J8X 4H2 Canada
Tél. : (819) 776-8320
Téléc. : (819) 776-8300

Au printemps 1995, la Salle de la Rivière du Musée canadien des civilisations a ouvert ses portes à une importante exposition de costumes autochtones intitulée : «Liens à la terre». Des articles vestimentaires provenant de collections de toute l'Amérique du Nord et d'Europe ont été rassemblés pour donner une vue d'ensemble des styles traditionnels caractéristiques des cultures de trois groupes autochtones du Nord-Ouest canadien : les Dénés, les Inuit du cuivre et du caribou et les Nlaka'pamux (peuple des plateaux de l'intérieur sud de la Colombie-Britannique).

Une part importante de la collection est constituée de mitaines, de gants, de bottes et d'autres accessoires. Toutefois, la partie de l'exposition qui s'est avérée la plus délicate, du moins en ce qui a trait aux ateliers d'exposition, est celle des parkas, tuniques, robes et autres vêtements de corps, soit plus de 150 en tout, pour lesquels il a fallu construire des mannequins.

Une technique employée précédemment en conservation pour fabriquer des mannequins, la méthode des «disques d'Ethafoam», ne semble pas convenir à la fabrication d'un si grand nombre de mannequins. En effet, mesurer individuellement le nombre de disques nécessaires prendrait beaucoup trop de temps. De plus, les disques produisent des mannequins cylindriques, ce qui n'est pas la forme naturelle du corps humain. Il faut faire appel à une méthode nouvelle, quelque chose de plus rapide et de plus simple.

Après avoir tâté plusieurs idées, on construit un prototype où deux silhouettes entrecroisées (vue avant et profil) sont découpées aux dimensions précises du vêtement qui leur est destiné, puis assemblées pour former la base du mannequin. Quatre pièces de remplissage sont ajoutées pour produire un torse complet; au total il n'a fallu découper que six morceaux d'Ethafoam. Le torse est ensuite rembourré avec un matériau stable comme la bourre de fibres polyester, puis fini à l'aide d'une épaisseur de tricot de coton. La bourre et le tricot s'insèrent dans des rainures pratiquées dans l'Ethafoam; ainsi, ils sont aussi faciles à poser qu'à enlever, advenant la nécessité de modifier le mannequin. Il suffirait alors d'arracher le tricot et la bourre pour découper l'Ethafoam ou y ajouter des morceaux, selon le cas, puis de réinsérer la garniture lâchement dans les rainures.

Après expérimentation, la technique des silhouettes entrecroisées devrait s'avérer une méthode rapide et (je l'espère) facile pour fabriquer un support d'allure naturelle et adapté à l'article vestimentaire auquel il est destiné.

Fabricating Ethafoam Disc Mannequins

Polly Willman

Preservation Services
National Museum of American History
Smithsonian Institution
Washington, DC 20560 USA
Tel.: (202) 357-1406
Fax: (202) 786-2154

Fabricating disc mannequins of Ethafoam is a very viable and affordable option for obtaining custom-made forms for the display of costumes. The process, however, for producing a form of proper size, proportions, and posture can be difficult and involve extensive handling of the costume object.

I will demonstrate a method I have developed which yields an accurate pattern faster with less handling of the costume. It involves pre-dressing the costume on a standard dress form, padding it out to approximate the correct body shape, and then taking measurements off this mocked-up form. This process is facilitated by the use of a flexi-curve which captures both the curved shapes and circumference measurement. It yields a pattern that correctly distributes front-to-back and side-to-side proportions and provides correct alignment of the adjacent patterns for stacking the discs.

The demonstration will be staged accompanied by several forms at different stages of completion. I will also have a handout of directions.

Fabrication de mannequins en disques d'Ethafoam

Polly Willman

Preservation Services
National Museum of American History
Smithsonian Institution
Washington, DC 20560 USA
Tél. : (202) 357-1406
Téléc. : (202) 786-2154

L'utilisation de disques d'Ethafoam est une méthode efficace et bon marché pour fabriquer des mannequins servant à exposer les costumes. Toutefois, il peut s'avérer difficile de réaliser un modèle des dimensions, des proportions et de la posture souhaitées, et il peut aussi y avoir manipulation excessive du costume.

Je fais la démonstration d'une méthode personnelle qui permet d'obtenir une silhouette précise plus rapidement et avec une manipulation moindre du costume. Il s'agit d'enfiler le costume sur un mannequin standard, d'ajouter de la bourre pour se rapprocher le plus possible de la silhouette voulue, enfin, de mesurer le prototype ainsi obtenu. Le processus est facilité par l'utilisation d'une «courbe flexible», qui permet de mesurer à la fois les courbes et la circonférence. On obtient ainsi un ensemble de mesures de profondeur et de largeur également réparties et on assure l'alignement correct des disques à empiler.

La démonstration montrera les étapes du processus. Je mettrais aussi à la disposition des participants un feuillet explicatif.

Functional Forms — Sturdy, Archival Mannequins

Patricia Silence

American Textile History Museum
Textile Conservation Centre
491 Dutton Street
Lowell, MA 01854-4221 USA
Tel.: (508) 441-4498
Fax: (508) 441-1412

The recent relocation of the American Textile History Museum to an 1870s factory building in Lowell, Massachusetts now provides gallery space to interpret the progress of textile production from pre-industrial time through the 1950s. The exhibits illustrate American textile history with wooden tools, industrial machinery, flat textiles, and three-dimensional textile products, including clothing.

The Textile Conservation Center has prepared a large number of textiles for the museum's opening exhibits. One aspect of this project was the fabrication of mannequins to display dresses with silhouettes reflecting a span of over 100 years. Collaboration between curatorial staff, costume experts, and conservators was critical to determine the correct silhouette of each historical costume and achieve proper support for long-term display. The forms had to be durable, archival, and yet more economical than the carved Ethafoam mannequins we normally provide for our clients. In order to address this challenging problem, we developed a method of producing sturdy cast forms.

These mannequins are relatively simple to make, and can be modified and reproduced.

This demonstration will focus on the materials, tools, and techniques required to make a reinforced cast mannequin. An existing form is adjusted to properly support and shape the garment, using padding and corseting as needed. This mannequin serves as a mold to cast the desired form in multiple layers of buckram. Reinforcing the interior of the buckram form with Ethafoam and inserting the necessary mounting hardware for the purpose of display provides stability for this lightweight form. A coating made of an acrylic resin bulked with glass microspheres is applied to the interior and exterior with a brush. This consolidant impregnates the buckram making the form very rigid and resistant to ambient moisture, which can deform and delaminate the layers. The form is then padded with polyester batting and covered with the selected show fabric. The finished product is an archival, supportive mannequin that is sturdy enough for long-term use or as a form for casting more mannequins.

Mannequins fonctionnels et robustes respectant les principes de conservation

Patricia Silence

American Textile History Museum
Textile Conservation Centre
491 Dutton Street
Lowell, MA 01854-4221 USA
Tél. : (508) 441-4498
Téléc. : (508) 441-1412

Le déménagement récent de l'American Textile History Museum dans une ancienne usine des années 1870 située à Lowell, au Massachusetts, a fourni la superficie nécessaire à l'interprétation des progrès réalisés dans la production textile, de l'époque pré-industrielle aux années 1950. Les objets exposés illustrent l'histoire américaine des textiles et incluent notamment des outils en bois, de la machinerie industrielle, des textiles plats et des articles textiles tridimensionnels, dont des vêtements.

Le Textile Conservation Center a préparé un grand nombre de pièces textiles pour les expositions d'ouverture du musée. L'un des aspects du projet était la fabrication de mannequins pour présenter des robes dont les silhouettes représentaient tous les courants de la mode depuis plus d'un siècle. La collaboration entre les conservateurs, les experts en costume et les restaurateurs s'est avérée critique pour déterminer la silhouette exacte de chaque costume historique et créer un support convenable pour l'exposition à long terme. Les mannequins devaient se montrer durables et respecter les principes de conservation tout en étant meilleur marché que les mannequins en Ethafoam sculpté que nous fournissons habituellement à nos clients. Afin de faire face à ces spécifications exigeantes, nous avons mis au point une méthode pour produire des mannequins

moulés robustes. Relativement faciles à réaliser, on peut les modifier et les reproduire.

La démonstration se concentre sur les matériaux, les outils et les techniques nécessaires pour fabriquer un mannequin moulé renforcé. On ajuste d'abord un mannequin existant pour supporter convenablement le costume et lui donner la forme voulue, en y ajoutant de la bourre ou en l'enveloppant, au besoin. Le mannequin ainsi modifié sert de moule pour former la coquille par application de plusieurs couches de bougran. On renforce l'intérieur de la coquille en bougran à l'aide d'Ethafoam et en insérant une structure de montage afin d'assurer la stabilité de ce mannequin ultra-léger. On applique ensuite un revêtement en résine acrylique renforcée de microbilles de verre à l'intérieur et à l'extérieur, au pinceau. Ce revêtement de renforcement imprègne le bougran et procure une grande rigidité, ainsi qu'une résistance élevée à l'humidité ambiante, susceptible de déformer et de décoller les couches. Le mannequin est enfin recouvert d'une matelassure de polyester et recouvert du tissu sélectionné pour l'exposition. Le produit fini est un mannequin respectant les principes de conservation, qui soutient convenablement les vêtements et s'avère assez robuste pour l'utilisation à long terme. Il peut aussi servir à mouler d'autres mannequins.

Fibre Optic Lighting Systems

Larry V. Bowers

National Park Service
Division of Conservation
P. O. Box 50
Harpers Ferry, WV 25425 USA
Tel.: (304) 535-6052
E-mail: larry_bowers@nps.gov

A variety of fiber optic systems will be presented with an eye toward the comparative merits of those systems displayed and their effective use. The appropriate use of fiber optics, and the inherent limitations of fiber optic illumination will be discussed.

Manufactured fiber optic illumination systems from the United States and England will be exhibited, with a concentration on those with a direct relevance to the museum field. Illuminators, lenses, light bars, etc. from Absolute Action, NoUVIR, and Lighting Services Incorporated will be available and will be demonstrated, as will hardware from component manufacturers such as Dolan-Jenner, Lumitex, etc. Although the focus of the demonstration will be on manufactured systems, the advantages and disadvantages of do-it-yourself systems, that is, marrying component parts from various suppliers to construct your own fiber optic illumination, will be briefly discussed.

Optical fibers of acrylic, glass, and thermoset resin will be demonstrated and available. Discussion will focus on comparisons of the three types, the advantages and disadvantages of each, and their appropriate use in museum exhibits. Wavelength transmission characteristics, attenuation, length of fiber run, ease of use, relative costs, and safety issues will be discussed.

At least five different fiber optic illuminators will be available for demonstration. Discussion will include advantages and disadvantages of halogen and metal halide illuminators, color temperature and color rendering index of light sources, use with occupancy sensors, and the most appropriate use of each type.

Output devices (lenses, light bars, fiber optic cloth, etc) will be demonstrated — from simple, homemade acrylic lenses to the most sophisticated, multi-element lenses capable of throwing a fiber optic beam across a room.

With the benefit of overhead projection, we will see detailed applications of various fiber optic illumination systems as used by the U.S. National Park Service over the last five years, with discussion of the efficacy of the system presented, its successes and failures.

An effort will be made to allow as much practical experience as possible. Participants will be encouraged to handle cables, lenses and illuminators.

Systèmes d'éclairage à fibres optiques

Larry V. Bowers

National Park Service
Division of Conservation
P. O. Box 50
Harpers Ferry, WV 25425 USA
Tél. : (304) 535-6052
CÉ : larry_bowers@nps.gov

Plusieurs types de systèmes d'éclairage à fibres optiques sont présentés; on compare leurs avantages et leurs utilisations concrètes. On traite des utilisations appropriées des fibres optiques et des limites intrinsèques de l'éclairage aux fibres optiques.

La démonstration portera sur des systèmes d'éclairage fabriqués aux États-Unis et en Angleterre, en privilégiant ceux qui trouvent des applications directes dans les musées. Des sources lumineuses, des lentilles, des barres d'éclairage et d'autres articles d'Absolute Action, de NoUVIR et de Lighting Services Incorporated seront mis à la disposition des participants et feront l'objet de démonstrations, de même que du matériel de fabricants de composantes tels Dolan-Jenner, Lumitex, etc. La démonstration sera principalement axée sur les appareils complets, mais on traitera brièvement des avantages et des inconvénients des systèmes à monter soi-même, c'est-à-dire des appareils assemblés à partir de composantes de divers fournisseurs.

Les fibres optiques en acrylique, en verre et en résine thermodurcie seront mises à la disposition des participants et feront l'objet de démonstrations. L'exposé se concentrera sur la comparaison des trois types, sur les avantages et inconvénients de chacun et sur leurs applications dans le cadre d'expositions muséales. Il sera question des caractéristiques de transmission de la lumière, de l'atténuation, de la longueur des faisceaux, de la facilité d'emploi, du coût relatif et de la sécurité.

Les participants pourront examiner au moins cinq sources lumineuses différentes, dont on leur fera la démonstration. L'exposé portera sur les avantages et les inconvénients des sources lumineuses à halogène et des modèles aux halogénures, sur la température de la couleur et l'indice de rendu de la couleur des sources lumineuses, sur l'utilisation en conjonction avec des détecteurs de présence et sur les utilisations les plus indiquées des divers types.

On fera la démonstration des dispositifs d'émission (lentilles, barres d'éclairage, textiles en fibres optiques, etc.), de la simple lentille acrylique maison aux lentilles à composantes multiples dont certaines permettent de projeter le rayon lumineux à l'autre extrémité de la pièce.

Suivra l'exposé détaillé, avec rétroprojecteur, des divers systèmes d'éclairage à fibres optiques exploités par le U.S. National Park Service ces cinq dernières années, accompagné d'une discussion de l'efficacité des systèmes, des succès et des échecs.

On s'efforcera de donner un maximum d'importance à la pratique. Les participants seront invités à manier les câbles, les lentilles et les sources lumineuses.

Case Lighting for Textiles

Stefan Michalski

Canadian Conservation Institute
1030 Innes Road
Ottawa, ON K1A 0M5 Canada
Tel.: (613) 998-3721
Fax: (613) 998-4721
E-mail: stefan_michalski@pch.gc.ca

In possible conjunction with an earlier paper on case lighting, this demonstration will consist of three display cases in a darkened room. One will be a wall case with a flat textile, demonstrating both common errors and low-cost solutions for even top-to-bottom lighting with a single fluorescent lamp. The other two cases will be free standing, displaying a costume on a mannequin. One will use very low-cost quartz halogen fixtures ($15) now sold for 12 volt systems. The other will use an energy efficient, long life, compact fluorescent lamp with mirrors. Both will be capable of multiple beams of light for even lighting over the entire costume, as well as small high-lights if desired. Viewers will be able to reach into the lighting compartments and adjust key elements to see how the lighting is affected.

Éclairage des vitrines pour les textiles

Stefan Michalski

Institut canadien de conservation
1030, chemin Innes
Ottawa (Ontario) K1A 0M5 Canada
Tél. : (613) 998-3721
Téléc. : (613) 998-4721
CÉ : stefan_michalski@pch.gc.ca

Dans cette démonstration, qui fait écho à un article antérieur, on peut voir trois vitrines d'exposition dans une chambre sombre. La première est une vitrine d'exposition murale contenant un textile exposé à plat où un éclairage égal verticalement est assuré par un seul tube fluorescent; c'est un exemple des erreurs courantes et des solutions à bon marché. Les deux autres sont des vitrines autonomes présentant chacune un costume sur un mannequin. L'une comporte des lampes halogènes très bon marché (15 $),

maintenant offertes pour les installations à 12 volts. L'autre est dotée d'une lampe fluorescente compacte à faible consommation d'énergie et à longue durée de vie, couplée à des miroirs. L'un et l'autre systèmes permettent d'éclairer également tout le costume et même, au besoin, de mettre certains éléments en évidence. Les participants sont invités à modifier la position des composantes dans chacune des boîtes pour voir les effets sur l'éclairage.

A Multimedia Exploration of Mounts for Textiles

Gail Niinimaa

25 Cathedral Road N.W.
Calgary, AB T2M 4K4 Canada
Tel.: (403) 282-5320
Fax: (403) 282-5320
E-mail: niinimaa@nucleus.com

Using the multimedia computer software HyperStudio on a Macintosh computer, this presentation will include a variety of solutions to mounting textiles showing case studies from both private collections and public institutions. Participants will have an opportunity to interactively explore a variety of mounting solutions for both flat and three-dimensional textiles. A discussion of materials and techniques will accompany each mounting technique. Images of completed mounts and diagrams of the mounting process will be scanned onto the computer screen and will be accompanied with text or voice. A variety of textiles and textile objects will comprise the subject matter such as: samplers, hats, costume, flat textiles and small three-dimensional textiles.

Multimedia, with its capability to capture voice and action, and to provide self-directed, nonlinear exploration of a topic can add an exciting dimension to the subject of textile conservation.

Exploration multimédia des supports de textiles

Gail Niinimaa

25 Cathedral Road N.W.
Calgary, AB T2M 4K4 Canada
Tél. : (403) 282-5320
Téléc. : (403) 282-5320
CÉ : niinimaa@nucleus.com

Réalisée à l'aide du logiciel multimédia HyperStudio sur Macintosh, cette démonstration porte sur toute une gamme de solutions de montage de textiles, illustrées par des études de cas menées sur des collections privées et publiques. Les participants auront la possibilité d'explorer plusieurs techniques de montage de textiles à plat ou en trois dimensions. Un exposé des matériaux et des techniques accompagne chaque méthode présentée. Des images des montages et des schémas du processus de montage ont été numérisés; ils sont affichés à l'écran de l'ordinateur et accompagnés par un texte ou une narration. Plusieurs types de textiles et d'objets textiles sont utilisés aux fins de la démonstration : échantillons, chapeaux, costumes, textiles plats et petits textiles tridimensionnels.

La technologie du multimédia, qui permet d'enregistrer la voix et l'action et d'explorer l'exposé comme on le souhaite et non de manière simplement linéaire et automatique, agrémente considérablement le sujet de la conservation des textiles.

Japonism in Fashion

Jun I. Kanai

The Kyoto Costume Institute
c/o Miyake Design Studio
3 West 18 Street
New York, NY 10011 USA

The Kyoto Costume Institute (KCI), founded in 1978, is the only Japanese institution specializing in the study of Western fashion in both cultural and artistic contexts. It has only been since the end of World War II that the Japanese have incorporated Western clothing into their daily lives, not only for its function but also for its modishness. The traditional kimono is now worn mainly for ceremonial and festive occasions. Therefore, it is especially important to study the social development of Western clothing, which is not part of the Japanese tradition. The study enables us to better understand the general evolution of Western fashion and to possibly foresee its future.

Since the KCI's inception, we have encountered many Western clothes strongly reminiscent of the decorations, patterns, construction, or overall sensibilities of the Japanese kimono. Because the goal of KCI is to study Western fashion, acquiring anything that displayed such similarities to Japanese traditional clothing was at first avoided. They seemed too close to home. However, we have come to realize that the KCI has a unique perspective from which to study the influence of Japanese tradition upon Western clothing — Japonism in fashion.

In the video presentation, the audience will see the KCI costume exhibition held in Tokyo guided by the chief curator, Akiko Fukai. Costumes from the 17th century to the present depicting Japanese influence are included in the video. Jun I. Kanai, curator-at-large, will translate and answer questions concerning the video presentation.

La mode du japonisme

Jun I. Kanai

The Kyoto Costume Institute
c/o Miyake Design Studio
3 West 18 Street
New York, NY 10011 USA

Fondé en 1978, l'Institut du costume de Kyoto (KCI) est le seul établissement japonais consacré à l'étude de la mode occidentale à la fois sur les plans culturel et artistique. Ce n'est que depuis la fin de la Seconde Guerre mondiale que les Japonais ont intégré la mode vestimentaire occidentale dans leur vie quotidienne, non seulement pour son côté pratique, mais aussi pour son style. Le kimono traditionnel est désormais porté principalement à l'occasion de fêtes ou de cérémonies. Par conséquent, il est tout particulièrement important d'étudier le développement social des vêtements occidentaux, qui ne font pas partie de la tradition japonaise. L'étude nous permettra de mieux comprendre l'évolution générale de la mode occidentale et, peut-être, d'entrevoir son avenir.

Depuis la création du KCI, nous avons examiné de nombreux vêtements occidentaux s'inspirant fortement des décorations, des motifs, de la fabrication ou des thèmes généraux du kimono japonais. Étant donné que le KCI a pour but l'étude de la mode occidentale, on a d'abord tenté d'éviter tout ce qui pouvait présenter des similitudes avec les traditions japonaises. De tels vêtements semblaient trop près de nous. Cependant, nous avons fini par comprendre que le KCI dispose d'une perspective unique pour examiner l'influence de la tradition japonaise sur les vêtements occidentaux, c'est-à-dire le japonisme dans la mode.

Dans la présentation vidéo, l'auditoire se fera guider par le conservateur en chef, Akiko Fukai, dans l'exposition de costumes du KCI qui a eu lieu à Tokyo. On y verra aussi des costumes du XVIIe siècle à aujourd'hui, qui illustrent l'influence japonaise. Jun I. Kanai, conservateur généraliste, fera la traduction et répondra aux questions sur la présentation vidéo.

9

**Posters
Affiches**

Pressure Mounting Textiles for Display

Thea Peacock and Monique Pullan

Textile and Fibres Studio, Organic Artefacts Section
The British Museum
Department of Conservation
Franks House 38-56 Orsman Road
London N1 United Kingdom
Tel.: 071-323-8087
Fax: 0171-323-8102

This poster illustrates a project recently carried out to re-evaluate the system for pressure-mounting textiles for exhibition in the British Museum.

The poster correlates some of the responses to a questionnaire that was sent out to several conservators in different institutions across the world asking about their considerations in the choice of mounting techniques and the range of materials currently in use. The aim was to gather information, opinions and practical suggestions to be incorporated into the mounting systems at the British Museum. The results were found to be useful and may also benefit others.

The poster also demonstrates some of the practical solutions that have been adopted in order to pressure-mount textiles for display in the Organic Artefacts Studio of the British Museum's Department of Conservation. Cross sections showing the construction of the mounts and samples of materials used are incorporated in the poster. Some ideas offered include the use of metal L-shaped mirror clips for attaching glazing to a backboard, the filling of cut edges of Aerolam F-board with polyester resin so that screws can be used to hold the glazing in place, the importance of constructing a "well" in the padding layer, and the use of Perspex as a glazing.

Montage à la pression des textiles

Thea Peacock et Monique Pullan

Textile and Fibres Studio, Organic Artefacts Section
The British Museum
Department of Conservation
Franks House 38-56 Orsman Road
London N1 United Kingdom
Tél. : 071-323-8087
Téléc. : 0171-323-8102

Cette affiche illustre un projet récent qui avait pour objet de réévaluer le système de montage à la pression des textiles exposés au British Museum.

L'affiche rapproche certaines des observations reçues en réponse à l'envoi d'un questionnaire à plusieurs restaurateurs de diverses institutions du monde entier, où on leur demandait ce qui a motivé le choix de la technique de montage et la gamme de matériaux qu'ils utilisent actuellement. L'objectif était de recueillir des renseignements, des opinions et des suggestions pratiques à intégrer dans les systèmes de montage du British Museum. Les suggestions recueillies se sont avérées utiles et pourraient très bien profiter à d'autres.

L'affiche fait aussi la démonstration de certaines solutions pratiques adoptées par l'Organic Artefacts Studio du département de la conservation du British Museum pour monter des textiles sous pression afin de les présenter. On peut y voir des vues en coupe montrant la construction des supports ainsi que des échantillons des matériaux utilisés. Certaines des idées proposées consistaient dans l'utilisation de pincettes métalliques en forme de L pour fixer une feuille de plastique sur un carton, dans le remplissage des bords coupés des panneaux d'Aerolam F avec de la résine de polyester, de manière à pouvoir utiliser des vis pour maintenir la feuille de plastique en place, dans l'importance de prévoir un «creux» dans la couche de rembourrage et dans le recours au Perspex comme vitrage.

Mounting a Teepee Liner for Exhibit

Shirley Ellis

Textile Conservation Service
Department of Human Ecology, University of Alberta
Edmonton, AB T6G 2M8 Canada
Tel.: (403) 492-4821
Fax: (403) 492-7678
E-mail: texlab@gpu.srv.ualberta.ca

Three teepee liners were selected for permanent display at the Provincial Museum of Alberta in Edmonton, Alberta, Canada. These liners, which line the inside of a teepee, are painted heavyweight cotton textiles in somewhat trapezoidal shapes with curved upper and lower dimensions.

These teepee liners posed an ambitious task to mount because of their size and shape, particularly when the exhibit case was a predesigned 1.2 x 2.4 m (4 x 8 ft.) shadow box. The liners were both too long and too wide for the exhibit cases. Not creating sharp folds in the fabric was challenging.

Because of their size and this being a permanent exhibit, it was desirable to mount the textiles on an inclined plane to provide support over time. This method was used initially for mounting one liner on padded heavyweight polyfluted plastic sheet (Coroplast, Hi-Core). It was unsatisfactory due to the display case's minimal depth and the liner's awkward shape.

A more successful method was devised for the remaining two liners. It used the curved shape of the teepee liner displaying it with a minimum of fullness inside the shadow box. Five centimeter wide (2 in.), loop-side Velcro was first stitched to cotton twill tape forming the Velcro unit, then hand-stitched to the upper edge of the liner. The Velcro unit did not extend the liner's total width so that each end could roll in, according to the final dimension established by the exhibit case.

The extra length of the curved lower edge was loosely folded toward the back. This was accomplished by hand-stitching a cotton band and drawstring along the bottom edge. When the extra length was folded up, the excess fullness could be drawn in so that it was evenly distributed. To keep the fold loose but supported, five or six lengths of twill tape were stitched vertically from the upper Velcro unit to this cotton band. Now, ABS pipes could roll up the excess width along each side giving the visual effect of an enormous scroll. When the final width was established, twill tape was used once again to secure the rolled ends. It was installed in the display case by fastening the upper edge to a corresponding length of Velcro, which was stapled onto a sealed wooden batten. The two pipes were fixed at each side with a wooden plug.

The final result provided a display of teepee liners that revealed their shape on a flat plane under a minimal amount of stress.

Montage de doublures de tipi

Shirley Ellis

Textile Conservation Service
Department of Human Ecology, University of Alberta
Edmonton, AB T6G 2M8 Canada
Tél. : (403) 492-4821
Téléc. : (403) 492-7678
CÉ : texlab@gpu.srv.ualberta.ca

Trois doublures de tipi ont été sélectionnées aux fins d'exposition permanente dans le Provincial Museum of Alberta à Edmonton, en Alberta. Ces doublures en lourde étoffe de coton peinte se placent à l'intérieur du tipi. Elles sont de forme approximativement trapézoïdale, avec les bords supérieur et inférieur arrondis.

Le montage des doublures représentait un grand défi en raison de leur taille et de leur forme, d'autant plus qu'il fallait les monter dans un coffrage de 1,2 m x 2,4 m (4 x 8 pi) déjà construit. Les doublures étaient à la fois trop longues et trop larges pour les coffrages. La principale difficulté consistait à éviter les plis trop marqués dans le tissu.

En raison de la dimension des pièces et du caractère permanent de l'exposition, on a estimé préférable de monter les tissus sur un plan incliné, pour assurer un soutien convenable sur une période prolongée. Cette méthode a été créée à l'origine pour monter une doublure sur un panneau de plastique cannelé lourd capitonné (Hi-Core). Elle s'est avérée insatisfaisante à cause de la faible profondeur du coffrage et de la forme trapézoïdale de la doublure.

On a donc eu recours à une méthode plus efficace pour les deux doublures restantes. Elle met à profit la forme recourbée de la doublure de tipi pour la présenter en lui donnant un volume adapté au coffrage. Une bande de velcro (côté bouclé) de 5 cm (2 po) de large est cousue à une bande de serge en coton pour former la fermeture velcro, laquelle est alors cousue à la main sur le bord supérieur de la doublure. La fermeture velcro ne couvre pas toute la longueur de la doublure, de sorte qu'il est possible d'enrouler chaque côté vers l'intérieur en fonction des dimensions réelles du coffrage.

La longueur excédentaire du bord inférieur arrondi est repliée sans serrer vers l'arrière. Pour ce faire, une bande de coton et un cordon de serrage sont cousus à la main le long du bord inférieur. Une fois le bord replié, la circonférence du bas de la doublure peut être réduite également en fonction des dimensions du coffrage en tirant sur le cordon. Pour maintenir le pli sans le serrer, cinq ou six longueurs de bande de serge sont cousues verticalement de la fermeture velcro supérieure à la bande de coton inférieure. Des tubes en ABS sont alors utilisés pour recourber les côtés afin de réduire la largeur, ce qui confère à la doublure l'aspect d'une énorme volute. Une fois la largeur définitive établie, le ruban de serge est utilisé une fois de plus pour fixer les extrémités recourbées. Il est posé dans le coffrage en fixant l'extrémité supérieure à une longueur correspondante de velcro, agrafé à une traverse en bois scellée. Des bouchons de bois viennent fixer les tuyaux à chaque extrémité.

Le résultat de cette opération est une présentation de la doublure de tipi qui révèle sa forme sur une surface plane, avec un minimum de tension.

A Possible Solution to the Rug Pad Dilemma

Steven Pine

P.O. Box 6826
Houston, TX 77265 USA
Tel.: (713) 639-7730
Fax: (713) 639-7740

Joy Gardiner

Conservation Division
Winterthur Museum, Garden & Library
Winterthur, DE 19735 USA
Tel.: (302) 888-4612
Fax: (302) 888-4838
E-mail: jwg@udel. edu

Anywhere historic rugs are displayed in period room settings, there is a need for a good, archival-quality rug pad. This is especially true where the layout of the room necessitates people walking over the rugs (which hopefully have runners in the trod-upon areas). Current commercially available rug pads have been found to be less than ideal. The hair-jute pads are a possible food source for insects and quickly degrade to become quite fibrous and dusty. Synthetic pads often contain rubber or other unstable, unacceptable materials.

A number of people have researched this problem including Steven Pine, conservator at Bayou Bend Collection and Gardens. He has come up with a pad formed from a 3 mm (1/8 in.) needle-punched polyester felt with an application of a silicon rubber, Dow Corning 732 RTV clear. The polyester felt cushions the rug, and the silicon rubber has enough tack to prevent slippage. This particular silicon has FDA approval for use with food.

The catalyst for this product is acetic acid which, in theory, will volatilize, leaving a neutral product.

A quantity of 182 m (202 yards) of this rug pad material was prepared by the conservation staff at Bayou Bend. It has been used in the collection for three years with excellent results.

Current and future work on this rug pad product include: investigating how long the acetic acid takes to off-gas; if there are any other similar products that would work better; if this product will work in buildings without climate control; and finding a commercial manufacturer to produce the rug pad.

The poster will feature samples of the rug pad, explanation of the materials used, photographs of the pads in use, and updating on the investigations currently underway.

Solution possible au problème des thibaudes

Steven Pine

P.O. Box 6826
Houston, TX 77265 USA
Tél. : (713) 639-7730
Téléc. : (713) 639-7740

Joy Gardiner

Conservation Division
Winterthur Museum, Garden & Library
Winterthur, DE 19735 USA
Tél. : (302) 888-4612
Téléc. : (302) 888-4838
CÉ : jwg@udel. edu

Partout où l'on expose des tapis historiques dans une pièce d'époque, il faut prévoir une thibaude de bonne qualité et respectant les principes de conservation, d'autant plus si l'itinéraire prévu des visiteurs les fait marcher sur le tapis (lequel serait préférablement recouvert d'un tapis de protection à cet endroit). Les thibaudes proposées dans le commerce se sont avérées peu efficaces. Les thibaudes en poils et en jute risquent d'attirer les insectes; de plus, elles se dégradent rapidement et deviennent fibreuses et poussiéreuses. Les modèles synthétiques contiennent souvent du caoutchouc ou d'autres matériaux instables et insatisfaisants.

Plusieurs personnes ont étudié le problème, notamment Steven Pine, restaurateur du Bayou Bend Collection and Gardens. Il a créé une thibaude formée de feutre de polyester piqué de 3 mm (1/8 po) enduit de caoutchouc au silicone transparent Dow Corning 732 RTV. Le feutre sert d'amortisseur et le caoutchouc au silicone accroche suffisamment pour prévenir le glissement. Par ailleurs,

ce silicone est approuvé par la FDA pour l'utilisation avec les aliments. L'acide acétique, son catalyseur, est censé se volatiliser, ce qui assure la neutralité du produit.

Le personnel de conservation de Bayou Bend a préparé 182 m (202 verges) de ce matériau. On l'utilise dans la collection depuis trois ans avec d'excellents résultats.

Parmi les travaux en cours et à venir portant sur ce produit, on compte : recherche sur le temps de volatilisation de l'acide acétique; existence d'autres produits analogues d'efficacité supérieure; comportement du produit dans un établissement dont le climat n'est pas régulé; repérage d'un fabricant commercial disposé à produire la thibaude.

L'affiche comprend un échantillon de la thibaude, la description des matériaux, des photographies de la thibaude installée et les derniers développements des recherches en cours.

A Sleeper of a Support System: Using a "Rope Bed" to Create a Slanted Mount for Temporary Exhibit of a Large Flag

Deborah Lee Trupin

New York State Office of Parks
Recreation and Historic Preservation
Bureau of Historic Sites
Peebles Island, P. O. Box 219
Waterford, NY 12188 USA
Tel.: (518) 237-8643 ext. 241

Kim Yarwood

State University of New York at Buffalo
Buffalo, NY USA

Dennis Farmer

Genesee County
The Holland Land Office Museum
Batavia, NY USA

Following conservation of its 7.2 x 8.4 m (24 x 28 ft.) War of 1812 flag, Old Fort Niagara arranged to temporarily exhibit it at the Castellani Museum, Niagara University, Niagara Falls, New York. The museum was selected because of its large, open gallery space. However, the size of the flag was still larger than the available gallery floor space, precluding flat display. It was fully lined, but its size and condition required at least supported display on an angle.

Working within the confines of limited time and budget, then Castellani Museum gallery manager, Kim Yarwood, and then Old Fort Niagara curator, Dennis Farmer, conceived of a temporary mount based on the design of a rope bed. Conservator Deborah Trupin reviewed the design and proposed modifications to make installing the flag on the mount easier and safer for both flag and people.

The support for the mount was constructed with 5 x 10 cm (2 x 4 in.) boards. The frame rose from a height of 15 cm (6 in.) off the floor to 1.8 m (6 ft.), in order to accommodate the flag's 7.2 m (24 ft.) height in the available 6.9 m (23 ft.)

space. The top of the support and the frame of the mount were bolted to the gallery wall. The frame of the mount was constructed of 5 x 15 cm (2 x 6 in.) boards. Holes were drilled through these boards at 30 cm (12 in.) intervals for the nylon ropes to pass through. Each rope crossing was tied together with a finer nylon string. The tensioned ropes created a grid to serve as the main support for the (fully lined) flag.

Once the mount was installed in the gallery, hook Velcro (corresponding to the fuzzy Velcro on the flag lining) was stapled to the sides of the mount. The flag was gradually unrolled onto the mount, arranged in place, and supported by the rope bed. The spacing of the ropes permitted installers to stand between ropes and carefully walk backwards supporting the edge of the lined flag as the installation progressed. The Velcro at the sides was used to tension the flag lining slightly to straighten and align the stripes on the flag. Black pleated curtains, like those used to disguise banquet hall tables, were also secured to Velcro at the sides and front edge of the mount for a finished appearance.

Utilisation d'un «lit à cordage» pour créer un support incliné pour une exposition temporaire d'un drapeau de grandes dimensions

Deborah Lee Trupin

New York State Office of Parks
Recreation and Historic Preservation
Bureau of Historic Sites
Peebles Island, P. O. Box 219
Waterford, NY 12188 USA
Tél. : (518) 237-8643 ext. 241

Kim Yarwood

State University of New York at Buffalo
Buffalo, NY USA

Dennis Farmer

Genesee County
The Holland Land Office Museum
Batavia, NY USA

Une fois terminée la restauration de son drapeau de la Guerre civile de 1812, qui mesure 7,2 x 8,4 m (24 x 28 pi), Old Fort Niagara a organisé une exposition temporaire dans le musée Castellani, à la Niagara University de Niagara Falls, dans l'État de New York. Le musée a été retenu en raison de ses vastes salles bien dégagées. Cependant, la dimension du drapeau dépasse encore la superficie disponible du plancher, interdisant la présentation à plat. Bien que le drapeau ait été entièrement doublé, ses dimensions et son état nécessitent un minimum de soutien pour la présentation inclinée.

En travaillant selon des échéances et un budget serrés, le directeur de la salle du Castellani Museum, Kim Yarwood, et le conservateur à Old Fort Niagara, Dennis Farmer, ont conçu un support temporaire inspiré du principe du lit suspendu par des cordes. La restauratrice Deborah Trupin a examiné le concept et a proposé des modifications visant à faciliter l'installation du drapeau sur le support et à rendre l'ensemble plus sécuritaire, à la fois pour le drapeau et pour le public.

Le support est fabriqué avec des planches de 5 x 10 cm (2 x 4 po). Le cadre s'élève d'une hauteur de 15 cm (6 po) à 1 m 80 (6 pi), afin de convenir à la hauteur du drapeau - 7 m (24 pi) - et à l'espace disponible - 6,5 m (23 pi). Le haut du support et son cadre sont boulonnés au mur de la salle. Le cadre est fait de planches de 5 x 15 cm (2 x 6 po). Des trous percés dans ces planches à des intervalles de 30 cm (12 po) permettent de faire traverser les cordes de nylon. À chaque croisement, les cordes sont attachées à l'aide de cordes de nylon de moins gros calibre. Une fois tendu, le cordage forme une grille faisant office de support principal pour le drapeau (entièrement doublé).

Une fois le présentoir installé dans la salle, une bande velcro côté crochets (correspondant au côté bouclé fixé sur la doublure du drapeau) est agrafée aux bords du support. On a déroulé progressivement le drapeau sur le support, on l'a réparti également, puis on l'a fait reposer sur le lit de cordage. La distance entre les cordes permet aux installateurs de se tenir debout entre elles et de reculer avec précaution en soutenant le bord du drapeau à mesure que progresse l'installation. La bande velcro latérale est employée pour tendre la doublure du drapeau légèrement, afin de redresser et aligner les rayures du motif. Des rideaux plissés noirs, semblables à ceux qu'on utilise pour masquer les pattes des tables dans les salles de réception, sont également fixés au velcro sur les côtés et le bord avant du présentoir, afin de parfaire la finition de l'ensemble.

Mannequins for Navajo Textile Display

Susan Heald and Gwen Spicer

National Museum of the American Indian
3401 Bruckner Blvd.
Bronx, NY 10461 USA
Tel.: (212) 825-4496
Fax: (212) 825-4479
E-mail: heald@ic.si.edu

A collaboration between Navajo weavers, textile conservators and exhibition designers led to the design of a mannequin that allowed 19th century Navajo wearing blankets to be displayed on three-dimensional forms showing them in a more accurate context than the usual two-dimensional wall display. During the exhibition planning, three Navajo weaver co-curators were consulted regarding the mannequins. The weavers wanted the forms to be more abstract and not look too human, yet at the same time evoke common postures. The weavers did not want "lollipop" forms (torso-on-a-stick), nor should they look ghostlike with no substance inside. Seventeen designs were created, representing different poses, ages and genders.

Several of the poses required extended arms, leading to the need for structural foundation to support the weight of the textiles. The solution to this problem was found by constructing an internal armature of 4 cm (1 1/2 in.) PVC tubing. Using these ready-made materials greatly simplified the construction. No custom structures were needed; the plumbing industry had done all of the work by fabricating every possible angle joint needed to create shoulders, elbows and even bases. A support stand was designed that allowed the mannequins to be installed after the bases were secured to the exhibit deck. Additional benefits in using the PVC include the ease in cutting and joining, the fact that no new carpentry trades were learned, or expensive tools were needed. The use of this type of armature could easily be adapted to other mannequin form materials.

Most of the mannequins were carved out of Ethafoam planks, and then were covered with 200 wt. beige color Polar-Fleece(g)[1] . The fleece provided enough padding to eliminate a layer of batting that is traditionally used. The seams were easily made by slicing an incision in the Ethafoam and pushing the fleece into it. Thus, only minimal sewing was needed.

During test dressing of the mannequins, it was discovered that the textiles clung quite well to the fleece, adequately supporting the blankets and preventing slippage. No Velcro needed to be sewn to the textile or the mannequins; only a minimum of security stitching was used to attach the blankets during display.

References

Bonar, Eulalie. *Woven by the Grandmothers.* Washington, D.C.: Smithsonian Institute Press, 1996.

Brako, Jeanne. Personal communication, 1996.

Heald, Sue. "Woven by the Grandmothers: 24 Blankets Go Back to Visit the Navajo Reservation," *AIC Preprints,* (1996), pp. 7-9.

[1] Malden Mills, 46 Stafford, Lawrence, MA 01841 USA

Des mannequins pour l'exposition de costumes navahos

Susan Heald et Gwen Spicer

National Museum of the American Indian
3401 Bruckner Blvd.
Bronx, NY 10461 USA
Tél. : (212) 825-4496
Téléc. : (212) 825-4479
CÉ : heald@ic.si.edu

La collaboration de tisserands navahos, de restaurateurs de textiles et de concepteurs d'exposition a rendu possible la conception d'un mannequin qui permet de présenter sous forme tridimensionnelle des ponchos navahos du XIXe siècle. Il s'agit d'une méthode plus vivante et plus représentative que la présentation murale à plat. Durant la planification de l'exposition, on a travaillé en consultation avec trois tisserands navahos assistants conservateurs pour créer les mannequins. Les tisserands souhaitaient des mannequins de type abstrait, pas trop réaliste, mais évoquant des poses courantes. Ils ne voulaient pas de mannequin genre «sucette» (torse sur une tige), ni des silhouettes fantomatiques, sans substance. Dix-sept mannequins ont ainsi été créés, représentant des gens de divers âges et des deux sexes, dans diverses poses.

Plusieurs poses nécessitent l'extension des bras, d'où le besoin de prévoir une structure interne pour soutenir le poids des textiles. La solution trouvée à ce problème a consisté à construire une armature interne en tubes de PVC de 4 cm (1 1/2 po). L'utilisation de ce matériel préfabriqué facilite grandement la construction. Il n'était pas nécessaire de façonner des structures spéciales; l'industrie de la plomberie avait déjà fait tout le travail en produisant tous les raccords d'angles nécessaires pour créer les épaules, les coudes et même les bases. On a conçu un piédestal permettant l'installation des mannequins après fixation de leurs bases à la plate-forme de l'exposition. L'utilisation du PVC a présenté d'autres avantages : la facilité de la coupe et du raccordement, le fait que l'équipe n'a pas eu à apprendre de techniques spéciales de menuiserie, ni à acheter des outils coûteux.

Ce type d'armature est facilement adaptable aux autres matériaux utilisés pour la fabrication des mannequins.

La plupart des mannequins sont découpés dans des feuilles d'Ethafoam, puis couverts de molleton Polar-Fleece(g)[1] beige de calibre 200. Le molleton assure un amortissement suffisant pour éliminer la nécessité de la classique couche de ouatine. Pour réaliser les joints, on pratique des incisions dans l'Ethafoam, pour ensuite y insérer le molleton. Cette technique élimine presque toute couture.

Durant l'habillage d'essai des mannequins, on a constaté que les textiles accrochent bien au molleton, qui soutient efficacement les ponchos et les empêche de glisser. Il n'a pas été nécessaire de coudre du velcro aux textiles ou aux mannequins; quelques points de couture tout au plus ont été réalisés à titre de sécurité pour fixer les ponchos aux fins de l'exposition.

Bibliographie

Bonar, Eulalie. *Woven by the Grandmothers,* Washington, D.C., Smithsonian Institute Press, 1996.

Brako, Jeanne. Communication personnelle, 1996.

Heald, Sue. «Woven by the Grandmothers: 24 Blankets Go Back to Visit the Navajo Reservation», *AIC Preprints,* (1996), pages 7-9.

[1] Malden Mills, 46 Stafford, Lawrence, MA 01841 USA.

"Wedding Belles"

Jane Holland

Ministry of Citizenship, Culture & Recreation
77 Bloor Street West, 2nd Floor
Toronto, ON M7A 2R9 Canada
Tel.: (416) 314-7154
Fax: (416) 314-7175

Linda Berko

London Regional Art & Historical Museums
421 Ridout Street North
London, ON N6A 5H4 Canada
Tel.: (519) 672-4580
Fax: (519) 660-8397

Almost everyone who works with museum textile collections has bemoaned the fact that there are far too many wedding dresses saved, and the collection of the London Regional Art and Historical Museums, in London, Canada, is no exception. But in the context of a community museum, the wedding dress is a powerful personal artifact of local social life. The focus of this exhibit was on the women who were married in or became citizens of London, rather than illustrating costume style. This was accomplished in three ways: by mounting the costume on mannequins in a naturalistic way; by completing the wedding outfit with reproductions; by accompanying the costume with photographs of the brides and newspaper accounts of the weddings; and by presenting the exhibit in the domestic setting of Eldon House, London's oldest house, now a museum and local landmark.

The exhibit started life with some liabilities of its own. As a smaller institution, the museum does not have specialist curators or an exhibit designer, so as former textile conservators with an interest in costume, the conservators became both. Also, the exhibit had almost no budget, which dictated a do-it-yourself approach. Conservation considerations carried equal weight to curatorial and aesthetic in the selection of artifacts and design of the exhibit. Inexpensive mannequins produced for the retail merchandising market were modified with custom-made arms, legs and hair. The exhibit room, originally chosen because it provided a ready-made backdrop, was comfortable and accessible to visitors. The use of the props of modern weddings, such as music stands for barriers and reproduction bouquets, enhanced its appeal. In the end, the exhibit was successful in bringing a new audience to the museum, and presenting documentation of the city's past that visitors responded to in a very personal way.

Le charme de la mariée

Jane Holland

Ministère des Affaires civiques, de la Culture et des Loisirs
77, rue Bloor ouest, 2e étage
Toronto (Ont.) M7A 2R9 Canada
Tél. : (416) 314-7154
Téléc. : (416) 314-7175

Linda Berko

London Regional Art & Historical
Museums
421 Ridout Street North
London (Ont.) N6A 5H4 Canada
Tél. : (519) 672-4580
Téléc. : (519) 660-8397

Presque tous ceux et celles qui travaillent avec des collections de textiles muséales se sont plaints à un moment ou un autre que l'on préserve beaucoup trop de robes de mariage. La collection des London Regional Art and London Historical Museums, à London, au Canada, ne font pas exception. Mais dans le contexte du musée communautaire, la robe de mariée constitue un objet personnel puissamment représentatif de la vie sociale. L'exposition dont il est question ici a pour thème les femmes qui se sont mariées à London ou en sont devenues citoyennes, et non l'illustration d'un type de costume. Pour atteindre les résultats escomptés, on a employé trois méthodes : monter les costumes sur des mannequins réalistes et compléter l'ensemble de mariage par des reproductions; accompagner le costume de photographies de la mariée et d'articles de journaux sur le mariage; enfin, présenter l'exposition dans le cadre résidentiel de la maison Eldon, la plus vieille de London, aujourd'hui un musée et un symbole pour la collectivité.

L'exposition a vu le jour avec certaines contraintes. Établissement plutôt modeste, la maison historique ne dispose pas de son propre conservateur, ni d'un concepteur d'exposition. Ainsi, en tant que restaurateurs de textiles s'intéressant au costume, les restaurateurs ont décidé de jouer les deux rôles. Par ailleurs, l'exposition n'avait pratiquement aucun budget, et il a fallu utiliser les moyens du bord. Les exigences de restauration ont pesé autant dans la balance que la conservation et l'esthétique dans la sélection des articles et dans la conception de l'exposition. On a modifié des mannequins abordables produits pour le marché de la vente au détail en y ajoutant des bras, des jambes et des cheveux faits maison. La pièce servant de salle d'exposition, choisie au départ parce qu'elle constituait une toile de fond déjà prête, était confortable et accueillante pour les visiteurs. L'utilisation, à titre de barrières, d'accessoires de mariage contemporains comme les pupitres à musique, et la disposition de bouquets artificiels ont agrémenté l'ensemble. En bout de ligne, l'exposition a réussi à attirer une clientèle nouvelle au musée, et à présenter une documentation du passé de la ville qui a personnellement touché les visiteurs.

King's Privy Chamber Throne Canopy ca. 1700, Hampton Court Palace

Val Davies

Textile Conservation Studios
Apt. 37 Hampton Court Palace
East Molesey, Surrey KT8 9AU United Kingdom
Tel.: 0181-781-9815
Fax: 0181-781-9813

The canopy formed part of the original state furnishings prepared for King William III's occupation in 1700. It has a framework box-like structure fixed to the walls by metal rods, and hangings of crimson silk damask decorated with applied silver gilt orrice lace and silver gilt fringing — a total of 17 textile pieces.

During the fire of 1986 which destroyed the King's Apartments, this canopy, already degraded from 286 years of continuous open display, was in the very seat of the fire, and incurred massive damage. The textiles were unrecognisable — stained, torn, encrusted with debris and splattered with molten lead from the roof, while the framework dangled from the wall.

The studio's immediate response to the disaster, the emergency flooding out of the textiles to remove particulate matter and allow identification of pieces, and the evaluation and selection of further treatments led to a conservation programme of support and display, which did not add appreciably to the weight the framework had to bear but which significantly reduced the visual disturbance caused by missing sections. Additionally, modifications to the original fixing methods were devised which were more conservationally acceptable and allowed for safe installation and display.

The particular requirements for the re-installation on-site of the canopy — scaffolding/handling/hoisting/etc. were tried out initially with fabric templates.

The major restoration project following the fire — rebuilding the structure and conserving the interiors — returned the damaged King's wing of the palace to a cohesive whole, the considerable research involved enabling the representation to convey the decorative schemes of the English court of 1700.

It had been vital that the throne canopy, commissioned for the Privy Chamber, and never having been moved from it, be conserved and returned for open display. Suspended 6 m (20 ft.) above the floor, it is now displayed with its patina of age, yet showing little of the damage it has survived.

Le dais de la chambre du Roi, vers 1700 (Hampton Court Palace)

Val Davies

Textile Conservation Studios
Apt. 37 Hampton Court Palace
East Molesey, Surrey KT8 9AU United Kingdom
Tél. : 0181-781-9815
Téléc. : 0181-781-9813

Le dais forme un élément essentiel de l'ameublement d'apparat du palais de Hampton, créé pour Guillaume III, qui y emménage en 1700. Soutenu par un cadre fixé aux murs par des tiges de métal, il se compose d'un pavillon en damas cramoisi à motifs d'iris et bordures brodés au fil d'argent, soit, au total, 17 pièces d'étoffe.

Durant l'incendie de 1986 qui a détruit les appartements du Roi, le dais, déjà altéré par 286 années d'exposition directe s'est retrouvé en plein cœur du feu. Il a subi de graves dommages. Tachées, déchirées, incrustées de débris et maculées de plomb fondu en provenance du toit, les étoffes étaient méconnaissables. Quant à la structure, elle se balançait sur ses fixations.

L'intervention d'urgence entreprise par le studio, soit le rinçage immédiat des étoffes afin d'éliminer les particules et permettre l'identification des pièces, et la sélection des traitements après l'évaluation ont mené à des décisions concernant le support et l'exposition qui n'augmentent pas de façon significative la charge du cadre, mais réduisent considérablement le choc visuel des sections manquantes. De plus, en ce qui concerne les méthodes de suspension d'origine, on a étudié des modifications acceptables sur le plan de la conservation, qui ont permis d'installer et d'exposer le dais en toute sécurité.

Les exigences particulières de l'opération de réinstallation du dais, soit la construction des échafaudages, la manipulation, le levage, etc., ont été mises à l'essai sur des modèles en tissu.

Le principal projet de restauration après l'incendie, c'est-à-dire la reconstruction de la structure et la conservation de l'aménagement intérieur, a redonné à l'aile endommagée du palais royal sa cohésion perdue. En effet, les recherches approfondies qui ont été menées ont permis de rendre avec fidélité les courants d'art décoratif en vogue à la cour anglaise vers 1700.

Il était crucial de restaurer et de remettre en présentation le dais, créé spécialement pour la chambre du Roi, dont il n'a jamais été retiré. Suspendu 6 m (20 pi) au-dessus du sol, il arbore fièrement son âge, en ne laissant presque rien deviner de la rude épreuve qu'il a traversée.

The Influence of Disaster Recovery on Reinstallation of Historic Wall Coverings

Deirdre Windsor

American Textile History Museum, Textile Conservation Center
491 Dutton Street
Lowell, MA 01854 USA
Tel.: (508) 441-1198
Fax: (508) 441-1412

A set of printed fabric wall coverings, part of the original library interior, was water damaged during a fire in a historic house, necessitating evaluating the feasibility of recovering the original materials. The Edgar Sawyer Mansion (known as Oshkosh Public Museum since 1922) was built in 1908 with interiors designed by Tiffany Studios. Disaster recovery was critical in the overall preservation of the material due to the prevalent environmental conditions during summer heat. The panels were immediately removed by museum staff, blotted, and then frozen to prevent fungal growth. The response of both disaster recovery and the following conservation treatment significantly affected the permanent exhibition of original materials integrated into a historic house setting.

The Textile Conservation Center (TCC) evaluated the frozen wall coverings for conservation treatment. The curator used our evaluation to determine if the original wall coverings could be recovered or would need to be reproduced. After cleaning a test panel, it was determined that the disfiguring water stains could be removed with a wet cleaning treatment. After the disaster, the library interior required extensive renovation that allowed the institution to reinterpret the room in its original configuration. During this process, it was discovered that several lengths of the wall coverings had been removed and lost during previous architectural alterations. Although many aspects of this successful treatment presented an interesting challenge, this poster focuses on manufacturing reproduction fabric to replace missing elements and the reinstallation process.

Organizing, preparing and fabricating reproduction fabric using both automated and hand-craft techniques, including custom dyeing and hand silk-screening, is illustrated during the presentation. Reproduction fabric was produced at the TCC working in collaboration with experienced textile machinery operators at the American Textile History Museum and a local yarn manufacturing company. The printed design was reproduced by drawing a stencil from the original fabric and transferring it to the silk-screen coated with a light-sensitive emulsion. The design was then printed on the reproduction fabric with dyes utilizing hand silk-screening techniques. The project plan for the hanging system was developed in consideration of the textile material as a wall covering rather than simply a textile. A collaborative effort between the TCC and wallpaper conservator, T. K. McClintock, has resulted in a method for reinstalling the wall coverings that closely emulates the original use of starch paste adhesive. Conservation techniques illustrated include attaching a supportive paper backing on both original and reproduction fabric panels in preparation for the corresponding walls.

L'incidence de la récupération après sinistre sur la réinstallation de panneaux de tissu

Deirdre Windsor

American Textile History Museum, Textile Conservation Center
491 Dutton Street
Lowell, MA 01854 USA
Tél. : (508) 441-1198
Téléc. : (508) 441-1412

Un ensemble de panneaux en tissu imprimé, éléments de l'aménagement d'origine de la bibliothèque, a été endommagé par l'eau pendant un incendie d'une maison historique. Il a subséquemment fallu évaluer la faisabilité de la récupération des matériaux d'origine. L'Edgar Sawyer Mansion (désignée Oshkosh Public Museum depuis 1922) a été construite en 1908 avec une décoration intérieure signée Tiffany Studios. Les travaux de récupération après sinistre se sont avérés particulièrement importants pour la préservation des matériaux en raison des conditions ambiantes liées à la chaleur de l'été. Le personnel du musée a immédiatement enlevé les panneaux, les a épongés, puis congelés pour prévenir la prolifération des champignons. Les méthodes employées pour les travaux de récupération et pour les traitements de restauration subséquents ont eu une incidence majeure sur le mode d'exposition permanente des matériaux d'origine dans le cadre de la demeure historique.

Le Textile Conservation Center (TCC) a évalué les panneaux congelés en vue du traitement de restauration. Le conservateur a utilisé l'évaluation du Centre pour déterminer si les panneaux d'origine étaient récupérables, ou s'il faudrait les reproduire. Après le nettoyage d'un panneau choisi à titre d'essai, on a décidé qu'il serait possible d'éliminer les graves taches d'eau par un lavage acqueux. Après le sinistre, l'intérieur de la bibliothèque a nécessité d'importantes rénovations, qui ont donné l'occasion de restituer l'aménagement initial des pièces. Au cours du processus, on a découvert que plusieurs bandes de panneaux d'origine avaient été retirées et perdues durant des modifications architecturales antérieures. Bien que de nombreux aspects de ce traitement couronné de succès ont présenté des défis particuliers, l'affiche se concentre sur la fabrication des reproductions visant à remplacer les éléments manquants et sur le processus de réinstallation.

Durant la présentation, on illustre l'organisation, la préparation et la fabrication des reproductions à l'aide de techniques automatisées et manuelles, notamment l'application spécialement adaptée de teinture et la sérigraphie manuelle. Le tissu reproduit est fabriqué au TCC en collaboration avec des opérateurs de métiers industriels de l'American Textile History Museum et d'un fabricant local de fils. Pour reproduire le motif, on a calqué au crayon le tissu d'origine, puis on a transféré le dessin sur l'écran de sérigraphie enduit d'une émulsion photosensible. Le motif fut alors imprimé sur le tissu à l'aide de teintures, selon les techniques de la sérigraphie manuelle. Le plan du système de suspension a été élaboré en tenant compte du fait que la pièce concernée est un panneau mural et non un simple textile. Un effort de collaboration entre le TCC et un restaurateur de papier peint, T. K. McClintock, a permis de créer une méthode de réinstallation reproduisant de près la technique d'origine, qui utilisait une colle d'amidon. Parmi les techniques de restauration illustrées, on compte la fixation d'un papier support à l'endos des originaux et des reproductions en fonction des murs correspondants.

Conservation of Costume for "In Royal Fashion": Time Management for a Large Project with a Small Staff

Barbara Heiberger

Museum of London
London Wall
London EC2Y 5HN United Kingdom
Tel.: 0171-600-3699 – Fax: 0171-600-1058
E-mail: bheiberger@museum-london.org.uk

"In Royal Fashion" is a major exhibition of the clothes and accessories of Princess Charlotte of Wales and Queen Victoria from 1796 to 1901. The conservation took four years (from June 1993 to May 1997), 5,000 hours, with two full-time conservators working on the project.

The numbers and types of objects conserved included: 19 dresses, 2 with trains; 1 state robe with kirtle; 2 coronation robes, 1 coronation canopy and 1 coronation cushion; 10 children's dresses, robes, etc.; 7 jackets, capes, etc.; 1 man's uniform; 2 pairs of drawers; 4 parts of dresses; 12 bonnets, hats and capes; 9 shoes; 5 pairs of stockings; 6 handkerchiefs; 3 gloves; 3 parasols; 1 piece of brocade, 1 collar, 1 cot cover, 1 samplebook containing 66 textiles; and 64 dolls.

In order to fit this amount of work into a relatively short time, several project management ideas were used, and conservation was fitted into the overall strategy of doing as much as possible in the time. The adjustments to treatments were: doing only what was structurally necessary; having no scientific analysis done; doing very little historical research; selecting a few objects only for fuller treatment; selecting a few large objects to contract out; and offering alternatives on treatments and display methods to curators where possible.

The benefits of this approach were that a larger number of objects were able to be conserved; and the photography for the book could be done after the conservation.

Restauration de costumes pour l'exposition «In Royal Fashion» : gestion d'un grand projet par une petite équipe

Barbara Heiberger

Museum of London
London Wall
London EC2Y 5HN United Kingdom
Tél. : 0171-600-3699
Téléc. : 0171-600-1058
CÉ : bheiberger@museum-london.org.uk

«In Royal Fashion» est une importante exposition des costumes et accessoires de la princesse de Galles Charlotte et de la reine Victoria, couvrant la période de 1796 à 1901. Les travaux de restauration ont duré quatre ans (de juin 1993 à mai 1997), soit 5 000 heures, et ont exigé les services de deux restaurateurs à temps plein.

L'inventaire des articles se dresse comme suit : 19 robes, 2 avec traînes; 1 robe d'apparat avec toge; 2 robes de couronnement, 1 dais de couronnement et 1 coussin de couronnement; 10 robes et autres costumes d'enfants; 7 vestes, capes, etc.; 1 uniforme d'homme; 2 culottes; 4 éléments de robes; 12 bonnets, chapeaux et capes; 9 chaussures; 5 paires de bas; 6 mouchoirs; 3 gants; 3 parasols; 1 pièce de brocart; 1 col, 1 couvre-lit pour lit d'enfant, 1 cahier contenant des échantillons de 66 textiles; enfin, 64 poupées.

Afin d'effectuer tout le travail nécessaire avec un échéancier relativement serré, on a mis en œuvre plusieurs idées originales en matière de gestion de projet. On a intégré la restauration dans la stratégie d'ensemble, qui consiste à effectuer toutes les tâches réalisables dans la période allouée. Il a fallu ainsi faire quelques concessions : se limiter aux interventions strictement structurales, en renonçant à toute analyse scientifique; n'effectuer qu'une recherche historique minimale; limiter le traitement en profondeur à quelques articles seulement; confier la restauration de quelques grands objets en sous-traitance; proposer aux conservateurs des solutions de rechange aux méthodes de traitement et d'exposition, lorsque la chose était possible.

Cette démarche a eu pour avantage de permettre la restauration d'un grand nombre d'articles. Les photographies du livret ont été prises après les travaux de restauration.

Examples of Stabilization and Display of Fragile Textiles for Museums

Vera Vereecken

Institut royal du patrimoine artistique
Parc du Cinquantenaire 1 - 1000 Brussels
Belgium
Tel.: 32-2/ 739 67 11
Fax: 32-2/ 732 01 05

Different types of intervention are presented in reference to specific textiles that vary in structure and degree of deterioration. The original qualities and the authenticity of the textiles were preserved as much as possible.

The poster shows the evolution from general methods of stabilization to more specific treatments.

Even in the case of serious deterioration, on three-dimensional or oversized textiles, stitching was the method used for treatment.

The materials are presented and their use is explained. The choices were made thanks to the collaborative efforts of a multidisciplinary team from the Institut royal du patrimoine artistique (Brussels).

Also on the poster, different ways of mounting textiles for exhibit or in preparation for storage in order to facilitate the proper handling of fragile textiles are presented.

Exemples de consolidation et de présentation des textiles fragiles à l'intention des musées

Vera Vereecken

Institut royal du patrimoine artistique
Parc du Cinquantenaire 1 - 1000 Bruxelles
Belgique
Tél. : 32-2/ 739 67 11
Téléc. : 32-2/ 732 01 05

Plusieurs types d'intervention sont présentés en fonction de cas particuliers de textiles de différentes caractéristiques et dégradations, en respectant au maximum leur origine et leur authenticité.

L'affiche montre l'évolution de la méthode générale de consolidation vers des traitements plus spécifiques.

Même en cas de forte dégradation, des textiles tridimensionnés ou de grandes mesures, le traitement s'effectue par couture.

Les matériaux employés sont présentés et justifiés. Ce choix est le résultat d'une étroite collaboration interdisciplinaire de l'Institut royal du patrimoine artistique de Bruxelles.

À cela s'ajoute des cas de présentation effectués à l'occasion d'expositions ou en perspective de stockage, pour faciliter et assurer la manipulation des textiles fragiles.